Wisdom
Notes

Wisdom Notes

Theological Riffs
on
Life and Living

*For Bill,
may these works keep
stoking the fires within.
Art*

*April 18
Lansing*

A. J. Dewey

Arthur J. Dewey

POLEBRIDGE PRESS
Salem, Oregon

Polebridge Press is the publishing arm of the Westar Institute, a non-profit, public-benefit research and educational organization. To learn more, visit westarinstitute.org.

Copyright © 2016 by Arthur J. Dewey

All rights reserved. Printed in the United States of America. No part of this book may be used or reproduced in any manner whatsoever without written permission except in the case of brief quotations embodied in critical articles and reviews. For information address Polebridge Press, PO Box 346, Farmington, Minnesota 55024.

Cover and interior design by Robaire Ream

Library of Congress Cataloging-in-Publication Data

Names: Dewey, Arthur J.
Title: Wisdom notes : theological riffs on life and living / by Arthur J.
  Dewey.
Description: Salem : Polebridge Press, 2016.
Identifiers: LCCN 2015006859 | ISBN 9781598151657 (alk. paper)
Subjects: LCSH: Christianity--Miscellanea. | Christian life--Miscella-
nea. |
  Life--Miscellanea.
Classification: LCC BR123 .D465 2016 | DDC 230--dc23
LC record available at https://lccn.loc.gov/2015006859

10   9   8   7   6   5   4   3   2   1

Contents

Acknowledgments

None of these commentaries would have seen the light of day without the invitation and support of Lorna Jordan, the former news director of WVXU. Mike Martini, Steve Hirshberg, Ann Thomson and Mark Heyne all assisted in recording the radio commentaries for the old WVXU. Gerry Donnelly and Maryanne Zeleznik brought my work aboard the new WVXU. I must also thank two technical experts, Jeff Johnson and Dave Stuart, who saved my bacon on a number of occasions. Nor can I forget the constant support and encouragement from my fellow commentator Rabbi Abie Ingber. All of these co-conspirators have become good friends and conversation partners as we aired these pieces.

Bob Miller not only enlisted me to write editorials for *The Fourth R* but has been a sharp-eyed editor of my work. Char Matejovsky knows well how to use a red pencil to enhance my essays. I am deeply appreciative of such collaboration and friendship.

I should also thank Steve Fortney for his ongoing encouragement and close reading of the material. Likewise I am indebted to Ken Overberg, S.J., who heard these commentaries often, even before they were written. Steve and Ken have been patient and unflagging friends. I must give a special word of thanks to Bill Benallack, who saw merit in my work and has long hounded me to publish these commentaries. I am much indebted to Cassandra Farrin for carefully shepherding this manuscript, to Barbara Hampson for her fine eye and wit, and to Robaire Ream, once again, for his ever creative touch and design. Of course, Larry Alexander, the publisher of Polebridge Press, cannot be forgotten. He recognized the possibility of putting all this together and encouraged me to move forward in this venture.

Finally I would like to thank all the listeners to WVXU and the readers of *The Fourth R*. Your continued interest has kept me going. Your comments have been gracious (with a few exceptions) and encouraging. You have affirmed that such a conversation was worth the energy and effort.

Introduction

There is an ancient rabbinic tradition in which rabbis were challenged to deliver the heart of Torah while standing on one foot. People did not have the time for technical niceties or philosophical parrying. They wanted what was significant for them pithily expressed. Fortunately I did not have that physical requirement in creating these commentaries. But I was constrained by time or space limits. Nevertheless, the task was ever present: to detect meaning in the ebb and flow of our life together on this planet. From the outset my commentaries were conversations with a listening audience. They offered a perspective that came from a personal response to a variety of fronts on which we live. I tried to explore the imaginative interstices of the everyday, the political and cultural tremors of our nation, and the possible resources of meaningful human life. Each engagement brought surprise, demanding nothing less than a constant ear for what was unspoken or unheard. I often found myself improvising, as words became "riffs," trying to sound out a fragile insight.

These commentaries span the last twenty years. They are truly "drive-by" reflections, designed to catch the imaginations of people on the go, and empowered by images I could not get out of my mind. Each piece represents a hunkering down, a decision on my part to stay in the little ease of the present to discover what has often been unspoken. So I make no apologies for the constraints of time and space. Rather, each commentary provides an imaginative frame to reconsider the mundane and maddening demands of life.

"God-talk" or theology is largely viewed today as a hothouse occupation, reserved for professionals or televangelists. Public discourse avoids any discussion that so many people desire. We want to talk about what is meaningful; we desire to detect and express those intimations of worth and value. But theology does not have to be a ghettoized patois. A contemporary theology attempts to reflect on the depths of our experience. Whenever we begin to explore the depths of our life together, we enter into what the ancients would see as a sacred realm. As moderns, we have jettisoned the mythic vocabulary of our ancestors. But that does not prevent an exploration of our experience, fears, hopes and dreams. It does not preclude recognizing the surprise of discerning meaning in the midst of our life together. It opens up new possibilities for a mature and exciting public conversation. In a very small way my commentaries have been "raids on the inarticulate," attempting to demonstrate that we can catch and share meaningful inklings—those Wisdom notes—as our planet tilts into a new dawn.

Origins—On the Way to Work

It started in a traffic jam. Usually the morning drive went smoothly as I dropped off my sons and then my wife before heading off to the university. But that morning's rain brought out the worst in drivers and in me. I was feeling rather claustrophobic in our family shuttle and exasperated by a recent local radio commentary. Then I heard Lorna Jordan of WVXU announce the station's willingness to bring in new voices from around Cincinnati. As we waited for the traffic to dissolve my wife challenged me, "If you think you can do better, go for it." Within a few days I had submitted a trial commentary and was soon contacted to record it. Two weeks or so later, I was asked for more. And so it began in late 1995.

From the outset the challenge was clear: to say something meaningful in "less than 60 seconds." The commentaries were squeezed into the concluding segment of the morning edition and often repeated for the afternoon drive time. Lorna left the subject matter up to me, but insisted that I consider what was current in Cincinnati and around the world. Each commentary became for me a composition in time and space. It was not simply a matter of counting words; rhythm and tone were critical. Opening lines had to grab. Each word, every inflection, had to have effect. Nothing extraneous was permitted. My sounds had to make sense. And, then, there was the recording. Lorna was exceedingly patient, allowing me a number of retakes. At times my mind would race faster than my sentences. Sometimes I lost the pitch and had to go back to square one. I began on Tuesday mornings as one of five new voices. Fridays were left to Nick Clooney, a well-known Cincinnati broadcaster (and father of George).

Then in 1996 Nick Clooney decided to move on, citing his travel and other commitments prevented him from doing his best on the commentaries. So, I was asked to alternate with Rabbi Abie Ingber on Fridays. This curious tandem lasted quite a few years. Each of us delivered a distinctive voice and direction. In the summer of 2003 I had the opportunity to teach Xavier students in London. Ann Thompson fitted me with a microphone and a recorder and the challenge to find a way to email the commentaries from London. From then on all my commentaries for WVXU were recorded and edited on that little machine. I was thus able to go "on the road" on a number of occasions. Only in 2005, when WVXU was sold by Xavier University to Cincinnati Public Radio, did I return to the studio to record my commentaries.

In 2006, after almost a dozen years on the air, I was asked by Bob Miller, the editor of *The Fourth R* magazine to become the regular editorial writer. *The Fourth R* has long been the public face of Westar Institute, the home of the national Jesus Seminar. Bob knew of my experience on the radio and suggested that I continue with an ear to the concerns of Westar Institute, dedicated to the quest for religious literary and critical conversation on matters of religion. This assignment continues.

The Collection

There are 252 essays (212 radio commentaries & 40 *Fourth R* editorials) in this collection. Chronologically they span late 1995 through the middle of 2015. I have been fortunate to comment on a multitude of issues and questions over the years. In order to bring some semblance of order, I have divided the commentaries into ten categories. Of course, these are rather arbitrary and readers will soon discover that most of these pieces could be placed in a number of sections. One can notice that the pieces tend to lengthen as each section develops. This is due to the fact that at times I was given more than a minute to speak (ninety-seconds, sometimes two and a half minutes). Additionally the longest end pieces are taken from *The Fourth R* editorials.

Despite the variety of pieces I can say that there has been from the outset a consistent method of composition. Many years ago I learned from the poet John Donne (in his "Holy Sonnets") that much can be done in a very small space. He took this discipline from the insight of Ignatius Loyola, who recommended creating an imaginative space for meditation. I did not have fourteen lines to situate my imagination. But I did have the time and space of "less than 60 seconds." That became my echo chamber in which to explore through words and images the questions that touched the life I shared with others. I was able to range far and wide, to look up close and personal. I could call upon cultural and personal memory to enrich my reflections. Indeed, I found much crowding in this crush of words. And I know from responses over the years that listeners appreciated the effort, sometimes staying in the driveway to hear where I was going in a commentary. Many wanted me to publish these attempts. More recently I have received numerous requests to reprint my editorials. I hope that this collection continues my attempt to get to the heart of things, allowing readers the opportunity to be surprised long after the broadcasts aired and editorials ended.

1

Around Cincinnati

I begin my selection with a potpourri that offers a variety of glimpses into Cincinnati. Since 1980 my wife and I have called Cincinnati home. In fact, my very first commentary, "Changing Stripes," concerned the Cincinnati football team's owner and civic responsibility. Since sports is Cincinnati's fundamental religion it was crucial to begin at the heart of it all. Readers will see that these essays go in various directions from dealing with traffic snarls to hospital crises, from Cinti's weather to the town's political climate. Some focus on personal loss and tragedy, others offer possibilities for the city. I have always been intrigued that the most negative reaction to my commentaries was reserved for "Paradise at Fifth and Race," when I advocated for putting an Asian Garden in a space that once hosted a now demolished department store. I thought a hint of beauty would be better for the city than another parking lot. Evidently I could say anything about the city's gods but to "get impractical" was going far beyond the pale.

Drive-by images 1998

Like many of you listening out there, I spend my weekday mornings in the car. There is no need to pick scabs, that is, to rehearse the fitful "stops and go's" of those labor intensive minutes. Instead, I would like to note something that can happen to any of us on the road.

I'm not talking about fender benders or five car pileups. No, it's something more subtle. It's what I call "drive-by images." These are the images that somehow make it through the shields of my scheduled morning run. Despite the fact that I'm "cribbed, cabined, and confined" behind the wheel, they register out of the corner of my eye.

There's the puzzling sight of a bare-chested man, at least in his fifties, pulling a barrel along Spring Grove Avenue in front of Spring Grove Cemetery. He would always wear an apron, sometimes a shirt in cold weather. I never saw what he was pulling, nor where he went. Only that determined pace. The myth of Sisyphus was alive and well.

Then there's the woman on Forest Street. Usually she would be sweeping furiously on the street in front of the Baptist Church. In all kinds of weather I would see this stubby woman wearing an enormous crocheted red hat as she flailed away at the debris.

Lastly, there is a homeless man, in dreadlocks and a lived-in down coat, who greets the sunrise on his knees in prayer. While traffic snarls on Gilbert Avenue, he remains serene.

I have no explanation for any of these people. But each, in just seconds, has shaken the snow globe of my morning world.

Changing stripes 1995

Just when an air of civility began to settle on downtown Cincinnati, when major businesses began to mount another corporate charge for the city, Mike Brown grumbles about not getting what some would call his protection money on time.

You may consider me nostalgic for a bygone era—when business leaders thought it an investment to give not merely to take from a city. Apparently P & G and some of the major banks still share that sense of the common wealth.

But what have the Bengals contributed to the common good? Besides the likes of Munoz and Anderson, giving up their free time for charity, what have the Bengals as a corporate entity done for the city?

Indeed, while the Public Schools a couple of years ago sought a few million dollars for education, Mike Brown made his initial demands. The Levy failed. Brown got his deal. Not the best impression.

Yet, after a few calls about the city, my thinking changed. The Bengals do much that is unheralded. The United Way, the Cincinnati Zoo, and Children's Hospital are only three of their numerous beneficiaries.

Perhaps more than modesty is needed now. What would happen if the Bengals tried an end run around public perception? What if they took the lead, carried the civic ball, and challenged others to get in the game?

It is time to get beyond the threats and postures of the present and build a partnership for Cincinnati. Maybe we'll find out that the snarling cats on both sides can change their stripes after all.

Reality in a Ranger's cap   1996

Last night I attended my son's high school registration. The Chair of the Science Department who guided us through the forms was a former student of mine. In fact, my son was born during that summer class almost fourteen years ago. Both she and I recoiled at the prospect of such a span of years, now sitting before us with a New York Rangers cap pulled down over his forehead.

I remembered how we sweated through the Gospel of Mark fourteen years ago, sifting for traces of an ancient community, itself dazed by the fall of Jerusalem and the destruction of the Temple, the linchpin of their religious world. We found inklings of their hope, set starkly against a sky that flashed apocalyptic promise for those nobodies of the Roman world.

I also recalled how another student, a hospital chaplain, wrote her final exam with tears welling in her eyes. Only hours before she had agonized with a couple who had just lost their newborn. She said afterwards that she needed to try to put something together in her distress. When I read her courageous exam I learned how humanity could be found in blue books.

Reality has a way of eluding our formulas, even the ways we would hold onto the past. My sudden recollections were interrupted by my son's murmur to get going. Once again I re-alized, in that moment of transition, that reality is ever on the move. You can't keep it in last summer's high-tops. But you can be patient and sometimes get close enough to be surprised.

▌ Hospital sounds 1996

▌ Cincinnati has been buzzing over the fate of University Hospital. Hearings, debates, editorials have reached enormous decibel levels. A newspaper article likened the future of the Hospital to the course followed by Boston City Hospital a short time ago. Somehow the noise of this latest brouhaha fell away as I remembered my days as an orderly on the floors of Boston City. Ironically, it was on the same ward where my Grandfather died ten years before.

An orderly is the lowest critter on the service totem pole. But between the bedpans and morning shaves, there was a chance to do something that few doctors attempted. I got to know the patients.

There was Mr. Baer, who decided to die. None of the nurses could get him out of his funk. So, they let me have a go at it. I went in and read him the riot act. "How dare you think of dying! Don't you know that we're worried about you?" Startled, he opened up. The medical team had rushed through that morning opening his wounds and talking as if he were not there. So he took the hint.

But Mr. Milan was most memorable. A World War I veteran confined to a nursing home, he arrived with enormous bedsores brought on by neglect. Mr. Milan's legs stopped at his knees but his nasty tongue was ever ready to skewer anyone who would try to do something for him. The nurses would do only what was needed, while being barraged by his blistering words.

Then one day I decided not to run out. He got quiet and I asked him about the War. For a moment the pain dissolved from his face as he broke into a French song and mentioned how he had received a medal from the French General Staff. He spoke of the Kaiser and Wilson, weaving a spell between him and myself until the head nurse cut us off, asking why wasn't I working. I stammered: "But this is my work too." But it was too late. Mr. Milan had slid quickly into his nasty shell. The next day he was transferred to a new nursing home.

8

Is it too late for such stories to be heard in Cincinnati?

Why wait for 2008? 1996

Cincinnati doesn't have to wait for 2008, we can go for the gold now! In fact, our desire to make a national splash can be combined with our misgivings over our schools. We can even do better than what our Law and Order advocates have been calling for. We can increase our prison space, turn our educators into true professionals, and nip educational downturns in the bud.

All we have to do is admit publicly what many of us fear: that there is nothing we can do to save those students from ultimate failure. Since they will eventually drop out and end up as criminals, why not build upon that probability?

Let us turn our schools into prisons. You might wince at that, but what do we already have? Recently a major announcement was made from the Public Schools—a new surveillance system had been set up. Why not go all the way? Instead of forcing teachers to keep the peace without the threat of corporal punishment, let them train as prison guards; principals can don the more respectable title of warden.

Think of what the city and county could save. We have the land and buildings. All we have to do is add dormitories, electrified fences, and we can contain the growing problems of drugs and violence. No longer would we have to worry about class size or providing for the needs of individuals. If there is any overcrowding, well, we can call it a "learning experience." And, to add to this, there will no longer be any need for separate levies on schools and prisons.

Best of all, we can give our children what they truly deserve—a life lesson about how fear and control make the world go around. I'm surprised no savvy city councilor has yet to call a news conference to suggest this.

The astonishing ambush 1997

Duke has been the University's first line of defense since long before I arrived seventeen years ago. Whether freezing in the winter or baking through the dog days of August in his guard house, Duke patiently greets faculty anxious over parking and wide-eyed visitors with dry humor, homespun proverbs, and a rising mountain accent. But unless you stop and let him adjust his cap so that he can meander awhile into a joke, you haven't met Duke.

Once he shared with me his major vacation worry. He was going out of town. His chief concern was water. Not for drinking but to rinse his glass eye. Seems he was so used to Cincinnati water that washing with anything purer would bring on a reaction.

Then there is his sketching. On slow days you might catch another side of Duke. He was commissioned to draw the University Christmas card a few years ago. A delicate nostalgia fills his West Virginia scenes.

But there is more. Recently he came back from the edge of death. On his ride home to Clermont County six deer sprang unexpectedly from the left of the median and, in two quick bounds, collided with his '75 Olds. The first deer hit front and center, a second bounced off the left front light, while a third rammed so hard into the left back side that the car spun around. The other three scampered away safely. Two cars behind him veered off to the right and left avoiding everything. They didn't even look back. Duke was left, scratching his head over his totaled Olds and deer parts strewn everywhere.

Even now our emblem of security staggers, relating what few really want to hear: the astonishing ambush of life.

▌A tempered wisdom 1997

The night before my jury duty began I was tempted to rent *Twelve Angry Men* at the local video store. Opting instead to get a good night's sleep, I had a hint that melodrama would not be enough to get me through the next three weeks.

After words of welcome by the jury commissioner and his staff, a film regarding your role as a juror, and directions for coffee, snacks and restrooms, you begin to realize that the hardest thing is adjusting to a pace far different from your daily rhythm. You can bring books, computers, reports, and pretend that you are still being productive, but that illusion soon vanishes when you realize that your presence intersects oddly with the fate of others.

Often decisions are reached just beyond your earshot, pleas are bargained, condemning someone unseen to five, ten years or more. Walking back to the jury pool after a defendant had agreed to a five year sentence, avoiding a possible ten year stretch if he lost a jury trial, I heard another juror wryly remark, "That guy knows where he's celebrating the Millennium."

My closest opportunity for an actual case occurred in the first week. I was in a pool of thirty prospective jurors sent to what was described as a complicated murder case. Since the defendant had already admitted killing the victim, it was a matter of determining the severity of the crime. After an all-day questioning of the prospective jurors, I was the first juror removed on a peremptory move by the prosecution. Was it my bow tie?

But I did learn from that day in court. Many of those thirty jurors were intimately acquainted with suffering and violence. Murder had touched the lives of two. No matter how the lawyers would maneuver, I sensed that the jurors chosen would bring what movies only suggest: a wisdom tempered in pain and seasoned to listen to one another.

▌ Dark night of the urban soul   1997

Last week most of Hamilton County lost some sleep. Around 1:30 a.m. sirens blared through what had been a pleasant Tuesday morning. Unknown to most of us, who were summoned from our beds, was that an acrid white cloud was forming at the Hilton Davis Chemical plant. Fifty-five gallons of oleum had leaked from a connecting line, exuding a smell like battery acid into the neighborhood.

Evidently the acid spill had occurred about two hours earlier. In front page news stories for the rest of the week, we learned that much confusion reigned in attempting to alert the public about this irritating situation. In brief, there seems to have been, once again, a failure to communicate.

However, before we hear nothing but some righteous demand for a witch hunt or a special committee to fix the problem, I simply would like to return to those moments soon after we were startled from our sleep.

I had gone outside, expecting turbulent skies, and found instead the early morning calm. The constant drone of the sirens sent me back in to the radio in hope of finding out what was happening.

When I learned at last some rough sketch of the trouble, I began to imagine those friends of mine, and all the countless others, in the endangered vicinity. Now, for some reason, I remembered that this was the habitual time for Lauds, when monasteries fill with sleepy chanters, whose bodies and souls sway in an eternal rhythm.

I went back outside into the dark night of the urban soul. Behind closed windows many of us waited, some annoyed, some anxious, all desperate for sleep. Yet, those of us awakened that night were caught up in something that escaped our grasp, eluded our technology, and rode on the bitter and balmy wind — in short, the unknown.

▌Northside parades again   1998

Tomorrow Northside parades again. Unlike corporate sponsored triumphs ballooning along downtown arteries or weaving through the tickertape of urban canyons, the neighborhood parade marches to a different drummer.

Here the raw ingredients of democracy come out to play. Over the asphalt tumble the flotsam and jetsam of our shared dreams and memories. It always begins with neighbors slowly picking their spots along the parade route. Some even find shade. Then the conversation is cut short by rapid bursts from a police siren, followed by the zigzag of a ladder truck.

After that, not a deluge, but a steady stream of people willing to put on a public face. Knothole teams in just-washed uniforms give way to wild grammas in jalopies. A local pharmacy's delivery truck rolls by boldly dressed in hand-painted signs. The Women's Lawn-chair Drill Team performs a flawless stomp. Bartenders dragooned to drive their pubs' pickups wave offhandedly, while our cosmopolitan hair stylist leads a company of her stunning models that bend the gender gap.

Add to this the white, yellow and brown of the talented Roger Bacon Band. How that many teenagers could have gotten up before noon on a summer day mystifies every parent along the route. The octogenarian Veterans of Foreign Wars some years ago marched away into memory. Now the graybeards of Vietnam take up their position.

Since this is an election year the candidates will be out in force. Plastic cups, magnets, fans, flags, and candy tossed mechanically will announce their arrival. Perhaps the most honest political statement was given a few years ago by Arn Bortz, who wasn't even there! A shapely blonde, perched on the back of a red convertible, held a huge black and white photo of Bortz. All you could see from the front was this massive mask held by two slender hands. Finally truth in politics: nothing but appearance!

▌As banal as possible 1998

▌ U.S. District Judge James Graham has ruled that the State of Ohio can display its motto, *With God all things are possible*, on the state seal in a sidewalk at the Capitol Square Plaza in Columbus. As long as the source of the quote is not named, there will be no favoring one religion over another.

According to the judge the words do not state a principle unique to Christianity. They are, at best, gestures to a generic God.

Meanwhile the American Civil Liberties Union ponders an appeal. Lawyer Mark Cohn thought his side had presented a persuasive case that the quote was from Jesus and that, as material from the New Testament, it was not appropriate as a motto for Ohio.

Although the Judge probably did not know it, that verse from Mark 10:27 is quite likely not from the historical Jesus. What is from Jesus is found two verses before: *It's easier for a camel to squeeze through a needle's eye than for a wealthy person to get into God's domain.* Scholars point out that the early Jesus communities had a difficult time swallowing such radical thought. Even the poor found it hard to believe that God's Empire opened freely for them and that wealth was no assurance of ultimate worth.

To get around this obstacle, the proverb *With God all things are possible* was invoked, allowing the rich a loophole.

And so, unwittingly, the Court continues this deflection away from a jarring vision. Keep our public discourse as bland and banal as possible. Just don't say anything with a bite to it. The poor might get the wrong idea.

A silent composition 1999

A mother, a father, a son. Whenever death comes it always takes a toll. Three of my friends, George, Steve, and Marv, in a space of days are staggering from death's blows.

Yes, we can coldly say that they are no different from any of us. We can concoct bromides about the human condition. But we all know that acid death easily eats these generalities away.

Death leaves a mark on us. A mother, a father, a son. Each death makes us realize how singular we are. The closer we come to death the more we are refined in its raw furnace. Our numbness, our grief, our guilt, our anger, our fright, burn through us in the intensity of loss.

And we know in our bones that the loss will never, never, never go away.

And our mourning comes in waves, sometimes blasting us like heat off a tarmac, sometimes more devastatingly in the gentle shock of a long familiar sound.

None of the coordinates of time and space work any longer when death comes close. Our words fall off the edge of the world.

And so, I would like to leave my friends with an image of silence—of walking among a forest of redwoods, of looking up and straining to see the tops of those ancient ones, of following the filtering light down to the ground, of noticing the shattered remains of moss covered giants dissolving along the forest floor.

And in that silent composition let them remember a mother, a father, a son.

Jesus and his Roman buddies 1999

If you drive long enough around Cincinnati, you'll find things passing strange. Recently my wife and I were driving along Hamilton Avenue. On the front steps of a church a crowd was gathering for a group picture. As I slowed down and stopped at the red light across from the church, a most unusual scene tugged at the corner of my eye.

On that early spring afternoon the tableau was set: a jocular Jesus was surrounded by his Roman executioners. The cast of a passion play had taken five for a few Kodak moments. Laughter and kibitzing replaced the well-known script.

Little did they know that this fleeting spectacle of a convivial Jesus and his Roman buddies embodied much of the shadow side of Christian history, where the cross not only followed the sword but tragically at times was turned into one.

Nor do many passion play audiences sense the tremors even today among their Jewish neighbors whenever the tale of Jesus' death is told. Riots and pogroms often followed in the wake of Palm Sunday invective.

But there is something at the very heart of things that is usually overlooked. Apologists and dogmatists have tried for years to cushion the blow. The earliest writers tried to paint over their embarrassment. Jesus the Jewish peasant died a godforsaken death like thousands of his countrymen. The Roman machine efficiently rubbed them out.

But now Jesus plays on the front steps of a church with the troops. Just a harmless coincidence. Who would want to make something more out of it?

The news you'll never hear   1999

And now for the news: This morning hundreds of thousands of greater Cincinnatians got up and went to work. Many left the comfort of their homes to go to jobs they regret or even despise. But their family's welfare, professional pride, or sheer stubbornness drove them past the orange barrel obstacle courses.

Earlier janitors, cleaning women, and security guards, shaking off another tedious night, got their kids' breakfasts before trying to find a few hours of sleep.

Meanwhile hundreds milled around in the already muggy dawn just for a chance at eight hours of work.

Secretaries kept offices and businesses afloat, juggling bosses' egos, triplicate mountains of paper, and endless clients' complaints.

Hundreds of high school students stagnated in summer school, patiently enduring a system that doesn't work along with the adolescent cruelty of their peers.

Drivers throughout the metropolitan area kept their tempers inside their vehicles as scores of SUV's insouciantly cavorted as if they owned the roads. Dozens behind the wheel stopped in time to let careless children cross—even against the lights.

Throughout the day poems were written, letters attempted, email sent, for no other reason than affection, sorrow and wonder.

Songs were overheard at odd moments. Uncertain smiles crossed unknown faces. Executives having second thoughts about downsizing sought to save jobs.

Chemists kept going despite the latest test failure. At the firehouse firemen hoisted kids onto the pumper in the afternoon heat.

All these stories and thousands more you will never hear on the News. You will hear each night the few times things broke down, when our silent decency is drowned out by sensational noise. Ratings and our blood pressure might go up. But the media haven't a clue about how a city really thrives.

▌ The Chasteen Chapel   2000

▌ At the University everyone's attention has been long focused on the new sports-dining hall complex rising like a giant bakery box on the northeastern side of the campus. Meanwhile the old student union is just about to meet the wrecking ball.

Unnoticed in all this hurly-burly have been the plans of Duke, who mans a black metal sentry box at the main entrance to the University. Designed with no human in mind, and equipped with a heater configured for a Los Angeles winter, the "black box" voraciously absorbs the summer heat. But Duke has made some cagey modifications to survive. Now, as he puts it in his Appalachian twang, he's "fixin'" to paint the ceiling, turning it into a "chasteen chapel."

Faculty who drive in have been enlisted as consultants. One artist has recommended latex paint and will help him choose a color scheme. But Duke is hankering to do more than coat the ceiling with a new color. He can already see a magnificent scene hovering over his head.

"Of course," he said, "there's no room to lay a board across and stretch out like Charlton Heston to get a close up view of the work."

After much deliberation he nixed painting an apotheosis of the retiring president, like the ascension of George Washington upon the clouds.

He's not cut out for such grandiose scenes. Now he's thinking of filling the ceiling with students, peopling the top of his little ease with those who never make the headlines, who simply come by and talk and eventually graduate. Maybe the job will never get done. But Duke keeps those faces fresh in his mind as he steals a few seconds to sketch before he regales the next visitor.

Paradise at Fifth and Race 2001

Christmas has come early to Cincinnati. Nordstrom put on its best Jim Carey impression and grinched us out of the sugarplum on Fountain Square West. The Queen City has been left, rephrasing Joni Mitchell, "We craved paradise but put up a parking lot."

Before the Whoville City Council commissions a master plan—one as predictable as the usual gang of suspects rounded up to write it—and before they attempt a desperate Heimlich maneuver, let the Grinch go.

Why not, instead, put a real gem in the crown of the Queen City? For once, let's get beyond the sports pages and the financial columns and design the beautiful at Fifth and Race.

Imagine passing through the portals of an Asian garden into a serene courtyard. See a covered path leading to a teahouse from which you could observe magnificent rockery teeming with waterfalls. Notice the interplay of trees, stones and water. Touch the delicate moss at your fingertips.

If we want to be a world-class city, we need more than a brand name. We need to be exceptional in discovering beauty in a devastated lot.

There is a Chinese story of a healer called the Gourd man. He carried a gourd around with him everywhere. One day a neighbor observed the Gourd man disappear into his gourd. The healer invited the neighbor to do the same. "But I'm so big and the gourd is so small, how can I fit?" Finally the neighbor in a leap of faith jumped into the gourd. What did he see? A paradise with pavilions, towers, trees and a lake. Heaven in a small space—just like a garden.

Even the invisible
go Krogering   2001

They are invisible to most of us in Cincinnati. But to the experienced eye they walk our streets. You can find them sleeping in the niches of our underpasses.

Along the river, in wooded areas, inside abandoned buildings, you might glimpse them. If, by some strange reason, you find yourself driving before dawn, you will see them shivering in front of temporary work offices, desperate for the chance of a day's pay. Even the lucky ones who find work every day cannot earn enough for both rent and food. Many of the subcontracted laborers who built Paul Brown Stadium, that monument of civic delusion, never had a place to call home.

But even the invisible go Krogering. One Tuesday about 1:30 a.m. I was getting some needed breakfast food. In the canyon of the soft drinks two Spanish-speaking men were debating what to get with their limited resources. One of the men wore a powder blue T-shirt under his work coat. I stood transfixed by the image on his shirt. A Ford pickup truck was printed to the right of our Lady of Guadalupe. I smiled and said to him that I liked his shirt. He graciously said thanks, flattered but puzzled by that gringo.

In 1531, ten years after the Conquistadors ravished Mexico, Juan Diego, a peasant poet, made a discovery that joined the Aztec heavens with the European mission. The compassionate image of an Aztec princess, pregnant and clothed with the sun, became an original American Gospel. Upon that peasant's tilma, the clothing of the poorest of the poor, was found the "inside of heaven."

For a brief moment in the artificial glare of Kroger's I caught a glimpse of hope, stenciled on cotton. But do we really want to be surprised by the invisible in our midst?

In this heavy air
we call Cincinnati   2001

Here in Cincinnati nothing seems to be going right. A smog's been smothering us for days, as reports of shootings pour in over our coffee cups. The cruelty of April still festers in July.

Even the woebegone Reds—our comic relief—have the IRS to worry about.

So, in this heavy atmosphere, even in the early morning hours, I sit in the dark. But something nudges me away from despondency. I recall those desperate summers when I was young, the house so hot that I could not sleep, and find the shadow of my father on the porch.

The baseball game has long been over. There are a few more puffs in his cigar. I sit on the step and listen to his play-by-play. Dramatically he rebuilds the game. For a few moments we are elsewhere. Lost in a story, caught in a rundown, digging in at the plate.

As a city, we are much in the dark. Despite the posturing of politicians and protestors, the manipulative rants of talk show hosts, the nervous assurances of those who do not walk the beat, we know that we are in the dark.

Perhaps it is time for Cincinnati not to grow up but to grow in. Time to meet what we resisted so strongly during those curfew days. Time to sit in the dark, not to explain, nor to pontificate, but to realize that others are breathing in the dark too. And we are all afraid of what might be there. And we are all afraid that there is nothing there.

To find out we shall have to listen for words murmured on the very edge of fear.

In this heavy air we call Cincinnati.

Cincinnati: The impossible dream? 2001

It may sound preposterous but I think I've finally begun to appreciate that republican Quixote Nick Vehr. For a while now many have been amused by his dogged drive to bring the Impossible Dream to the Queen City. More recently, however, he surprised his critics by finding enough financial support to get to the recent round of Olympic inspection. And so we wait to see if Cincinnati makes the short list.

But focus on what Nick Vehr has done. He has refused to see Cincinnati as a backwater victim, a residue of history, condemned to predestined Midwestern mediocrity. His vision, shocking though it may seem to some, is religious. Vehr has offered a public vision that transcends the narrow assumptions and prejudices of our city. He would draw on the cooperative energies of people throughout the Tri-State area. He sees interconnections, where many in recent months have seen only opposition. He paints a rainbow, rather than dabbling only in black and white.

Vehr is the most visible theologian in Cincinnati. He challenges us to imagine how our hometown would look if it were made with care.

Are there limits to his transcendent vision? Sure. But that two week sports package teases us to a deeper level.

What if we learned from Vehr and took our religious impulses seriously? What if we stopped embalming our hope and saw in the chaos our city poised, on the brink of creation? What if we realized that we don't have to wait for a starter's pistol to find out that life is only lived when we give it away? That our life together is too important and too interesting to be left to professionals? What if we surprised ourselves by creating Cincinnati again, for the first time?

▌The devil is beating his wife ▏ 2002

Two days ago the weather was typical for Cincinnati. The variable sky, as James Joyce once wrote, was "as uncertain as a child's bottom." There was even one period of meteorological flux when it rained while the sun was shining.

An old folk saying explains that odd confluence of sun and rain: "The devil is beating his wife."

That atmosphere provided a perfect backdrop for a boycotted city.

We have been in a state of siege since the riots of April last year. And since last July African-American activists and church leaders have called for an economic boycott of Cincinnati. Recently entertainers Bill Cosby and Smokey Robinson have indicated they would honor the boycott.

Talk radio celebrities have long stoked the homegrown prejudices. The business community laments that the boycott will do no good but punish an already beleaguered economy. Our new, strong major last Tuesday tried to put a positive spin on what even the Vice-Mayor considered a disappointing account of what the city is doing to empower the poor in Over-the-Rhine and the West End.

Meanwhile fear leaks through the city. Politicians are sweating for their political lives, while activists become more frustrated. "The devil is beating his wife."

Is there a way out of this? Evidently, September 11 has made little impression on us. Don't we see that we cannot get away from each other? That our common humanity demands more than public relations finesse or outraged posturing?

There was a man back in a Birmingham jail, who imagined a third way, beyond complacency and hatred, beyond cynicism and despair, beyond the stereotypes of class and poverty of imagination.

He trusted in the theatre of truth, where love sits right down with you at the lunch counter.

Isn't time for us to stop beating each other up and surprise ourselves with each other's company?

▌A friend in darkness 2003

Diabetes, as far as I can recollect, was not part of Dickens' vocabulary. But Dickens knew the human cost of disease. He also was quite aware of the darkness that descends on human lives, the fog that snarls about us, keeping us from shaking out any glimmer of light.

It is no wonder that Dickens often wrote ghosts stories for this time of year. Here we are at the farthest turn from the sun, and, even in our post-industrial age, we sense that primordial shudder. Light's loss coldly touches a deeper fear—abandonment. Through all the centuries those bonfires and Yule logs, those frenetic ravings against the night, now boosted by twenty-four hour cable, have helped us bluff our way through the dark.

A friend of mine sits at home today in total darkness. A life-long diabetic with only one eye left, he underwent a procedure to stave off the final loss. A laser cauterized some capillaries in hope of slowing the advance.

Christmas has come and gone in darkness for my friend. It's easy for his friends and family to tell him to be patient. We think that the darkness abates. But my friend is an artist, who knows when and how the heart trembles. And now he is on the far side of the moon. Which ghosts gather to gnaw on his heart? Or is it even worse there?

A critical moment 2004

Just over a week ago a remarkable meeting took place. Convened by the *Cincinnati Enquirer's* editorial board, a group of religious thinkers ate box lunches as they opened up over the Gibson Gospel.

The conversation began timidly and predictably. Some Christians declared that they saw the film through their eyes of faith, while the Rabbinic students calmly reiterated their concern for the anti-Semitic tone throughout the movie. Then the biblical scholar weighed in, describing Gibson's work as a Christian snuff film that failed on three counts—as a movie, as history, and as theology.

What could have happened didn't. Despite disagreements listening prevailed. It became clear that even the editors, who had waded into water far above their heads, were caught up in the discussion.

On the twentieth floor on Elm Street people began to consider the social consequences of religious imaginings. It became clear that religious issues are not something that can be treated as "local matters." There is a need for a disciplined public discourse on questions of religion. It is time to recognize that the televangelists and Mother Angelica do not reflect the majority of Americans, who seek out meaning for their lives.

It is time for all of us to grow up and become responsible for the dreams and damage of our particular traditions. It is also time for the *Enquirer* to take the next step to further this public conversation by hiring a full-time writer who has a critical appreciation of the development and diversity of religions.

It's a jungle out there 2004

Two Fridays ago, as many of us watched the obsessive anxiety of Adrian Monk, the TV San Francisco detective, Douglas Robinson of Northside spent his first night in jail. Earlier that day he had phoned police to say that he had shot his wife, Patricia.

Later it was learned that the former court reporter believed that he and his wife would soon be homeless. A bank mix-up started a woeful avalanche. While their apartment manager offered various agencies for assistance, Robinson heard only that they had just two months to get things in order.

Robinson, a one-eyed diabetic, living on disability, saw little hope—especially for his morbidly obese wife. He thought she would never survive on the street.

The County prosecutor, doing his best Inspector Javert imitation, declared that he has no sympathy for someone who should have sought a power higher than a gun.

In our American meritocracy such failures no longer have a Steinbeck to underwrite their human dilemma. Our moral calculus shields us from what we instinctively fear: that most Americans are only one catastrophic step away from the abyss.

It's a jungle out there
Disorder and confusion everywhere
No one seems to care ...
People think I'm crazy, 'cause I worry all the time
If you paid attention, you'd be worried too
You better pay attention
Or this world we love so much might just kill you ...
It's a jungle out there*

---

*Randy Newman, "It's a Jungle Out There," theme song for *Monk*.

March of Folly 2004

Twenty years ago the Pulitzer Prize winner Barbara Tuchman penned *The March of Folly*. In it she documented that throughout history woodenheaded leaders, refusing advice, willfully pursued policies that ran counter to common sense and even the security of a nation.

Tuchman called this stubborn adherence to counterproductive policy by its true name, "folly." When one operates by fixed notions and ignores any contrary signs, when one does not allow one's wishes to be deflected by the facts, then the stage is set for another round of delusion.

What was said of Philip II of Spain—"No experience of failure of his policy could shake his belief in its essential excellence"—sadly survives the sinking of the Armada.

Tuchman came back to me this week as I walked among rows and rows of military boots. Each pair had the name of a soldier who had been lost in Iraq. "Eyes Wide Open," a program of the American Friends Service Committee, encamped on a grassy mall at Xavier University.

For three days and nights people slowed down. They stooped to read the names. The boots had a human scent. One mother found her son's name and saw that the boots were not his size. So she returned with his boots and tied his picture to them.

I wondered why leaders—so adamant to stay the course—will not hear those boots falling in this new march of folly.

O, the horror, the horror, Ohio 2004

You know that this is a crazy election year when Sheriff Simon Leis turns into a democratic watchdog. Recently he emailed a terrorist alert to thousands of businesses and schools. Lame duck Luken, mayor of Cincinnati, was caught off guard and understandably confused that the Sheriff has become a loose cannon, firing his warning shot without any priming from Washington.

But connect the political dots. If Ohio is the "heart of it all" in the upcoming election, then Cincinnati is its right ventricle. Leis in the role of Paul Revere set out to warn the good-hearted people of Hamilton County that blood clots are coming.

In fact, Leis's scattershot may have hit something; for he joined the chorus of alarm that the election in Ohio is imperiled. Remembering his Shakespeare, Leis "from indirection, finds direction out." The major threat to the election not unsurprisingly comes from the "enemy within," that is, from political shenanigans.

The Republican Secretary of State has been doing his best to raise "80 pound stock" to the historical rank of "chads." Meanwhile the write-in election of Hamilton County Prosecutor not only will slow the results but may also justify throwing out any number of ballots.

Oh, the horror, the horror! Ohio, the new heart of darkness—the Florida of the Midwest!

High stakes Texas gamble 2005

Yes, I am still in Petra. Still stunned by the rose stone city. Still awed by the exhibition's fragments that will be gone from Cincinnati after tomorrow.

In my mind's eye I keep returning to those muted rooms. The most haunting piece is a sliver of a face, a male forehead with a suggestion of hair, a left eye and part of an upper lip. That is all. But more than enough to capture an unyielding strength.

Then there is that limestone carving. Nike, winged victory, holds aloft a zodiac circle that bears the seasons in familiar and surprising signs. Open-eyed and smiling enigmatically, Tyche, Lady Luck, stares from the center of that eternal round of fate.

The ancients knew that Lady Luck was fickle. Cultivate her as you would, she will always leave you in the end. Her face was beautiful, but you could never count on her.

Tomorrow, half a world away, people will risk their lives. Their children, their country, and their hopes spin on a wheel of fortune. From a safe distance we can only detect the bits and pieces of their anxious lives.

Whichever way they turn they are caught in a web not of their doing. Yet who else will pay for any losses the imperial high rollers deem acceptable in this high stakes Texas gamble?

Mind the gap 2005

"Mind the gap." Visitors to London soon are acquainted with this well-known British caution. You notice the yellow words painted near the edge of the platform. Pre-recorded voices intone the warning as the tube doors open.

"Mind the gap." These words have followed me back to the States, even to Cincinnati. Not only do they echo a happy summer but even suggest what might be described as a Zen koan. I've played with the ambiguity of these words. How can one be attentive to a gap, to what is not there? And what of the mind itself, is it not the gap par excellence? The ghost in the machine?

Oddly those words hovered about as I pondered another Cincinnati tragedy. A young mother killed her three-year-old daughter for wetting her pants. Reports registered the horror. Sympathy naturally flowed for the victim.

But my mind stayed with that mother. I detected a gap. That woman went over the edge. She had fallen beyond the lines of respectability. And yet I decided to stay in that gap, sensing the sheer terror of a mind completely at a loss. Perhaps only briefly, we have all been there, stretched, bewildered, apparently abandoned.

In that wild, drowning state, we lash out, keeping our fears at bay. The lucky ones catch an unexpected lifeline: "Mind the gap."

What do you say after goodbye? 2005

Nine years ago I took a chance with words. Former News Director Lorna Jordan offered listeners an opportunity to emerge from silence. After an initial commentary, she called me back. Soon Abie Ingber and I tag-teamed on alternate Fridays. After reporting from London two summers ago, I found a weekly niche on Saturday mornings.

My words to you have been drive-by images, fragile attempts to make some sense of this kaleidoscopic cosmos. Your thoughtful listening and responses have meant much.

Who knows what the next incarnation of WVXU will bring? I fear that, as elsewhere in this land, local accents will disappear.

Yet it is precisely now that different voices, even curmudgeons in Cincinnati, must be heard.

Our nation is on the brink. The middle class evaporates. News media fail to cross examine. No one, except the top 1 percent, trusts themselves and their children to the future. "Corporate interests" are another name for "high stakes gambling." A war, born in deception, begets hideous offspring.

As the X-Star satellite breaks up in its final minutes, I send out a last word: Will unexpected voices shake us from our silence, or shall we become comfortable with fascism, so understated in business suits?

At the end of the world 2005

What is left when your world ends?

We have all been thinking such desperate thoughts—more than we would admit these days. The plaintive voices from New

Orleans do not need any accompanying instrument. They turn us over and over in those muddy waters.

But we don't have to leave home to detect how vulnerable we are. A leaking tank car quickly shook us from our summer lethargy. Mayor Lame Duck sprang into action as families around Lunken Airport wondered if and when they could go home again.

Even this week, as work crews began to dig a block away from my house, the unimaginable came home to me. Thinking of the city's infrastructure crumbling daily beneath our streets, just for a second, I wondered ...

The ancients gave us a word for all of this: apocalyptic. Second-century Jews thought their world was over. A Syrian monarch would give Israel a Greek makeover. Traditions and heads were lopped off.

Out of this historical vertigo came the scroll of Daniel, where visions and revisions gave hope to those who would hang on.

From the whirlpool of our days there is a clue for us.

Beneath the spin and cover-up, beyond the numbing totals, human voices still reach us. They have come from the end of their world. With nothing left but stories.

Perhaps it is time for us to look up into the clear September sky, time to size up the sum of our fears, time to share with one another stories that come out of the blue.

Questions on Genesis   2007

Once again the greater Cincinnati area has become "the heart of it all." Not sated by the never-ending saga of the aging exile and hustler Pete Rose or the erstwhile fireworks of Marge Schott that brought back uneasy memories of brown-shirted parades on Fountain Square, or even the legendary crusades that lumped the photography of Robert Mapplethorpe alongside the centerfolds of Larry Flint, Cincinnati is entertaining another surge in publicity. Last Memorial Day the Creation Museum opened right across the Ohio River in northern Kentucky.

Dedicated to the "truth of the Bible"—that God created the heavens and the earth and all living things in six consecutive twenty-four hour days, six thousand years ago—and founded by private donations to the sum of $27 million, this museum has brought the wonders of Disney to Paradise. Adam and Eve not only talk with God, they stroll with dinosaurs. As home-schooled children, sheltered from the godless reach of public education, walk past the exhibits, just a nod from a dinosaur is enough to confirm their myopia. Pseudo-science and biblical literalism have found not only a home but a headquarters.

Now that the opening ribbons have been cut and guards patrol with guns and dogs, now that news crews from Europe and the States have gotten their fifteen minutes of sensationalism, it would be helpful to get some perspective on this event.

The mastermind behind this museum, Ken Ham, has constructed a modern ark against the inundations of the secular humanists. For him and his followers it is a matter of biblical truth sailing against the destructive influence of a godless world.

Yet, despite the dramatic allure of reading both the Bible and the earth along animatronic lines, there are some questions that will not be found in that museum, which finds all its answers in Genesis.

First, there is no wonder about the location of the creation story of Genesis within its own historical context. Indeed, the success of this museum comes only when visitors are ignorant of the contributions of the last three hundred years of biblical scholarship. Scholars have long known that the first chapter of the Bible did not fall out of the skies; indeed, it is a dramatic response to an earlier creation myth, the Enuma Elish. This was the prevalent creation story of the ancient world—or, at least, among the overlord Babylonians.

In the Enuma Elish the god Marduk wins dominion over the other gods by savagely gutting Tiamat, the Mother of the gods. Order is maintained by controlled violence. And human beings are then created to serve as slaves and playthings to the gods.

This story was celebrated every New Year's Day in Babylon. The exiled Jews, deported to Babylon in the early sixth century BCE, shivered within the triumphant echoes of this story. Then a priestly Hebrew poet composed an alternative reality. He retold the story imagining the world as coming into being not through violence but by the simple act of communication. The world was not populated by overriding gods, who kept humans underfoot. Instead, air, sea, and ground were fit for humans who embodied God's creative touch.

This was not a scientific account. Rather, it was a poetic response of a devastated people to the default story of an oppressive empire. The priestly author of Genesis 1 obviously did not know about nineteenth-century scientific empiricism out of which the Creation Museum reads the Bible. Rather, the writer paints a world where communication and reliability are the basis for human life.

But even the biblical poet had yet to contend with what we face today.

We do not live in the sixth century BCE; nor do we live out of its cosmology. In fact, we are still living in the fallout from the sixteenth century, when Galileo brought down the known universe with his telescope. Before Galileo the stars and planets burned as celestial spirits. When Galileo peered through his telescope, he realized that what he saw above was what he saw below. But this insight is yet outstanding for many observers of the skies. The heavenly world is still falling in slow motion like an aging satellite.

Moreover, only since the nineteenth century have we gradually begun to imagine the enormous age and size of the universe. We have yet to come to grips with the consequences of living in time, with recognizing the implications of the historical imagination. We would dearly live in some ideal virtual reality, yet even that is embedded in space and time.

The task before us is to reclaim our religious traditions within this still very much unimagined universe. But some prefer to live in religiously gated communities. If the matter is simply black and white, why worry about the gray?

The seven wonders of Cincinnati 2007

Perhaps you've heard of the contest to name the new Seven Wonders of the World. If you haven't there is still time to get your vote in. The deadline is July 6. You can vote by internet or phone. The winners will be announced on July 7 in Lisbon.

Bernard Weber, a Swiss adventurer, who heads a foundation to promote cultural diversity by supporting, preserving and restoring monuments, began this campaign in 1999 to bring the world together through pride in our global heritage.

Now United Nations Educational, Scientific and Cultural Organization (UNESCO) had already designated 830 places as World Heritage Sites. But Weber wanted to focus world attention and so gathered nominations for two hundred sites. Then the list was whittled down to seventy-seven, and then to twenty-one.

The Taj Mahal, Stonehenge, and the Pyramids are in competition with (among others) the Statue of Liberty, the Kremlin and Easter Island.

Pardon me for my provinciality but there was nothing of Greater Cincinnati on the final list. You might think it a bit cheeky to even imagine our Queen city on such an august ticket, but, in a town where our horizon often stops at the Ohio, that should not keep us from launching our own contest. Flying Pigs, here we go again!

What better way to honor this fair city than to list its wonders! Even better, why be burdened with our multitudinous marvels and monuments? Let's think outside the box, beyond the pedestals, and throw the contest into the future. Let's not settle for what the Seven New Wonders contest is content with—namely, the status quo. Why worry about the facts, when we can indulge in the American dream? Let's name wonders that we would like to see in Cincinnati. Despite the fact that we are not constitutionally disposed, let us imagine the Seven Wonders To Be of Cincinnati:

I begin with the religious base of our city: A Cincinnati Reds Farm system that actually produces a continuous crop of players who know how to pitch.

Two: a commodious new multi-purpose jail conveniently located near Paul Brown Stadium.

Three: a Fountain Square that is not under eternal construction.

Four: a Metro System that runs east-west as well as north-south, that runs frequently all day, has local and longer lines—even light rail—and accommodates the majority of commuters.

Five: public high schools that attract more students than they can hold.

Six: an Asian Garden beautifying the heart of the downtown—a jewel in our crown.

And last but not least: a public radio station with contributions from over 85 percent of its listeners.

2

Rounding the Bases

I continue with a section on baseball. This material follows closely on the first selection. For there is no Cincinnati without baseball—without the Reds. At the same time, as a displaced Bostonian, I came with my own brand of misery. Baseball, too, was in my blood. In fact, my commentary skills derive from listening to my parents: to my mother's narratives of family and incidental encounters and to my father's detailed description of the latest Red Sox disaster. I preferred his account of what happened over actually listening to the game. I could never ask what the score was. No, he would provide the background and frame for the play-by-play. Remembering this, it is still a soft summer night on the porch with my father drawing out the plays with puffs of a cigar.

Up close and personal 1996

This marks the fifth season's opening without my father. You see, for those of us growing up in New England, a passionate obsession was passed from father to son. Talking ourselves through those endless winters we conspired to hope again and again for more than the clear light of reason would ever allow: we dared to imagine that the Sox might go all the way. We choose to forget Updike's dictum: for the Red Sox fan there is always the agony in the garden but never a resurrection.

Dad's final season came in 1991. A severe pancreatic attack in May kept him from focusing too much on the early self-destruction of the Sox. His surprising recovery was mirrored by Boston's rise in the standings. And, even when he suffered a relapse, there seemed to be hope. Just before the Sox began their inevitable plunge into nowhere, Dad died.

Some of you might wonder why I would wrap words about my father in this seasonal ramble. I do so not only because we shared these words but because his death halted that cycle of words. Our seemingly endless round of games flattened out on the heart monitor.

Dwelling upon all those futile volleys against Fenway's Green Monster, I realized he gave me more than I imagined: he gave me words and the chance to speak. Baseball no longer holds its feverish fascination for me. But dreams do, and wanting to learn how people live from the stuff of hope, that electric surge from within. In short, I am my father's son.

The not so Splendid Splinter 1996

There he was again! Staring at me from the Sports Illustrated cover, gripping a bat slung over his left shoulder, Teddy Ballgame—no longer the lanky Kid, nor the swaggering forty-year-old batting champ; no, it was the not so Splendid Splinter at seventy-eight.

Three strokes have taken 75 percent of that phenomenal vision. The man who could read the seams of a fastball now sees through a glass darkly. Encountering him again on a magazine cover sobered me considerably. Here was the icon of my youth grown old. Those moments of exacting beauty, of those hips turning, wrists bringing the bat head around, the crack of solid contact, and the deafening roar of approval as the ball arced into the visitors' bullpen, those frozen moments began to melt.

I must admit that Ted Williams was never a role model for me. Unlike athletes today who give lip service to such nonsense, Ted was too complex to imitate. How do you respond to someone who wins a game one day and then throws a tantrum the next? I learned how to hit from a man concentrated on his craft, knowing at the same time that his private life shattered in his hands from such fierce intensity. Indeed, only recently has he finally found the worth of his children. The discrepancy between his performance and personality was what ballplayers call a "nagging injury."

That volcanic rage to perfection smolders still amid the debris of age. But now it vents in surprising ways. A wheel-chaired girl he met while rehabilitating receives his tender care, while a thirty-five-pound salmon, that took his cast, fought him hard, and then slipped away when he pulled too much, occupies his waking dreams.

Even now that "foolish, fond, old man" rudely discovers that he is much too difficult to be simply the greatest hitter of all time.

▌In the light of the gods ⠀⠀⠀⠀⠀⠀1997

In less than a fortnight Baseball will begin again. Having grown up in Boston, that hotbed of baseball futility, where masochists are weaned on the many splendored ways of defeat, especially in the seventh game, I have been forced repeatedly to ask what is really going on down there between the lines. The realization that, as John Updike put it, for the Red Sox there is no Resurrection but only an Agony in the Garden convinced me some time ago to seek a theological resolution not in Jerusalem, nor in Rome, but on Olympus.

Just open up Homer's *Iliad*. There the basic operating procedure of the divine is quite clear. In the heat of battle, at the critical point, suddenly one participates in the blessed life. For a fleeting moment excellence is sensed, a decision is made, the goddess smiles. Human and divine action coalesce in a sphere of significance.

But there is a price for this understanding. Again and again we are warned not to measure ourselves against the gods. For gods and mortals are of different breeds. Thus, while the gods might come close, that very experience carries with it the cost of knowing one's mortal limits. Moreover, as Hector's death scene shows, divinity flees the doomed individual. At best we gain a glimpse of a realm the Olympians inhabit forever.

So for me the boys of summer play in the fragile light of the gods. It is this Homeric perspective which gives me the equanimity to see the baseball forever running past a hobbled Bill Buckner, or Bucky Dent's cruel homer over the Green Monster, or Eric the Red's staggering First Game home run off Dave Stewart and then his body crumpled on the grass after attempting a catch in the final game of the '90 World Series.

More than I ever expected   1997

There I stood looking down at Cinergy Field on opening day. This was not supposed to be the way my birthday turned out. The plan was simple: pick up my older son after school, buy a couple of scalped tickets, and spend some quality time with my fifteen-year-old.

The only thing that worked was getting into the six-dollar stadium parking lot. Couldn't scare up a ticket. By the time we reached Fountain Square sporting its pink froth, it was clear that the April Fool's joke was on us.

Then Geoff suggested Carew Tower. In my seventeen years in Cincinnati I had never performed that pilgrimage. So, we made the ascent. That magnificently clement weather seemed to hold the city spellbound. We heard the roar from Cinergy Field even before we turned south on the observation deck to peer down on the stadium.

But soon the game lost its charm. We turned east and then north and imagined what Cincinnati looked like a century ago. Our mutual reverie was interrupted, however, by a young man leading with a Boston accent, "How are the homeless treated in Cincinnati?"

As we talked I learned that he worked with various social coalitions persuading cities to give the homeless a chance to own their own homes in the inner city. The monumental debate over Broadway Commons versus the riverfront grew minuscule in light of genuine need. My eyes scanned the horizon from the

West End to Over-the-Rhine. The buildings below took on a fragile flesh tone in the late afternoon sun. Voices as silent as the stadium was thunderous reached my ears.

He left by saying that he was going back east, probably to be arrested in a couple of days in another protest. My son, who had been listening, said, "That's a good thing that he's doing, isn't it?" Those compassionate words were more than I ever expected from opening day.

An impossible dream? 1997

I never imagined that our County Auditor Dusty Rhodes would be part of my midsummer dreaming. But there it was. With a sense of fiscal responsibility and wit, Rhodes proposed the obvious. Why spend hundreds of millions building a stadium for a team that, given the carpetbagging of modern sports, may well pack up and leave, when controlling interest in the team could be purchased by the people?

I know that the team is not up for sale. But when has that stopped unwanted suitors from wooing some vulnerable company? And now is the time to swoop, if recent financial reports of red ink are to be believed. Indeed, why can't the Reds be owned like the Green Bay Packers? You want to swell the ever-dwindling crowds at Cinergy? Make all the seats from the red to the blue owners' boxes! The players would literally be playing for us! Such a move would bring the capitalism of baseball back to its democratic roots.

But, as I said, this is part of my midsummer dreaming. And with dreams come frightening possibilities. What if the City Council wanted to get in on this? Especially in an election year. A painful image comes out of the dugout of my mind: collective management à la the Cubs of the mid sixties. The brain trust of Qualls, Heimlich, Tillery, Sterne, et al, in pinstripes is too appalling to contemplate.

But that rogue image should not dissuade us. For a moment dream the impossible dream: Cinergy to the people! The Braves may be a fictive America's team, but the Reds can be really ours. Let Lasorda bleed his Dodger blue; we'll even hemorrhage in red ink until we get the farm system going again. If we own it, we will come.

Where the game is truly played   1998

I thought I was all over it. The midwinter announcement for opening day '98 made little impression on me. No telltale hankerings to go out to the old ballpark. No desire to get a first day fix.

And this from someone who had seen Bobby Kennedy throw out the inaugural ball at Fenway, the day when Tony Conigliaro smashed his first home run into deep center field. When I moved to Cincinnati, I began to see another side to the team that defeated the Sox in '75. I could not help myself. Soon I was caught up in the civic liturgy of the Reds' opener. I saw Tom Seaver bend his knee on every pitch, marveled at Mario Soto's fast ball, chuckled delightedly when the Reds turned on Nolan Ryan, or predictably took out Mike Torres, now laboring for the Mets, by the second inning.

But those memories have been dislodged by that headless hypocrisy, euphemistically called Major League Baseball. Interest fades when sports pages turn into People Magazine or the Police Blotter. Alienation sets in when star players garner financial packages greater than many university endowments.

As I said, I thought it was over. But then my older son decided to go out for his high school team. He got me running in January. By early February we were playing catch. Then we hit the batting cages. Meanwhile there was practice at six in the morning. No long term contracts here. No guarantees. Just the familiar rhythm of throwing and catching. Every now and again you marvel at making a play or jack the ball with the sweet spot of the bat. God, I love this game.

So there will be baseball for me this year. Not in the concrete cavern of Cinergy but on the sandlots, where, even in the mud, the game is really played.

If we own it, we will come!   1998

Last August I shared with you my midsummer musings: if we own it, we will come. Yes, I called for the sale of the Reds to the people of Cincinnati. Want to swell the ever-dwindling crowds at Cinergy? Make all the seats from the red to the blue owners' boxes! The players literally would be playing for us!

But now the dream does not seem so far-fetched. A curious constellation hovers over Cincinnati, and I don't mean the moon and stars of P&G. Reports abound that the dysfunctional owners of baseball would prevent the return of Marge Schott to active status. Indeed, they would prefer to give her an outright release.

At the same time the ratings of WLW have gone south. In what might simply be a ratings ploy, Gary Burbank, Andy Furman and other talk personalities threw out the possibility of Jacor Communications buying the Reds, with the proviso that Jacor would then offer 49 percent of the team's stock to the people. An executive at Jacor, Randy Michaels, has indicated the company's interest, although nothing was said of the people's ownership.

Meanwhile, Bill Koch of the Cincinnati Post has publicly appealed to Marge Schott to sell the Reds for the sake of the fans.

Certainly things are very much in flux. But consider this radical possibility for the people of Cincinnati and the Tri-State. What would happen not only if Jacor could convince Marge to sell but, even more, if Jacor went beyond its own self-interest? What if Jacor became the middleman in a deal which ultimately would give the people of Cincinnati ownership of the team? Even 51 percent?

Too wild a thought? Could it be that capitalism and democracy could work together? Let's dream the impossible dream: Cinergy to the People! If we own it, we will come!

In the spirit of Cincinnatus   1998

As advertised, the battle for Ohio takes place at Cinergy Field this weekend as the Reds host the Indians. This is but shadow boxing compared to the struggle behind the scenes.

For many the issue is simply about where the Reds should play. Too familiar is the controversy over the future site for the Reds. It's been two years since Hamilton County approved the stadium funding proposal. While the Bengals gained the lions' share of the spoils, the Reds maintained a pat hand, countenancing nothing other than a Riverfront wedge.

Neither the enormous groundswell of support, nor the arguments that an Over-the-Rhine site would arrive sooner and at less expense, nor even the City's recent offer of a $20 million incentive package, has had any noticeable impact upon the Reds' front office.

It is precisely this refusal to look at the larger picture, to imagine the public good, which reveals the deeper issue. For, whatever the resolution, there remains a fundamental problem. Not even a nostalgic ballpark can remove the likelihood that one day the Reds owners could decide to move or indulge in further urban blackmail.

As I mentioned recently, this might be the opportune moment. Others have sensed this, including Hamilton County Treasurer Robert Goering, who raised the possibility of Marge Schott's selling her general partnership shares to the County. Although County Commissioner Bob Bedinghaus predictably rejected this suggestion, the Cincinnati Post took a page from the Cleveland Indians' portfolio and called for a public stock offering for Reds fans.

The key in all of this is majority ownership by the people, not by the government; otherwise, Cincinnati will always be at the mercy of those who could take the team, the money and run. Wouldn't it be amazing if the Reds' partners acted in the spirit of Cincinnatus and returned their interest to the people?

Still dreaming that, if we own it, we will come—Cinergy to the People!

Late afternoon squall in Cincinnati 2000

Tonight begins the final series for the Reds. Before this season slides away in a flood of disappointment for many, I would carve a scene from last Saturday. My favorite pitcher, Pete Harnisch, was slated against the Astros.

Things did not go well. Dmitri Young played the lead-off batter's fly ball into a double. Bagwell soon brought him home. Back-to-back home runs gave the Astros a three-run lead two innings later. Although the Reds fought back to get within a run, time and luck seemed to be running out.

Then, as the bottom of the eighth began, the heavens opened. For two hours we contemplated the late afternoon downpour. It was as if Hiroshige, the famous Japanese woodcutter, had worked his magic on this field of dreams. Slanting lines of rain cut down on humans scurrying for cover.

Finally the skies cleared. Only the faithful were left. Out of the thirty-two thousand about two hundred remained. My son Nick and I stood behind the visitors' bullpen. We watched Franklin the left-hander and Slusarski the righty warm up. Franklin's ball was moving. You could catch up to the righty's.

After Franklin got Casey to ground out, Slusarski was brought in. He promptly gave up homers to Ochoa and Stynes.

This was baseball at its purest. For the space of an inning something occurred that does not happen often in the major leagues. This was not for those fans who believe a baseball game is a constant grazing event.

This was for the resolute. Nothing was left. No title. No championship. Just the game itself. I cheered each pitch, each pop of the glove, each crack of the bat. It was beautiful. It was Zen.

George Brett and the Supremes   2005

In his initial at bat before the Senate Judiciary Committee, John Roberts likened his prospective job to that of an umpire's. He doesn't make laws but applies the law. He will "call 'em as he sees 'em."

What would George Brett say about such legal theory? Brett is famous for the "Pine Tar Controversy." Billy Martin, the manager of the Yankees, waited until the right moment to mention to the home plate umpire that the pine tar on Brett's bat went too far up the barrel. Only after Brett had hit a ninth inning two-run homer, did Martin make his case. The umpires agreed, cancelled the home run, and called Brett out, thereby ending the game. Upon which Brett leapt ferociously out of the dugout to dispute the decision.

The controversy did not die. The Royals protested the game. Then the American League president, as the final arbiter, declared that, while the decision was technically correct, it had actually violated the spirit of the law. The only reason for the rule was the stinginess of baseball owners. Tired of replacing baseballs, scuffed from pine tarred bats, they had constructed this rule to save money. It had nothing to do with giving any player an advantage.

So MacPhail reversed the umps' decision, restored Brett's homer and ordered that the Yankees play the Royals from that point in the game.

MacPhail's decision demonstrated what so-called strict constructionists want to deny: that every legal decision is an interpretation, that one can never wash one's hands of a judgment. When you call 'em as you see 'em, you should be honest enough to admit that the ump isn't blind.

3

On the Road

Before my summer in London (2003), I had already made a few "on the road commentaries." Because of academic commitments I have had occasion to travel throughout North America and Europe. With my sojourn in London I actually began recording, editing and transmitting the commentaries. The dozen pieces "from London" gave me great pleasure. Somewhat idiosyncratic, they capture what captivated me during that serendipitous summer. I have often been fortunate to have been led astray by friends, who have introduced me to situations and people I would never have found on my own. The final essays suggest my ongoing love affair with Greece.

Montage of memory   1996

Recently I visited an antique mall in Indiana. In the midst of the debris of the past, I came across a homely, white, wooden frame containing a faded photo collage of a family spanning four generations. The photos ranged from early twentieth century to the sixties.

In the upper left hand corner Dad and Mom Grottle proudly posed, probably outside their home. To the right stood a photo of their son Fred clad in the uniform of the Great War. As my eyes followed along the rows of photos, the family of Fred Grottle took form. Fred and his wife (shown in various bathing suits over the years) had a daughter and son. Both of them seemed to have married and Fred's grandchildren stared out hopefully in grammar school poses.

In many ways there was nothing terribly remarkable about this collection of faded aunts, uncles, autos—even a silhouette— that crowded into view. Indeed, what principally amazed me was that it was being sold. Upon inquiring, I found out that the seller's wife had picked up the item solely for the yard-long frame, since its dimensions were prized by many who would construct their own photo collages. I then found out from the seller's wife that she had purchased the item at an auction in Hamilton, Ohio, and that the members of the family were there. She had asked them if they really wanted to part with the piece and was taken aback when they allowed the purchase.

Now I do not know why the Grottles parted with these pictures. Finances may have dictated, perhaps they were intent to avoid a family feud, perhaps the memories were just too hard to bear, or maybe they had more photos than they could handle. But I do know this: their letting go of their family's images into the hands of strangers is an intimation of what we must all do someday.

Where theologians fear to tread   1996

The good news is that I shall be in New Orleans in two weeks. The bad news is that I shall be at a convention of biblical scholars. For those of you who never travel among the academic tweed, let's just say that the intellectual flight of a biblical convention is very much like that of Howard Hughes' Spruce

Goose—the wooden plane that flew once and then was relegated to a museum.

Even the seven deadly sins have much less bite. Pride postures superciliously behind a podium. Envy bites a lip and takes down illegible notes. Covetousness looks longingly at those with jobs; while lust preoccupies itself among the book displays. In sum, our sins tend to be as mediocre as our salaries.

That is why, after sitting through the daylong tortures of the mind, I shall slip away to Preservation Hall. I shall stand in line and then find a space on the dusty floor in that dilapidated jazz room.

Four years ago my friend Max introduced me to this intimate exchange of sound. There I sat as the ancient Humphrey brothers, Percy at trumpet and Willie at clarinet slumped in their old press-back chairs between sets. The eighty-seven-year-old Percy was handed a clump of dollar bills from the gatekeeper and he slowly sorted them out for each member of the band.

But it was Willie at ninety-one years of age, sitting there in silence, who left an indelible impression upon me. His broad brown face seemed suspended in long-suffering. Was this the face of God?

Then Percy's trumpet sounded and we were off. For the first time in my life I realized that jazz could take us where theologians fear to tread—especially when Willie slowly rose from his chair, reared back with his clarinet, and played as if the notes would never end.

▌Among giants   1997

Recently I walked among giants. Not that I had intended to. But a former student of mine and her boyfriend, having picked me up at the San Francisco Airport, led me astray once again into ecstasy.

For the last few years, whenever I come to the Bay area for a seminar or convention, Cindy and Richard generously pick me up. The only thing they ask for is that they shanghai me for the afternoon. Before dropping me off at my destination, they delight themselves in introducing Dr. Dewey to another facet of their California.

Usually we first find some obscure place to eat, like Ma Ma Ya's, a Japanese breakfast and lunch hole-in-the-wall (which unfortunately has since closed with Ma Ma Ya's marriage and migration with her husband to Oregon), or Babette's, a singular restaurant in sleepy Sonoma. Both Richard and Cindy bring their considerable analytical skills to bear upon the area's cuisine and vineyards.

And they do this all in an absentminded joy. I have watched them tease each other, recounting one another's foibles and mutual comedies, as we careen along Route 101. But more, I have been able to mark their growth and affection for each other.

And so, when we spent a quiet afternoon in Muir Woods, where the ancient redwoods soar as high as football fields are long, where you can lose your balance by simply gazing up at a seven hundred-year-old tree, I took another look at Cindy and Richard and marveled how, in that silence and sunlight and mist, they were tutoring me in the gentle art of life.

Boston Common at twilight   1998

By the time you hear these words, I shall be back in Boston. A biblical convention brings me back to my birthplace. But it will carry me back to far more than the ruminations of scholars.

For me Boston is November. Especially at gaslight. I know that I will escape the posturings and pontifications of learned colleagues some afternoon, catch the 'T' to Park Street and then turn south along Tremont Street, turning right onto Boyleston. And there, at the southeast edge of the Common, if all the elements fall alchemically in place, I shall glimpse what Childe Hassam painted over a hundred years ago.

Hassam's perspective quietly draws you in. On the left trolley cars shuttle along Boyleston as a horse drawn cab disappears into the focal point of the scene. On the right a steadfast array of wind-ruined trees carries your line of vision to the emotional center of the piece.

There on the trodden snow, slightly left of center, in front of numerous pedestrians, a young woman, well-dressed in browns, watches her two daughters in their fir-trimmed coats throw crumbs to eight flittering sparrows. As the sun sets fire to the trees on the right, warming the brick-faced background, the woman's profile turns golden as she and her young ones are lost in that forgetfully fragile moment.

Almost thirty years ago I fell into that scene. Even before I encountered Hassam I knew the aching nostalgia of a November afternoon. But Hassam gave me a way to see why I felt such unexpected pain. He drew me to the heart of it: a flickering of tenderness as the sun goes down.

Tending a fire   2001

The smell of smoke is still in my hair. Three days after returning from the mountains of West Virginia I can detect residues from the fire tended over the Memorial Day Weekend.

It was good to get back—not just to nature—but to those habits that have characterized humanity for millennia. Building a fire and keeping it going are not automatic. It is not simply a matter of throwing logs in the fireplace and lighting a match. You really have to work for a fire, especially if the logs are damp. Paper, kindling, and well-positioned logs are essential. You can't overlook the airflow; the fire has to breathe. What is not seen is as crucial as what builds before you. Interstices count.

Now you enter a world of care. A fire must be tended. How different it is from the focus of the modern hearth—the TV. Tending a fire demands sensing real changes, noticing the subtle turns and hungry vagaries of the flame. For most of us the television hearth is at best predictable; at worst, a numbing ghost-watch.

Yet why bother with all that work, that mess of smoke and spark? Because it still can teach us much. It gives us the occasion to indulge in reverie, in dreams that fly up with the sparks, as voices huddle by the flames.

It reminds us that there is no magic. No burning bush. Except those necessary, small, human steps in learning to build and be surprised. A holy moment. Get it started and, if you have built well, the chemistry of flame takes over. Loosed from the logs, long-ago sunrises and sunsets pour out wildly, coruscate and vanish in our care.

Alice Kurtz, flight 509   2001

What do you do when a portrait, painted in 1903, comes to life, walking down the aisle of a 757? I had just secured my seatbelt when I saw a young mother with her two children and husband settling themselves down eight rows forward in the plane, bound for San Francisco.

What was Alice Kurtz doing on Flight 509, seat 30C? Had time and space been tampered with? Those high cheek bones, that slender neck, brown hair drawn back, and those thoughtful eyes, should be on the wall in the Fogg Museum back in Cambridge.

Thomas Eakins painted not what should be but what is. With an eye tutored in anatomy, Eakins rejected the flattering art of his sensational contemporaries and got deeper than bone and sinew — he dared explore the dark side of the mind. He caught his subjects exhausted, somber, or defiant, at the very edge of sadness.

Alice Kurtz sits in a play of golden light and shadows, with her eyes staring off to the right, transfixed in a moment that shimmers in sorrow. There is still resolve left in her cheek, lips, and delicate neck.

But there she was in front of me. An orange T-shirt instead of a lace blouse. And in my notebook a copy of the Eakins' portrait. Should I ask if she knew the work? Perhaps a descendent?

An hour before we landed I interrupted her return from the lavatory. She looked at me warily. But, on viewing the reproduction she became pensive, even puzzled. Her daughter then started to wake; she handed the portrait back.

Will she return to that image of no illusion? At least, I got to see Alice Kurtz finally smile.

From London
London on the Fourth 2003

The English traditionally follow the lead of old King George who noted in his diary of July 4, 1776 that nothing very much important happened that day.

At home in Cincinnati the bottle rockets would have been engaged for two or three nights before parade day.

But in London on the fourth it is business as usual. And that's fair enough. We might have won that war, but the Brits have more than one disastrous foreign war to fall back on and out of which they will spin a dramatic tale. Just visit the Tower of

London for an afternoon and see what the Yeoman warders, Beefeaters to us, can do with the mayhem of royal history.

But impressions of America do seep out even in the tube. An airline add plays to the cost conscious English by advising that "When every waitress, barman, taxi driver and bellboy in America is expecting a tip, you need a cheap flight."

Meanwhile BBC Radio Personality Annie Nightingale helps those of us whose first language is not English. She published the results of her survey to determine the biggest "div" on earth. A "div" is a silly boy, a daft bloke, an uninspired adult who just doesn't get it. With three times more votes than any other person in this category our George W. finally won an election.

Of course, if Yanks need fireworks on the Fourth, they can enjoy one of the hottest tickets in town: *Jerry Springer: The Opera*, where three-nippled cousins and lesbian trailer trash make us proud to be Americans.

From London
Groundlings 2003

We were groundlings for the night. For five pounds I got to stand with almost six hundred people in the new Globe theatre to hear Christopher Marlowe's play *Dido Queen of Carthage.*

If you saw *Shakespeare in Love,* recall the theatre with an open roof, where Gwyneth Paltrow disguised herself and her love, where Judi Dench as Queen Bess sat in the Queen's box. That's where I was. Not in the box, but on the ground, two feet from the stage.

But the play was not just a retelling of the tragic love of the Punic Queen for the duty-driven founder of Rome. This play helped usher in the birth of English blank verse. Consider how a school play—yes it was performed originally by choirboys— helped launch wave after wave of the "wonder of our speech."

I did not count the time. Nor did my ankles cry. I stood enchanted on that summer eve.

The next night my teenage son went with friends to see *Richard II.* They gambled and got in on no-show tickets.

For the first time in their lives my son and his best friend heard Shakespeare. Imagine two American teenagers, more at home in video games, standing spellbound for almost three hours.

When they got home, they did not retire to their rooms. Instead of isolating themselves with their earphones, they sat around the kitchen table and became animated as they detected what the "airy nothingness" of words can do.

From London
Moonrise 2003

There I was in summer shorts, freezing as the wind off the Thames picked up, waiting for the moon to rise. I was looking to the southeast in anticipation, because of the startling claim by Don Olson, a Texas astronomer. He had done his homework and made a convincing argument that tonight would duplicate the conditions of that evening 114 years ago which Vincent van Gogh captured in a painting known as "Moonrise."

Because I could not get to Saint-Remy to experience the lunar event, I decided to watch the moon emerge over the Globe Theatre as I stood on the Millennium Bridge. The sunset slowly coruscated away, leaving glimpses of flame on high-rise office windows. It was after ten, the lamps along the Thames brightened. But the moon had yet to show.

I walked over to the Globe and there met three of my students who had heard of my mad moonwalk. I recalled John Lyly's sixteenth-century play *Endymion*, about a man who fell in love with the moon. We began to see ourselves in the role of Linus, waiting in vain for the Great Pumpkin.

We walked back across the bridge. Then almost around eleven the moon rose over the Globe. It was hugely full, golden, and magnificent, with a slight nimbus surrounding it.

Van Gogh and Shakespeare fell into alignment, as did the words of Keats' "Endymion":

> A thing of beauty is a joy for ever:
> … it will never
> Pass into nothingness; but still will keep …
> Yes, it will keep.

From London
Stones 2003

One of the best-kept secrets in England is Scotland. We're all familiar with the blaring stereotypes of that land—the kilts, bagpipes, burr and wild red hair, romantic glens, misty lochs, and craggy mountains. But Scotland is not itself without its stones.

Edward the First knew this. That scoundrel packed off the Stone of Destiny, the Stone of Scone, upon which Scottish kings had been invested with power. Longshanks had a coronation throne constructed that would entomb the Stone of Scone. Only recently did the British government relent and remit the Stone of Destiny back to Edinburgh.

There in Edinburgh Castle I saw it along with the crown jewels or honors, as the Scots would call them. They were simple enough: an enormous sword, once broken in half, a scabbard cracked in three places, an arching crown, and the Stone of Destiny. Modest in comparison to the jewels in the Tower of London. But a thrifty Scot would say enough for a king to get a grip.

As I walked through Edinburgh I became acquainted with the silent witness of stones. I found damp alleyways and the underground where the poor and outcast had shivered their lives away.

I walked to Regent Park and found a ring of stones, sent from every region of Scotland. As the poet Hugh MacDiarmid puts it, "all the loose ends of Scotland" are gathered there. For some time I sat with those stones and slowly grasped the patient power of a people.

From London
Madness of George Dubya 2003

Free speech, bound and gagged in America, is alive and well in London. *The Madness of George Dubya*, written and directed by Justin Butcher, launches a stealth satire, flying merrily under reactionary flak.

It begins happily enough. Secure in his plaid jammies, superman T-shirt, and cowboy gear, while hugging an enormous teddy, Dubya shares his dreams. The War on "Tourism" and his expert handling by gangster men in black—including Colin Dick and Donald Duck—are keeping the world safely at gun point.

Then everything goes to hell. The shades of Dr. Strangelove haunt the dream of Dubya. A lower echelon American Air Force officer decides to maintain the purity of the world by unleashing "Ultimate Justice" on "Iraqistan." The PM, Tony "Blear," hyperventilates at the growing realization that he cannot spin this idiocy away.

With updated lyrics from Tom Lehrer, Butcher punctuates his play with uproarious music. Even Mina "the Cleaner," gets down to basics, shedding her smock to bump and grind her terrorist sympathies in a black leather bra, trimmed with timers for her strap-on dynamite.

I shall not give the ending away, except to say that it is far more unnerving than Kubrick's devastation.

Writing fine satire is always a risk, as it builds on the madness of the moment. Butcher's company brings us to the wits' end of the world.

Even Dubya has some wisdom for America: "Ever have a dream where you know something bad is going to happen and you can't move?"

From London
California dreamin' 2003

For many Americans California is a state of mind. The recent recall initiative that has Governor Gray Davis scrambling for his political life suggests this once buoyant dreamland has begun to crack along predictable fault lines.

But in London California is an oasis on the Tube. During afternoon rush hour, we wait sometimes two and three deep for the next un-air-conditioned car. Computerized messages countdown the minutes to the next stage of the ordeal. In the fetid heat, we have only energy enough to stare numbly across the tracks. And right over there is a panorama of heaven itself!

A prizewinning chardonnay anchors the right corner, while the subdued crowd can only gaze at Ernest and Julio's vineyard, decked out in green and gold and stretching right up to the foothills of the Sierras. Hovering clouds in a brilliant blue sky signal a perfect day. "California dreamin'" instantly crosses the Atlantic and the tracks.

Yet even paradise can come to a jarring halt. Inside the car, four girls from UCLA, barricaded by suitcases, were engrossed in their own bubble gum conversation. The entire car heard their opinions on the great matters of life, namely hair and color preferences.

Valley speak had taken its toll. As they got off at Russell Square, a woman looked over plaintively to me and said, "California girls! Americans I usually can take, but these four haven't shut up since they got on at Heathrow, over an hour ago!"

From London
Boudica 2003

Many Americans coming to London are surprised to learn that it started off as a Roman town. With no evidence of any settlement in pre-Roman times, fragments of the Roman Wall still can be seen on the streets today.

Julius Caesar made two raids on Britain, but it was only ninety-seven years later in the year 43 CE that the Emperor Claudius, needing a military victory, invaded with four legions. Colchester, in what is now East Anglia, became the Roman capital, Londinium a staging area and port.

An East Anglian tribe, the Iceni, tried to walk the tightrope as a semi-independent client kingdom of Rome. When their king died, the Roman procurator decided that this proud people was not submissive enough. Roman grants of money were now re-named loans and immediate repayment was demanded. Queen Boudica was flogged, her daughters raped.

But Boudica did not submit. She rallied her people. A Roman historian describes her as tall, with red hair flowing to her waist, wearing a gold neck-ring and clutching a spear. Colchester with its imperial temple, London and St. Albans went up in flames.

Then a fatal mistake: Boudica faced the legions in a pitched battle in the Midlands. Emotion and ferocity could not carry the day over disciplined troops.

Yet Roman occupation did not erase Boudica's brave memory. You can see her still, on Victoria Embankment, across from Big Ben, riding her war chariot into history. A disturbing reminder to the empire mongers of today.

From London
Recipe 2003

Perhaps the best way of fathoming London is by getting lost. Not only must you ask someone for guidance but also you come upon such unexpected things.

There we were wandering about in Soho, sniffing our way along Old Compton Street, renowned for its eclectic shops and restaurants. The sun had finally set. There in the half-lit window of a café stood two Christmas trees in white and dark chocolate. They towered over us as we stood in awe on the sidewalk.

We had chanced on Patisserie Valerie, a Hungarian owned café.

Fortunately, one of my companions, Sharon, a co-owner of a Cincinnati bakery, knew exactly what these towers were and how their flowing skirts were confected. She revealed the recipe on the spot. Melt chocolate, either white or dark, with corn syrup. Then knead it until it gets like clay. When it is workable, roll it out, like homemade pasta. Cut it evenly, crimp the edges. Attach each piece in ascending order with icing or egg white. Shake powdered sugar or cocoa on top. Voilà.

The simplicity of the recipe was inversely proportional to its dramatic effect.

I mused on the care and precision in Sharon's voice. Here was an artist leading the rest of us into the mysteries. Out of chunks of chocolate and gobs of syrup came something beautiful. A baker is truly a sidewalk artist, creating, not with chalk, but with much more awkward elements, a fleeting wonder for our days.

From London "Over There" 2003

Back in the frenzied days of World War II, with America recoiling from Pearl Harbor and anticipating marshalling troops in England for an invasion of Europe, an unknown writer in the War Department penned "Over There: Instructions for American Servicemen in Britain, 1942."

The London Times wryly noted that this pamphlet should become a best seller since it gave an unusually direct view of how others see the British. In sixteen pages the writer described the country, the people, their customs and manners, their quiet determination in war, as well as some oddities of language.

Americans were well advised to "look, listen, and learn" before entering into a conversation. Size or "being the biggest" meant little to the English. But age and tradition spoke volumes. Servicemen should remember that these Britains, so soft-spoken and polite, had been in a war zone since 1939. Even their women have died at their gun posts as other girls stepped forward to "carry on."

So, look before you speak.

Especially in pubs. Americans must realize that a pub is a neighborhood gathering place, not a service station.

I wish I had this booklet a week ago. Twenty-two of my students descended on a pub in Salisbury, thinking they could order, then catch the train to Bath in twenty minutes. An hour later their orders still dribbled out. The request for chocolate milk took the longest, since the bar tender had to go out back to milk his goat!

From London
From knickers to saris 2003

You can get to Leicester from St. Pancras Station in a little more than an hour. But the trip from London to that Midland city is more than a simple translation of time and space.

Recently a friend, Alan Race, an Anglican priest, long engaged in interfaith work, invited me up for a day.

Once famous for its manufacture of stockings and underwear, Leicester is undergoing a cultural sea change: from knickers to saris.

Immigrants from India now form a substantial portion of the population as Leicester contends with Birmingham to be, within the next decade, the first city in England with a south Asian majority.

Leicester seems to be handling the transition well except for incidents festering from pockets of poverty and unemployed youth.

We visited three religious communities before enjoying a late lunch. We attended the devotions in a Jain temple, heard the sacred text of the Sikhs chanted, and watched elderly Hindu women pay homage to Krishna. Each temple left me with a different aspect of serenity.

And Alan left me with a parable. The Hindu Temple was once a Baptist church from which the missionary William Carey went off decades ago to India. He brought both the Bible and a social conscience. Now the very people he would have converted have arrived at Leicester, purchased the church, and transformed its dark and somber wooded sanctuary into a lively riot of light and color that the Baptists would never have dreamt possible on earth.

From London
Rikki
2003

My chat with Rikki began innocently enough. The maintenance man had come to catalogue my hot water heater. Evidently all the building's new machines were defective and would eventually produce losses in the thousands of pounds.

He was quietly documenting this probable catastrophe. His somewhat smothered accent was vaguely familiar. From where? Yes, Australia. Hasn't been there since 1985.

What brought you to London? "Body snatchers."

At that I froze. Was this long-haired, mustached man some sort of ET freak?

Then I learned. Rikki Shields is an aborigine, whose early life was spent in a Catholic mission, where they "cut his mother tongue out of his head." Then he began a walkabout of thirty years that took him throughout all of Australia. At Mantrika, the blue rock, the place of dreams, he discovered his mission. He then went through the country photographing his people and land. Leaving his "Land of Broken Dreams," he became his people's voice in "London Town where Clay People dwell."

A video made from his photos, "A Journey of the Spirit," was awarded the Golden Knight of Malta. Through his poetry and photographs he calls out to England to return the remains of his people, encased in Museums, or on some royal surgeon's shelf.

Rikki still hopes that "there is humanity in this hostile jungle city." Didn't they remember the "Dusky Cricket Warrior" King Cole? Meanwhile, his protests will not die down. Nor will he forget the water heaters.

From London
Taking leave
2003

When I leave London I shall not go quietly. But, like any good Tube rider, no one will know it!

As they wave me through customs, as I buckle in for the nine-hour flight, the better part of me will still be sitting on a bench in Green Park under a canopy of London Plain trees.

On the other hand, friends may have to perform an intervention and pry my still good BritRail Pass from my hands. Just the thought of returning to frontier conditions where the mere notion of public transportation turns the oil industry apoplectic sends shivers up my spine.

Days before I take off I know I shall become nostalgic, like Garbo in Queen Christina, memorizing every nook and cranny. Even tourists will wonder about me staring at the sky, trying to absorb the blue of the late afternoon.

Everything that I see will be for the last time. But isn't that what life is? Always seeing things for the last and the first time?

So, as the Thames flows under me at Blackfriars Bridge, and I direct my gaze west to catch the sunset's glint off Big Ben and Westminster, I see what Dr. Johnson meant three centuries ago:

> Why, Sir, you find no man, at all intellectual, who is
> willing to leave London. No, Sir, when a man is tired of
> London, he is tired of life; for there is in London all that
> life can afford.

From Baton Rouge
Two silent islands   2003

As the year creeps incrementally into the dark, after the trick or treat of Halloween and recent elections, I'm haunted by a story almost ten years old. You may remember the headlines of November 1, 1994: "Japanese student killed on Halloween by home owner."

Here in Baton Rouge there is a church that remembers the exchange student Yoshi Hattori. As you drive up to the Unitarian Church of Baton Rouge, you notice two things. On the left you see a striking circular window opening onto the sanctuary. On the right you see an expanse of lawn and there, yonder, near a line of trees stand two boulders, one red, the other purplish gray. They lie there like two silent islands on an untroubled green sea. Walk over to them and they draw you into their stillness. You stand, perhaps you even sit on the grass, and you listen.

Later you hear the story. From a friend of the family who cared for Yoshi. He got lost and was asking for directions. A woman who answered the door misunderstood, panicked. Her husband came to the door and fired blindly.

The response of Yoshi's parents was too hard for Americans. They sent these huge stones as symbols of reconciliation to the city of Baton Rouge. City officials were uncomfortable with this inexplicable gesture of peace. Only the Unitarians could imagine a public venue for them.

As I stand near these weathered stones I wonder when we Americans will ever comprehend genuine overtures of peace.

From San Francisco
An honest man   2003

Unless my itinerary changes drastically before year's end, this was the last time I talked with Allan Fong. But Asian folklore warns about thinking that a story is over. To my delight since 1991 he has been running a yogurt stand just to the right of the security checkpoint for passengers boarding Delta Airlines at SFO.

A native of Canton, he worked for years as a busboy in San Francisco. Then one day he found a package containing $277,000. Instead of pocketing the cash, he sought and found the eighty-two-year-old man who had no trust in banks. That man left Allan without a thank-you or a tip.

But then good will kicked in. At the urging of the then mayor, the airport landlord extended a $180,000 loan to Fong to open up a yogurt stand.

Yet now this honest man has "had it." He's worked long enough to pay off the loan. He's getting tired, especially of the lack of human contact, for since September 11 his business has plummeted. Customers evaporated for months. But the coup de grace actually came from the office of Homeland Security. His shop is to be reconfigured into an expanded checkpoint.

For twelve years he's filled cones and cups, celebrating his good fortune with mini-Dragon and Lion Dances in the Terminal.

But the times now call for sacrifice. Who will miss a grateful Chinese yogurt maker or even remember an honest man?

From New Hampshire
Candidate Ed   2003

I never thought I'd be having breakfast with a presidential candidate. But there he was gulping down orange juice just two seats away. This gray-haired, ruddy faced fellow, still boyish in his mid fifties, didn't mind being seen with his suit jacket tossed over two extra-long T-shirts and miss-matched pajama bottoms. It had been a bitter cold morning throughout the inn.

The night before Senators Kerry and Lieberman had absorbed most of the glare from the eleven o'clock news. Now I was sitting with Ed O'Donnell, a genuine "unknown," yet making his sixth presidential run. As he poured milk onto his cereal, he declared why he was running. He wanted to help the people at the bottom: prisoners, mental patients, the homeless, those who have made mistakes. He criticized the people at the top of American society for becoming more intolerant and critical of those underneath.

In the midst of his passionate assessment of our gun culture, feckless politicians on both sides, and the unnatural stress borne by the ordinary worker, he asked if anyone was driving over to Manchester. It seems that he could not afford the thirty-mile cab fare.

Who'd have thought Don Quixote was alive and running in New Hampshire? I didn't have the heart to tell him that since 1958 every presidential candidate I've actually met or heard — whether I supported him or not — lost. The last thing Ed needed was an albatross on the presidential seal!

From Beaverton, Oregon
The insulated life 2004

Ever since an elderly lady spilled hot coffee into her lap and won her suit against MacDonalds, businesses have decided to assume that people are too stupid to see what's right in front of them.

Starbucks, for example, now wraps its coffee cups in environmentally correct insulating sleeves that pre-empt lawsuits by announcing the obvious:

Careful, the beverage you're about to enjoy is extremely hot.

As I stared into my tea I wondered: What if life came with insulating sleeves?

Then mothers and TV weathermen could rest easy. Gratuitous advice would never be far away, just read the sleeves of a custodial cosmos:

Careful, the sand you're about to walk on is extremely hot.
Careful, the match you're about to strike is extremely hot.
Careful, the woman you're about to kiss is extremely hot.
Careful, the iron you're about to strike is extremely hot.
Careful, the dress you're about to put on is extremely hot.
Careful, the watch you're about to buy is extremely hot.
Careful, the boss you're about to ask for a raise is extremely
    hot.
Careful, the woman you are about to scorn is extremely hot.
Careful, the branding iron you're about to feel is extremely
    hot.
Careful, the electric chair you're about to sit in is extremely
    hot.
Careful, the lava you're about to be swallowed up by is
    extremely hot.
Careful, the sun you're about to fall into is extremely hot.

From Troutdale, Oregon
Where mirth is on tap 2004

As a visitor, you often only begin to enjoy a place when friends from the locale open your eyes to something that tourists rarely see. Since we had time for lunch before my lecture, Al and Barbara took me to the former County Poor Farm in Troutdale, Oregon.

Actually things got even more curious. For Al explained that the present owners, the McMenamin brothers, have a remarkable talent. Somehow hitting upon the idea that historic buildings need not fall to the wrecking ball, they've enlisted local artists to help rejuvenate theatres, pubs, taverns, hotels, a Masonic Lodge, as well as a neighborhood school, throughout the greater Portland area.

Soon I was walking around Edgefield, transformed from Poor Farm to restaurants, a winery, distillery, lodging and gardens. The halls were lined with photographic fragments of its history. Minute attention was paid to the poor who long ago lived out their days with dignity. Now a riot of paintings completes the human dimensions of the place.

After lunch we walked the gardens and came upon what looked like a hobbit house. Out of the sunlight we entered a candle-lit cigar and port bar. There was a side room where mirth was on tap. In the middle sat a tall, white bearded man, with laughing eyes. Bill McMenamin got up to greet us and I thought of Tolkien's preposterous master of the woods, Tom Bombadil, who provided lodging for Frodo and friends, at a time when the world was in shadows.

From New York
At the epicenter
of our age   2004

Two and a half years after the world we knew ended, I finally visited the epicenter of our age.

Last Sunday I took a cab from Times Square to Ground Zero. There was no need to give the driver any other directions. On the way I began to sense that this visit would become my Sunday devotion.

Dropped off in the chill morning air, I stood in front of what has become a construction site. Of course, this is New York, where buildings are ever coming down and going up. Shiva of Manhattan, the creator and destroyer, the breaker of concrete and layer of bricks, left telltale signs—even on her day off.

Through the chain link fence I stared at the still gaping wound. The sky was not as blue as that long ago Tuesday. I walked the perimeter, went down into the train station, and contemplated the iron cross relic set up on the east side.

I cried remembering the lives that disappeared on that day. For weeks I had read every touching recollection in *The Sunday Times*. And I took heart recalling what no politicians can now manipulate—that on the first day of our new age the decent instincts of the people emerged. For some time the miracle of democracy took place. The people needed no leaders; they knew what had to be done.

As the wind blew in from Battery Park off the Hudson, I wondered if we would continue to remember what warmongers would have us forget.

From New York
What the churches could
hardly imagine 2004

If you've ever been at a public discussion, you know what can happen when someone from the audience gets hold of a microphone.

There we were in a hotel near Times Square in the midst of a critical conversation over the ethical life of the churches today, when a man in his fifties got up.

Although he identified himself as gay he did not use the opportunity to defend the rights of gays and lesbians to marry or to be ordained bishop.

Instead he told us a horror story—his story about the attempt to live a good Christian life.

He began by mentioning that he has been in a loving relationship for the last thirty years. Both he and his partner grew up in Christian homes. Each was committed to the Gospel.

But because of the church's stance and their own internalization of that understanding, both of them felt that their growing relationship was wrong. So they attempted to pray their way out of their feelings for each other. That did not work. Neither did a thorough scouring with the Bible.

So, for the sake of their religious commitment, they did what they felt had to be done. Weekly for three years he and his partner underwent electroshock treatments.

Fortunately he and his partner survived the therapy and have thrived for years. He raised his voice that day in witness of his finding a mystery the churches could hardly imagine. He found that at the heart of things there is no discrimination, only surprising life.

From New York
The end of the world at
Times Square 2004

It was fitting that it happened on Times Square—that intersection of neon dreams and concrete reality, with those insistent icons, flickering ever between disappointment and hope.

The Jesus Seminar played Broadway. For four days over three hundred people from all over this nation and the world met at the Marriott Marquis to ponder the future of the Judeo-Christian tradition. Speakers such as Karen Armstrong, James Carroll, Richard Holloway, Bishop Shelby Spong, Marcus Borg and Elaine Pagels set the stage for the critical conversation.

At a time when religion seems to be a theatrical blood sport, when the media, both print and electronic, fail to recognize the religious roots of our political life, when lip service is paid to the quests multitudes are making towards the interior, when politicians cynically play the piety card, it was quite startling to experience an occasion where neither the mind nor the heart was sacrificed.

Instead, people moved beyond the scandalous headlines of the day. They asked about the possibility of ethical existence in a global perspective. Taking seriously that humanity is no longer where our ancestors have been, they realized that the historical imagination brings with it unexpected possibilities. What do we do with our religious scripts that have ended in the heavens—now that we look through the Hubble Telescope? What happens when people finally realize that their religious worlds have come to an end? Is the memory of Jesus still dangerous as this planet spins into the next millennium?

From O'Hare
Airport Talmud 2004

When she approached my row, I had a fleeting sense that we had met before. But my lack of sleep kept some of my synapses from firing. A forty-five-minute delay on the tarmac helped bring me to my senses. We fell into a lively conversation and discovered that we, indeed, did know each other. Some years ago Donna and I had served jury duty together. It seems that we meet under trying circumstances.

Since Donna mentioned that she listened to me on Saturday mornings as she drove to her synagogue, I asked her opinion.

What do you think—a book filled with pages blank except for a wisdom saying centered about an inch below the top margin of each page? You pick up this book in the airport and leave a comment on whatever saying provoked you. Then you drop it off upon your arrival. As more and more people pick up these volumes their words would add layer upon layer of unexpected wisdom.

Donna immediately saw I was describing a Talmud. All that's needed is an Airport Gideon Society to distribute and collect these unfinished commentaries.

Air travel has become a tedious endurance contest with civility so poor that one airline gives free tickets to passengers that surprisingly act human to others.

What if we were to take things into our own hands, use well that interlude of air, where we are neither here nor there, and find a human connection as weak and as strong as words?

From Houston
In the crossfire   2004

Right now I'm in Houston. Not to pick up all-star paraphernalia, nor to catch the latest on the Enron scandal, nor even to hobnob with the Republican elite; no, I'm here at a seminar of Bible scholars and storytellers. Indeed, what we are about has a direct connection to the political conversation of our nation.

Both presidential candidates will continue to embody a choice for the American people. Each presents a story of what America is and can be. Beyond the mindless attack ads and jingoistic rant, an attempt is being made, as Arthur Miller writes, "to find the magnetic core that will draw together a fragmented public."

Centuries ago a British king asked his council whether to listen to a foreigner's story. One advisor compared human life to the momentary flight of a sparrow, which one night flies into a banquet hall, briefly finds warmth, and then flies out forever into the dark. The king's advisor noted that any story able to throw light on our uncertain existence should be heard.

In this election year we stand in the electronic crossfire of the world. Will we listen to the voices and stories that are lost in the uproar? Who will ask whether the stories prepackaged for us are more than shadow boxing? Will we have the courage to deliver a story that sheds more light than fear? What story can we tell our children that will give them all a chance and not a life sentence?

From Schenectady, New York
The toilet paper church 2004

Last weekend I visited with a Methodist community in Schenectady, NY. We puzzled together over sayings of the historical Jesus. Unlike our faith enraptured president, they actually hand wrestled with the uncomfortable repertoire of that peasant artisan.

As we got to know each other, I found that this community, so teeming with social conviction and ongoing projects, so alert to theological ideas, had almost been torn apart over a very profane matter.

The Church has an open door policy. Since they are in the heart of downtown, the poor often make use of their bathroom facilities. No one had a problem with this until elderly ladies in the congregation complained about the lack of toilet paper on Sunday mornings. This issue soon reached biblical proportions. Liberals wanted the doors to stay open. Conservatives maintained the right to keep the bathrooms stocked.

Finally a woman asked: "What are we here for? Why can't we provide for what these people need? Let's set up a basket of soap and toilet paper for them."

And so it was done. The people take what they need and the elderly ladies sit comfortably. I playfully tagged the community "The Toilet Paper Church." And one woman responded, "We shall wear that name with honor." Long ago James counseled that faith without works is dead. Indeed, in our world faith without toilet paper leaves only a mess.

From Vero Beach, Florida
Encore, for the first time 2005

After two hours of lecturing and answering questions on ancient and modern cosmologies, I drove back exhausted and empty to the hotel.

Earlier that afternoon, in the process of getting lost in Vero Beach, I had happened on a classical radio station. So, when I switched on the radio in the rental car that night, I caught the tail end of an introduction to Schumann's *Piano Concerto in A minor*, Opus 54.

I had heard that piece many times before. But that night I heard it truly for the first time. From its very abrupt beginning, through the gentle repetitions, joyous declarations, and delicate fingerings, I was swept along. Wave after wave cascaded over my heart, caught in that passionate undertow.

The music did not let up. Relentlessly it kept climbing, then falling back into those signature moments of aching tenderness, where the heart will either burst or break, then back up into an exultant joy and then all over again.

On reaching the hotel I could not turn off what was sounding deep within my heart. I sat stunned in the parking lot to the very end. When I got out I noticed the night sky and the waves along the beach and sensed why Dante could sing about love's subtle music in the stars.

From Santa Rosa, California
Paul—in translation 2005

Right now I am flying to a translation meeting. For the last few years a group of dedicated scholars has been working on a new translation of the authentic letters of Paul. For some, Paul represents the one who turned a reform Jewish movement into the Christian church. For others he is a traitor to his heritage. Still others see Luther the monk haunting his sentences. For many women Paul is a patriarchal misogynist. In short, Paul often comes across as an arrogant, self-righteous, unpitying control freak.

But that is not the historical Paul. What we have discovered under the layers of interpretation and assumptions is a Paul very different from his ecclesial press releases. Here is a Jew who was amazed that the God of Israel would remember a "nobody," and worse, a state-executed criminal.

Paul saw himself not as a convert but called like a prophet to go to the sub-human of the world. For that was how gentiles were seen by observant Jews. His world of ethnic distinctions and cultural advantages was undermined by the uncanny realization that God does not play favorites; instead, refuses to give up on the lost.

Paul's God was so unlike the gods of Empire. Who could handle an alternate reality where trust, not takeover, was the tissue of human life?

From Toronto
The greatest jihad 2005

Invited to give two lectures last week in Toronto, I met a remarkable Muslim woman, Raheel Raza, a media consultant and writer, originally from Pakistan, who brought the suicide bombings in London dramatically home to me.

Raheel has two sons, the same age as the bombers. In Canada they have grown up in an atmosphere of respect for other faiths and life.

Saif, Raheel's twenty-year old visited Birmingham, England, earlier this year. He was shocked at the rhetorical fire from the pulpit. Once, on a drive with friends, a tire went flat. Saif suggested that they take the vehicle to a gas station they just passed. But the three British-Muslim lads would rather walk for miles than have any business with a non-Muslim. Saif returned home alarmed and frustrated by such views.

Raheel wants people to know that "moderate Muslims are alive and well, working around-the-clock to undo the damage done by the indoctrination of hate."

She knows no amount of surveillance or targeted profiling will solve matters. It goes right to those deepest relationships where some teenagers find hope and others only despair.

If there is to be a jihad, she says, let it be the "greatest of all": the struggle to respect the dignity of human life.

From Philadelphia
Off to see the wizard 2005

A week ago on a trip to Philadelphia I was eager to take in the new Harry Potter film. My Friday night was free. So, when two former students called to take me to dinner, I thought that we might see the movie afterwards.

But the moussaka and retsina caused us to linger—in catching up and spying into the future. Then, upon leaving the restaurant, they decided to lead me astray.

They took me east on South Street to see—even in the dark—a maze of marvels. In an alley an entire wall of a building danced in a glitter of broken glass, ceramics, bottle parts, and cement. Words floated upside down and right side up, tumbling among the debris.

Then we encountered the entire front of a three-story house. It literally buckled and waved in the lamplight. I marveled at the enormous effort.

But there was more. We came upon the "Magic Garden." Unfortunately, the gate was closed. But even the walls were part of this outrageous compounding. Glass bottles shot out alongside broken plates, ceramic interludes, and even pre-Columbian like figures.

As I peered through the gate I was stunned by what appeared to be an endless piling of poetry in plaster.

The next afternoon I had to return. This time the gate was opened. In the soft November sunlight the entrance became a brief tunnel, twisting in a fiesta of fragments. At the end I saw a workbench with scattered debris that would soon become beautiful once more.

Turning left, I entered the workshop and met Juan. He told me the story of Isaiah Zagar who, since 1969, has been turning South Philadelphia into a living labyrinth. Then he asked, "Would you like to meet him?"

Isaiah Zagar left his work in his back room, rubbed the dust off his hands and shook mine. Flowing white hair and a beard surrounded his gentle face. I thanked him for choosing to make his home so many years ago in what was then a half-deserted area. He and his wife had returned from the Peace Corps in Peru. But the discrepancy between what he had lived and American life proved too much. A breakdown kept him unable to put anything of his experience on canvas.

Then he remembered what he had learned long ago from the environmental art of Clarence Schmidt. He tried working with the detritus of the town. Broken bottles, glass shards, ceramic and porcelain fragments, all these and more began to figure into his vision. He would go outside the lines of a confining canvas. His space would be nothing less than the city.

And so, he began. What he has done is nothing short of wizardry. But it is not simply his quixotic art; it is the resolve that he and his beloved Julia have shown in staying in an urban desert. They have been part of the rebirth of the area. Their work, their life, and their love have delivered a garden in the city.

Miami tea 2006

There I was, thinking I had things in hand. I had fled the opening reception to the conference to get some distance and gain some time to think. The room service order arrived. Grilled fish, veggies and a pot of tea to fortify my reading of the seminar's papers.

But then I discovered that in Miami tea is not a drink of choice. Understandably coffee—in all its varieties is.

The teapot was actually a coffee carafe—half full of tepid water with a lingering coffee aroma. Neither lemon nor milk was served alongside. The milk would require an extra tip.

So I had time to think as my tea—such as it was—steeped.

There is an age-old wisdom in the protocol of tea. As you let the tea steep, you take part in a delicate, world-wide composition. From the tea fields of Asia, from the hands that picked the leaves to those that boxed them, through the intermediaries of the market, to the setting of cups and dishes, you have to take time to assemble things, to become patient, and in those moments, memories often filter in.

I recalled my first cups of tea. Not the half-milk and half-tea baby steps. But those late Thanksgiving night snacks. Turkey sandwiches and tea. There I was initiated into those adult sounds while my parents and grandmother shared with me the family gossip and the talk of ghosts. As I sipped my tea, I felt part of something larger, as if long lost ancestors had gathered with us around the kitchen table.

As the tea steeped, I thought of a recent tea with newfound friends. I met Shelley and Bruce Richardson at a recent crafts fair in Northern Kentucky. They were selling their teas and books on tea. We chatted and found much in common. This led to their invitation to tea at the Netherlands downtown.

With Christmas carolers in Dickensian dress strolling about the tables, Shelley and Bruce poured out the story of their ministry of tea. Musicians and students of theology, they restored the Elmwood mansion as it tottered on the verge of oblivion. For fourteen years they brought the art of tea to the heart of Kentucky. Now they are expanding their scope. Bruce has become a skillful writer, publisher and wholesaler of tea. Meanwhile Shelly has gone from recipes to poetry. She brings the art of tea to congregations and groups.

I marveled at this kind couple. They provided me with more than tea that day. They reminded me how civility comes about. It comes through care, care for the little things, like leaves or those who harvest them. It comes through taking time to set the table, to heat the water, and to wait. It comes with listening for the kettle's whistle, with sipping words along with your tea. It comes in slowing down and in finding in the fragile moment how our lives are truly steeped in silence.

The adventure of a garden   2006

The helium birthday balloon tethered to the mailbox was our only sign. We turned down a gravel path between two houses. We soon saw on the left a wide expanse of lawn, then we pulled around the house and disembarked onto a back yard that was unexpected and immediately intriguing. What I had imagined would be a congenial birthday celebration for a friend at his sister's, near the Indiana border, with the usual cornhole games and cake, became an entrance into a secret garden.

After the initial welcome and offering of beer, a few of us could not help wondering about the landscape before us. A fire pit to the right with a wisteria backdrop, in the center a constructed playground and tree house, at its left an apparent miniature topiary garden, beside that a stand of trees with gnome-like faces posted ten feet above eye-level. There were two paths right of center, begging for exploration.

So we started down one path and found defined areas with flowerbeds, grottos, even a bench under a gargoyle guarded trellis. We walked all the way to the end of the property and then doubled back along the other trail. There we met Bev, who began to fill us in on her husband's dream.

About thirty years ago they had bought what had been a tree nursery. Her husband John found what he had always wanted. His diverse experience in gardening and engineering allowed him to design a plot that would take a lifetime to build.

When I finally got to sit down with him, his eyes lit up as soon as I described his garden as "an adventure." He does not see his work as finished. No, it continues to be a work-in-progress. He is happy that he has enough to last through and beyond his coming retirement.

When he was in high school, he took care of a woman's property on a sloping Clifton hill. She trusted that this teenager could do things and he did. She also taught him how to appreciate growing trees. "You can put your arms easily around the ones you have planted. But in thirty years you won't be able to put your arms all the way around."

John learned that tree-hugging means that you're there for more than a season; you're in for the duration. You see that your work takes time and that this is how you find out what time can be. And so, he tells of the trees that line the eastern side of the garden; once spindly saplings and now stout barriers and shade-givers. He took care to plant them so that they would not encroach on his neighbors' yards. He recounts how his wife found that she had a knack for scrounging tools and materials for rebuilding their modular box into an eclectic chalet. He tells how their children played in the tree house and made—through their bicycling—the paths that we had walked on. And now—with the children grown—the neighbors take walks in the evening along with the inevitable, interloping deer.

Towards midnight we sat around the fire pit and gazed at Polaris. In contrast to the daily bombardment of the media, everything around us in that garden had been designed with patience and care. Who would have thought you could find such an unlikely Eden tucked away down a gravel path under the stars?

From Logan Airport
The Terror returns
2006

The Terror has returned. Distracted by the interminable Iraqi fiasco, we were lulled into imagining that we could keep the Terror half a world away.

And so, I stand in line, ready to go through inspection at Logan Airport. Bereted National Guardsmen stand nearby in desert fatigues. Water bottles are confiscated and tossed into bins. The names of nineteen suspected terrorists flash across the CNN screens.

A calm, nevertheless, prevails under this red alert. I begin to look around. I notice the incredible variety and complexity of those faces around me. There is more than some nervous tic or anxious stare. I suspect I'm detecting faces rather than profiling fellow passengers because of what happened to me just a few nights ago. I was introduced to a remarkable woman by my brother. There was some degree of difficulty in getting to know her, since she died in 1842.

But Elisabeth Vigée Lebrun left many clues for those who would know her. She painted over seven hundred portraits, thirty of which were of Marie Antoinette. Her works are found today throughout the globe in major and minor museums. Her career stretches from the Ancien Régime through an exile of twelve years, and a return to her native France. She has left us in her *Memoirs* a lively glimpse not only of the lives she painted but also of how she worked.

Her success as a portrait painter came from her sense that her painting was a conversation. She and the sitter performed a remarkable duet, so that what you saw on the canvas was a revealing aspect of who that person truly was. Marie Antoinette's daughter, the Duchesse d'Angoulême, for example, said that a particular portrait was a "speaking likeness" of her mother.

At first glance portraits appear mute. Yet you only need to spend a few thoughtful moments with one of Vigée Lebrun's to be stunned by the person confronting you through the ages. Whether it is some German baron or an unknown waif, you are brought up short by what Vigée Lebrun coaxed out of her subject. Even nobles gain a common touch.

In fact, when you see her painting of Sainte Genevieve and slowly realize that she has painted her recently deceased daughter, you begin to understand what she called the "cruel grief of her daughter's death." That mother rushed to her dying daughter only to find her eyes falling "dreadfully on that sunken face." The next day she was childless. Then she adds: "I saw her again. I still see her in the days of her childhood…. Why did she not survive me?"

In the face of the Revolution's Terror Vigée Lebrun refused to overlook those features which make us human. She would converse with her subject until the undetectable emerged. Later, even with the loss of her daughter, she would not give up on her vocation to discover the tender shoots of our humanity.

All these thoughts came home to me as I stood, waiting to be scanned. I wondered if we shall have the courage and the imagination not to give in to the forces of fear and diminishment.

Will we still be able to see in the faces that we meet more than a recipe for terror? Will those lines, those unnoticed twists and turns, those failed and foolish faces, those human lines, stagger us with more than what we would imagine?

▌ On the edge of things 2007

▌ As I write this, Greece is burning. Since flying out of Athens on the first of August, my memories of a fantastic voyage through time have been morphed and recombined by the daily input of horrific images from the Peloponnese. Those of you who have traveled in Ellada by bus or car or donkey know the treacherous mountain passes, the amazing vistas over farms and olive groves, the ruins that sometimes appear without a warning. And then there are the people: villagers who bring their produce and their products to the roadside, waiters at the local taverna who know "what you wouldn't like," and mothers who will tell you their opinion (and every Greek has at least one). None of these are types anymore for me. I know them by name. I worry for their fate.

Amid all the smoke and political backbiting over the unprecedented number of fires throughout Greece, I've tried to navigate through this crisis like the Greeks I've met. It's not the simple response of "no problem" you get from a guide or a hotel manager; rather, I learned this particularly from a shopkeeper in Crete. Zeta is a middle-aged mother, who prefers to engage her customers in conversation, entertaining questions about what is important rather than simply selling her souvenirs. Her colleagues in the neighboring shops think she is crazy. But, no matter. And so, one hot July Sunday afternoon, she spent her time telling my son and me her story. Unmarried and pregnant by a fellow who left her, she raised her daughter with the aid of her family. One day a young business man entered her shop. He did not shy away from a woman with a six-year-old. They've been married over thirteen years. (She smiles at the thought of those years together.) Then, she adds, one day her husband's accountant found that some mistakes had been made in the taxes and they owed the government (about €60,000). It was then that I caught what must be the classical strength of the Greek woman. "What was I to do? If I worried, what good would it do? I told my husband, 'I've figured it out. No vacations for the next three years.' So, here we are now. We got through it. Paid it off. And I still have a chance to talk with you." I stood stunned by this smiling woman.

Indeed, it is such residual strength that gives me hope, despite the terrifying news reports. No one who has ventured stumbling in the heat over ancient archeological sites can fail to recognize that the Greeks have learned to live from disaster to disaster. They have survived somehow even when armies looted their shrines and devastated their cities. Perhaps this comes with the experience of sailing on the "wine dark" sea to islands unchartered and often unwelcoming. Even the experiment of political life in the golden years of Athens was always in jeopardy. The land has known a sad litany of occupiers: Romans, Turks, Franks, and Ottomans.

Nowhere is this illustrated better than by the sanctuary of Delphi. This was for Greeks the center of the world. Demetri, my waiter at a local taverna, and Gianni, the merchant who took pride in his silver work, know the story by heart. Once Delphi was rich in renown and monuments; now, its debris is staggered along the slope of Mount Parnassus. The Temple of Apollo is a sorry sight. Here suppliants once came to ask Apollo questions of life and death, war and peace. Inside the Temple was housed the famous oracular chamber, where the prophetess would give responses by delivering utterances under the influence of the vapors streaming from underneath the shrine.

But now, no more. No longer do the proverbial lines ("Know thyself," "Nothing in excess") echo from the walls. The emperor Nero, declaring himself a lover of Greece, once carted off many valuable pieces to Rome. Since the late fourth century the oracle has been stilled. A century ago a French archeological team, despite finding what probably was the "forbidden area" (the *adyton*) of the oracle, rashly judged the whole oracle enterprise to be a fake and the notes of Plutarch (the late first-century biographer and priest at Delphi, who wrote extensively on the Oracle in *Moralia* 5) a fable. They sealed up the entrance on the southern side of the Temple and published their reports.

But recently a geologist and archeologist have demonstrated that the oracle rests on two intersecting and very active fault lines and that ethylene gas percolated up from the limestone formations below. The oracle did become intoxicated. I did not smell any of that sweet gas when I visited. Nor could I budge the seal left by the French. But I did find an opening on the south side. It was large enough to crawl into. So, I did. I realized that I had crossed the *temenos* (boundary) of Apollo's temple. It occurred to me that I should ask a question. Isn't that what rulers and politicians, citizens and farmers, ventured so long ago? Then it hit me. This is what made this sight a religious center. It was not the gas, not the intoxication, nor the monuments, nor the ceremonies. *It was the asking of the question.* For in asking questions that have consequence, questions of life and death, health and marriage, you are brought to the edge, to the very precipice of being human.

How fitting on the very edge of Mount Parnassus, people sensed the precariousness of life. Then the proverbial lines of the Temple came home to me. As you ask questions of import, you truly come to know yourself as a fragile creature. You see immediately that you do not know the depths of your existence and so you cry out, hoping for an answer. You also sense that you must tread carefully, "nothing in excess," for that would keep you from recognizing your human limits. When I crawled out of the hole in the Temple wall, I stood in silence. Despite the heat, breezes from two sides converged as I stood. There were no signs. Only centuries of ruins. I hadn't asked a question. Instead, I discovered why questions are important: it is how we humans live on the terrifying edge of things.

▌ "No Turks!" 2008

▌ Last summer one of my students in Greece, assigned to do a site presentation on the Turkish Quarter in Athens, was running into difficulties. He couldn't find it! He knew that Greece had been occupied by the Ottomans for over four hundred years. In desperation he asked an Athenian policeman where the Turkish Quarter was. After contemplating the question a good five minutes, the policeman pronounced, "There are no Turks, no Turks!" That declaration was so dramatic that we included it into our running slogan for our extended trip to Greece: "No clouds, no Turks, no problem!"

Despite the policeman's remarks, the situation (as anything in Greece) was not that simple. In fact, all we had to do was to stroll down to the Roman Agora, located just north underneath the Acropolis, to notice two buildings in disrepair. Indeed, just sit down for a salad at the Acropolis taberna abutting the Roman Agora and you can look over your feta cheese to see the remains of a madrassa (Muslim seminary) just outside the Agora and a fifteenth-century mosque occupying a good portion of the northern side of the Agora. Neither building had been kept up or restored. Only a wall and an entrance of the madrassa stand, while the mosque has been long since shut up and fenced in.

The policeman, on the other hand, did have a point. There was no significant Turkish presence in Athens. But even this was due to the brutal transference of peoples in the years after World War I. Emboldened by the Ottoman's losing alignment with Austria-Hungary in World War I, the Greeks attempted to liberate their fellow Greeks in Anatolia (present day Turkey). After an initial success the Greek forces made for "the City," Istanbul, only to be thwarted by the military genius of Kemal Atatürk (who had been born in Thessaloniki). The loss was so thorough that all Greeks living in Anatolia were forced to leave the new nation of Turkey; in return all Turks were transported out of Greece. Hundreds of thousands of lives were affected. Even to this day many descendents of those Anatolian Greeks are still hard-pressed to survive in their "homeland."

This brief incident impressed upon me the problematic assumptions of what we take to be "history." It is ironic that a city devoted to its classical past (as the tedious and exacting reconstruction of the Parthenon bears witness) could neglect a sizeable layer of its history. Of course, from a Greek point of view, centuries of oppression and humiliation are not desirable objects of contemplation. In contrast, the long, hard road to independence is well-documented in statues and street names, government buildings and museum sections.

Indeed, the very appearance of "Greece" in the modern world was due in large extent to the forces unleashed by the revolutionary movements in America and France. The possibility that people could take control over their political fate struck a corresponding note throughout the mountain and valleys of the Peloponnese. The rest of the story of the fits and starts of the Greek Revolution is, as they say, history.

But "history" is actually an ambiguous word. It is not merely the assemblage of facts, or even a narrative connecting how things came to be. The idea of history comes out of various and intricate negotiations of humans wherein they use specific ingredients not only to envision their past but also to construct a future. If it weren't for the romantic vision of an ancient classical Greece, the modern Greeks would have had a harder time fabricating a nation state. It was crucial for the fledgling nation to wrest Athens from its Ottoman backwaters and recast it as a symbolic testament to the glory that was Greece.

And just as every translation both discloses and covers up, so also does the construction of history. Each choice brings with it an angle on the past as well as the inevitable forgetfulness. That is why a critical, cooperative approach is the only way to keep from falling victim to the myopia of one's own self-interest. Historical investigation becomes a complicated art of detection, where claims are checked, where what isn't said is just as important as what has been spoken, and where the historian constantly realizes that he or she might be wrong.

It is the same for the Jesus Seminar's investigation of Christian origins. Well aware that the data and narrative of the Christian tradition have been selectively and intentionally framed, the Origins Seminar has begun casting about for more material evidence (such as recent archeological findings) as well as exploring the very assumptions of such inquiry into origins. We obviously cannot predict the results but we can be sure that the beginning of the Christian tradition will probably not look the same again. Already in the first phase of the Jesus Seminar we had begun to re-imagine the historical Jesus as a non-apocalyptic peasant sage. What will result when the public becomes apprised of the various and competing Jesus communities, when people realize that communal life in those early years was not prescribed from on high but that growing and competing communities made it up as they went along?

As it was with the Athenian policeman, it is easier for many to stick with the established story. But the inevitable problem is such that such a quick fix can be undone by a few loose stones.

▎ A letter from the Galatians   2010

Almost heaven, Anatolia, ...
Life is old there
Older than the trees
Younger than the mountains

Growin like a breeze
Country Roads, take me home
To the place I belong
Anatolia, mountain momma
Take me home, country roads.

All my memories gathered round her ...*

It was not until we approached ancient Ephesus, taking the winding road up the mountain to the home of Meryemana (Mother Mary) that the words of John Denver's song began to mingle in my mind.

Things had not been so suggestive upon our arrival in Izmir. Our guide had failed to meet us in the terminal. So, along with fifteen students, here were two scholars, adept in ancient Greek and able to maneuver in modern, quite at a loss for words. Our bus driver Tyfoon bey could get us to the bus but could not manage anything more in English. So we sat, wondered, and waited, until our guide Ahmet bey, who had intended to be on our flight from Istanbul, showed up, having taken the next plane to Izmir.

All of that initial confusion and bafflement fell away as we climbed the mountain. Our guide treated us at first like other tourists and had taken us to the House of Mary, where pilgrims, Muslim and Christian, streamed into the tiny stone building, then gathered for outdoor services, lighted candles and left petitions in knotted pieces of white cloth. But we were not the usual tourist group. Already we had been connecting the earlier phases of what was Ephesus to this modern manifestation. What we would see and reconstruct in our imaginations told of a numinous place, which, despite the shifts of time and sediment, maintained a special hold for generations. The Anatolian Mother of the Gods had undergone many metamorphoses: from Cybele and Artemis to Theotokos. But in every time the "Mountain Momma" was there calling her devotees home.

Some would stop their reflection right here. They would be satisfied at discerning an underlying religious behavior lasting over thousands of years. Certainly that is more congenial than the specifically apocalyptic tale of some Orthodox (who tell of the priests that disappeared into the walls of Hagia Sophia at the conquest of the Turks will emerge out of those same walls) or the lingering hope for some Muslims for a return of the Caliphate.

WISDOM NOTES

Both tales would regain the imperial advantage over the other.

But even the more modest reflection on religious behavior may miss a most important factor: this is twenty-first-century Turkiye. We no longer have the luxury of earlier scholars who romanticized the Ottoman world. This is a secular state (the majority of its seventy-five million people are Muslim) that has chosen to set its face towards the modern world. In fact President Obama recently was strongly criticized in the Turkish press for characterizing Turkiye as an Islamic democracy. While the president was attempting to complement Turkiye, the Turks immediately asked: Would you call Israel a Jewish democracy?

In a country of over 100,000 mosques only 5 percent of the population is devout. Many would have the government cut the funds given to personnel at mosques to 20 percent and devote the remainder to education. The West hears of right wing religious enthusiasts; we do not hear the ordinary citizen. But go beyond the ancient sites to Istanbul, a city of fourteen million. Look at the thousands of apartments, at the skyscrapers beyond the outskirts of the old section of the city. Get out of the bazaars and detect the sounds of a young (60 percent of the population are under thirty) and growing nation. Listen to the dreams that never reach Western media outlets. Walk into small towns and take in a corner restaurant. Or lunch in the college town of Canakkale. Over the eggplant and stuffed zucchini flowers you will begin to intersect even with those whose language is as complicated as Japanese. As you sip your raki in a roadside cafe, your Turkish friend will point out that you are holding the results of globalization in your hand, as Americans own over 30 percent of the largest raki company.

Throughout my time in Turkiye, I continued to reflect on the prospect of a "God Seminar." If Westar is going to hold such a seminar, we shall have to come to grips with the "context on the ground" and go beyond usual theological tours and apologetics of the past. We need to challenge our imagination so that we can transcend the established definitions of what constitutes the matter of religion. Indeed, our older brother Paul can add to this discussion. Long ago he recognized the limits of the religious habits of the Galatians who were devoted to the Mountain Mother as well as their situation as "nations" under Roman dominance. His letter continues to ask: what makes humans truly "cosmopolitan," what liberates us all? Indeed, Mustafa Kemal

Atatürk, greatly influenced by the Enlightenment, pushed Turks in this direction.

As we enter what some have called the "Third Axial Age," the human search for meaning is nothing if not global; at the same time, it has become increasingly secular, roiling in economic and political waves, all the while teeming with complex residues of religious habit and narrative. I would submit that those fragile attempts to maneuver in the warp and weft of this enveloping complexity, daring to cross the no man's land of being at a loss for words, will continue to surprise us with new ways of weaving our "God-talk" (*theo-logia*) into patterns we have yet to imagine. Perhaps we shall even break out in song.

*Adapted from "Take Me Home, Country Roads," Words and Music by Bill Danoff, Taffy Nivert and John Denver.

▌ The Choros of Zalongo 2011

▌ Writing from Greece is not easy these days. I think Paul would have sympathized. The electricity is out for an hour or two each day. The trains and the buses will not run in protest tomorrow for two days. The Internet is intermittent. The people are understandably upset for the wizards of European finance have spun their fate. No one knows what will happen. But everyone is certain that things will grow worse. Indeed, if the only thing you know comes from the newswire, the situation is dire: anarchists rule the streets, the government founders, awash in incompetence and uncertainty. As I stood near the ancient cemetery of Athens recently and noticed a portion of the wall of Themistocles propped up by rusty iron poles, I could not avoid thinking that this was a fitting commentary.

But that is not Greece, not the heart of Greece. Get to know a Greek and you will see beyond the ticker tape. There is more here even in such straits. Indeed, in the very face of financial collapse, the people continue to eat and to dance. Yes, to eat and to dance. This is not a frantic escapism but something as deep as life itself. For the Greeks have lived through so much for so long. Five hundred years of Turkish domination has not been lost on their national psyche. Indeed, the words of Paul still ring true: "I have learned the secret of dealing with circumstances of every kind" (SV Philippians 4:12). I have been taught this especially from the women of Greece, from Niki the waitress to Irini the guide. Indeed, a shopkeeper from Crete demonstrated the remarkable strength of Greek women. Her husband had been assessed for an extra sixty thousand euros due to their accountant's incompetence. She calmly declared no vacation for three years and a severe regimen. They survived and danced at their daughter's wedding last year.

These are the stories no one hears from Greece. Even the Special Olympics' opening in Athens did not make the Sunday *New York Times*. Yet how fitting that these Games should be playing at this time. Timothy Shriver, the head of the Special Olympics, provides a telling perspective:

> The Special Olympics Movement is here saying, "You forgot someone." Even Plato forgot someone. He wrote the right words, but he forgot someone. Like Jefferson, he wrote the right words, that all men are created equal, but he forgot people, he forgot the slaves. Plato forgot our people. Now we are here to say he forgot somebody, one more group.... This is the contribution of modern Greece, to say that even the ancients had forgotten someone and now we are saying in Athens that you too are included.

An old story is being retold. The Olympic Games take on an added chapter with participants who would never have been noticed in the ancient world. The stadium will be run again. But this time those who have been humiliated, told not to try, laughed at, excluded and passed over take the field. The flood lights that dance through the Athenian night now shine on their efforts. They remind Greece and all of us that if those who have no address, no bank account, no home, can take up the challenge to come to these Games, then there is hope. In this painful time these athletes bear witness to the national anthem of Greece, a call to memory out of a life of desperation:

> From the sacred bones of the Greeks,
> you rise, valiant,
> as once before!
> Freedom, I greet, I welcome you!
> You lived there within
> the bitterness, the shame,

waiting for someone
to say to you, "Come back!"
　　—Dionysios Solomos

When you are suffering, you can lose hope. You lose hope when you forget, forget the simple memories that stirred you to life. We need each other to help us remember not only who we are but who we can be.

So, when I turned to a friend, Nicos Nicolaou, a teacher of ancient Greek for more than thirty years, and asked how he would describe the current situation, I was not surprised by his answer. "It is a tragedy," he said. But Nicos did not mean our usual sense of loss. We talked of how the Greeks experienced tragedy. The plot is already known. What is important is for the chorus to dance through the words. The audience is caught up not only in the rhythm but in the recognition of something deeper. Insight brings a relief in the very midst of catastrophe.

Yes, the people continue to dance. But don't miss the tragic downbeat in all the exuberating. When the women join hands in a circle dance memories are linked and reforged. This is how the Greeks read things by "knowing again" (Αναγνώσις). Recognition comes from catching what the rhythm signifies and leads you through great suffering and pain. The artist Giorgos Zongolopoulos captured this strikingly is his heroic sculpture of "The Choros of Zalongo." Four giant-sized women in profile, descending in size, linked hand in hand on a cliff in Epirus, represent fifty-seven women of Suli who plunged to their death with their children rather than being captured by the Turkish forces on December 18, 1803. A smaller version stands in the presidential garden in Athens, just a street away from where all the demonstrations are taking place.

Yes, the Greeks continue to dance. Democracy is still afoot. How many of us who claim a part of this heritage would risk catching the downbeat of this dance?

▌ What grabs us 2014

"That grabbed me!" This or some similar expression has been on our lips. A dramatic incident, a painting, a beautiful body, a wonder of nature, even a horrific accident, might have been the cause of such a declaration. The ecstasy may be momentary but we know, even if only for that moment, that we have been taken beyond the little confines of ourselves. We also know that this can happen at any time. Neither predictability nor inevitability has anything to do with this experience, which, as we often say, "comes out of the blue."

This happened to me some years ago in the ancient cemetery of Athens. I was struck by the poignancy of a scene from classical funereal steles (upright stone monuments). The sculpture was quite simple: the deceased is sitting and saying farewell to a beloved spouse, son, or daughter. A final handshake is frozen in the stark loss of death. Indeed, in some museums in Athens you come upon fragments of these steles: just two hands in that final farewell. Those fragments alone stun me. I am caught up in the endless relay of mortality. The warmth of human touch reduced to stone. The handshake shrouds the devastation of abandonment.

But Greece has more to offer. In the eighth century CE a new ikonic tradition emerged. What was to be known as the *Anastasis* (the "Standing Up," the "Resurrection") appeared. In this ikon Jesus, in white robes, bearing the imprint of his wounds, has just broken through the prison of the Underworld. Behind him is the surrounding womb of the blue heavens (indicating second birth). To the left and right in the background the rocky walls have been pushed away, while under his feet lie the remains of the door to the Underworld, now shattered and forming a Greek *chi* (the letter X). Various elements of confinement, keys, and shackles are strewn on the ground, and Satan lies bound in the debris.

The focus, however, is upon the hands of Jesus, which reach out, grasping the wrists of Adam on his right and Eve on his left. Behind Adam stand the royals of Israel and John the Baptizer. Behind Eve stand Joseph and the prophets. Now it is that act of grasping which concentrates your gaze. Despite the static nature of the ikon, the scene is filled with an extraordinary energy that pulls you into the action. Light and motion have broken through the desperate and dark confinement. This is not some scheduled visit with a prisoner, not even a jailbreak. It is an utter devastation of the forces of despair and diminishment.

This scene has no biblical basis. 1 Peter 3:19 mentions that Jesus "preached to the imprisoned spirits." But this ikon surpasses that remark. The Apostles' Creed affirms that Jesus "descended into the Underworld." Yet there is nothing of the crashing presence of the "One who lives." In fact, if one can find any traces at all it is with the Greeks, who told stories of journeys to the Underworld. Odysseus made a trip. (Of course, Virgil makes sure Aeneas makes one too, thereby holding up the Roman side.) Perhaps the most famous is that of Orpheus, who musically charmed his way into the realm of the dead to bring back his beloved Eurydice. But here the story ends in loss. Orpheus could not keep from looking back and his beloved was lost from his grasp. Their story adds another delicate lamentation to humanity's mournful repertoire.

And then there is Plato's cave. One man escapes a shackled and shadowy condition only to escape and see the light. The task of the philosopher is to bring this enlightenment back to his former cave-dwellers. But even Plato would admit that this is a story. In fact, today we would call all of these artistic expressions "myths" and then go on to dismiss them.

But that would be a tragic mistake. For such mythic expressions are not attempts to keep us from the real. The mythic imagination was invoked when people found themselves in conditions beyond their control. Mythic language gave the ancients a way to take seriously the powers of destruction and dissolution, of creativity and surprise. Today we are still beset with the sense of powerlessness, of being shaken by events and forces outside our control. But we suffer from a poverty of imagination. We do not have an appreciation of mythic speech. Now without mythic language there is no adequate perception of power. We do not have words or images to address the depths and orientation of our existence.

I have displayed the images of the Greek funereal steles and the *Anastasis* to many groups. Each image captures the audience. They easily pick up this silent language. The power of these images goes beyond a blunt bottom line assessment and comes home again and again. There is something that continues to speak to us in that final farewell. And there is something unsettling and wonderfully wild in those hands holding on in the debris of the Underworld. It grabs you.

Seasons
& Feasts

In many respects these are mood pieces. I had tried to hover around certain times of the years, certain memorable days. They often begin in simply observations and move deeper into the interior. A number of these commentaries center on Independence Day. They gave me a chance to focus on our fundamental liberty and responsibility. There is also a piece on 9/11 set in terms of the art of memory.

Leftovers 1996

Thanksgiving has a habit of running out on us. Yes, there are the obligatory Norman Rockwell scenes, crowded with relatives, cranberry sauce, and after-dinner naps, that seem to repeat themselves year after year in dyspeptic spasms throughout the land.

But even the most horrific travel narrative soon begins to lose its frantic shape, dissolving eventually alongside replays of the Dallas Cowboys, Pilgrim hats, and Aunt Dorothy's relentless heartburn. Already by the morning after, Thanksgiving retreats before the Christmas rush. Its Kodak moments fade into forgettable stereotypes.

There is a way, however, to keep yesterday from vanishing completely: simply notice the leftovers. I'm not referring to the debris of turkey and pie. But to the empty spaces created by life's musical chairs.

I learned this early as a boy. Instead of sleeping off the feast I would creep down the stairs and listen through the banister to the muted conversation of my parents and grandmother. Nothing terribly important (like Christmas presents) was ever mentioned.

Except one year, my mother heard a creak and found me on the stairs. That night I had my first leftover sandwich and a cup of tea. That night I entered an enormous world and heard the stories of my ancestors. That night I found that memory leaves a lasting taste.

Ghost stories 1996

For Christians the days after Christmas are terror-filled. The feast of St. Stephen conjures up a frenzied public stoning, while the memory of Thomas à Becket's bloody murder in the cathedral falls four days after angelic strains of peace on earth.

If you think about it, Dickens may well have captured the spirit of the season's best, since a number of his Christmas tales are mobbed with ghosts. For every Christmas candle there is a lurking shadow, for every glimmer of light, a numbing darkness.

But the most haunting memory of all is that of the innocents. As the legend goes, astrologers from the east unwittingly step on the royal toes of King Herod, alerting him to the possibility of a pretender to his throne. Finding himself duped by those foreigners, Herod issues a death warrant for all males two years and younger within the vicinity of Bethlehem.

Scholars dryly note that this story and the accompanying flight into Egypt recapitulate both the Exodus and the Babylonian Exile of the people of Israel. But how do you respond to the trembling note of Rachel crying for her children, who are no more?

The only answer for me is another story of stunned innocence. This was told to me by a survivor. One day an old Jew emerging from a boxcar saw his granddaughter being selected for death. Sensing disaster he begged the officer in charge to take him instead. The officer smiled cruelly, "Alright, if you can tell which of my eyes is real, I'll let you take her place." The old man stared into the officer's unmoving eyes and finally declared, "The left one." Upon being asked how he detected this, the old man said, "because the other one looked human."

The old man was led to his death, and, some days later, his granddaughter, reprieved as a plaything, met the same fate.

The horror story of the innocents did not end two thousand years ago, it still stalks our streets. And even as we joyously sing, "What child is this?" Rachel will not be consoled.

▌Two Christmas carols   1997

In the spirit of the season, here are two drive time carols:

The theologian and the class conspire
with shepherds tending flock about the text
that gives a strange democracy to knees.
More sudden than a star, the mind ignites,
while angels sing the footnotes to the lines,
a thrill to thought, an end to argument,
a fugal final to the firmament,
omega couched within the alpha bed.
Love's tent is set to tease the intellect.
For, weaving in and out, an innocence
draws on the untold tapestry of thought,
a frankincense forgotten by the brain,
a many-colored melody to clothe
the heart in nothing other than a song.

The second:

Child star, you only had a one night stand,
a vaudeville of the lion and the lamb,
and then the show was on the road again.
Augustus booked you down at Bethlehem.
The cast was filled with extras, summer stock,
a chorus line of kicking ancestors,
while angels handled the publicity.
Nostalgia crowds the shepherds in the act
and plays my heart in that old pantomime.
The stage ("If only we were young again")
is set beyond my orchestrating mind
where nothing stops the show from going on,
from flesh's bringing down your Father's house—
O silent entertainment, unsung star!

Incense of the season 2000

Every now and again, our electronic culture breaks down. The static buzz and neon glare are invaded by nothing more than a familiar smell.

Particularly at this time of year when the earth begins to tilt us into the dark, we slow down, take walks, and kick wildly at leaves. That is where the intrusion often occurs. The earthy incense of the season entices us.

Most of the time we are dominated by the visual. Sounds also can occupy us, penetrating to the bone, leaving us fixed upon a word.

But a smell surrounds us, coming in like fog, catching us off-guard, sometimes transporting us through our bodies into a realm beyond ourselves.

When I was young the good and not so good sisters spoke movingly about the odor of sanctity. But what does a fifth-grader know except the leather scent of a baseball glove and the sweet cut of grass?

Actually I did know another smell. Sometimes when I pick up the scent of freshly baked bread, the memory of riding on an early morning train comes back. As the train turns a corner on the trestle tracks, the car is filled with the smell of bread fresh from the bakery below. Through the dreadful shrieks of those turning cars a sweetness infiltrates. Right there among the drowsy commuters I sensed *panis angelicus*—the bread of angels.

Even now I am inclined to see the wisdom in the wry remark of a friend, who likes the Orthodox Church because it is the only denomination still with a smoking section.

▌Letting the shadows fall   2000

It was a perfect October afternoon. We drove under the crisp blue sky, with the angles of autumnal light putting every leaf into focus. The radio brought an ancient pinstriped script to my mind, for the Yankees were again contending for a post-season championship.

There has been much comment over the lateness of the World Series, as it moves closer and closer to November's freezing winds. But that media tempest was far from my thoughts. I remembered why the "fall classic" was so important to me, so long ago.

Those rituals, intoned by familiar voices and imagined between the lines, focused my mind through the slow burn that is always autumn. Mel Allen's voice still carries through the rustling of leaves. We would hurry to the sandlot to get in another game before the increasing advance of night. It was not the televised games that were important. No, it was that background sound, that commonplace chant, which brought a note of urgency to every play we made.

And isn't that what autumn is? A moment when our world wobbles. When light begins to play tricks on us. When the painter's hour becomes painfully condensed. When passing things become finally, achingly beautiful.

My son and I played catch on that perfect October day, with the fresh air repeating the pop from his throws. I cherished the arc I put on the ball and that final, blistering pea into my glove. As we walked home I saw so clearly how baseball in October is a way of letting the shadows fall.

▌Mixing memories   2001

Perhaps T. S. Eliot was right to call April "the cruelest month." Although we might be inclined to assume that he was thinking of taxes, he was intimating something much more unnerving.

Nor was it the dread that chills every Red Sox and Cubs fan on opening day. For they know that despite all the hype those teams will come crashing down—some years sooner than others. As I said, Eliot was suggesting something else.

April, the "cruelest month," mixes "memory and desire, stirring dull roots with spring rain." Each season brings its memories. With spring memories are mingled. Spring comes in crocuses, arrives eager with magnolias, which too often are destroyed defying the rain, wind, and cold.

As I let my memories of spring mix and mingle, images of my father and baseball come back with the crack of the bat. And now my two sons take their turns to swing away. Those fragile moments, those promises of spring, linger. And in the cold light of an April morning we catch a glimpse of mortal beauty. We shiver as our children grow.

And our memories continue to stir. Some of us still recall the words of a Jewish peasant, caught up in the power plays of the Roman Empire. While others wince at how his death has been used. Pogrom replaced passion, as the death of an innocent man became the excuse to murder innocent people.

Yes, spring comes with mixed signals. Each time we turn the earth, each seed we plant, we detect our own ambiguity. Memories overrun us like daffodils. We find forever in a glance, as we stand transfixed at the uncertain insistence of life.

▌ Liberté in dungarees 2001

▌ Tomorrow is Bastille Day—le 14 juillet. The fall of that Parisian prison recharged the shot of minutemen heard round the world.

Only slowly have we learned that freedom cannot be contained. For centuries we thought that only the few, the proud, the elect, could exercise their sovereignty. But the slave murmurings were always there. Moses. Spartacus. Peasants, like Jesus, throughout time shrewdly imagined breakouts.

In the late summer of 1968 I caught the scent of Lady Liberty. King and Kennedy had fallen. Johnson avoided a political snake pit, while Nixon smugly advanced on Washington. At a time when idealism should have died, I fell in love with the face of freedom.

I saw her in *Life Magazine*. There she was on the shoulders of a fellow protester, her left arm raised with the students' colors. French students had taken to the streets against the government's inhumanity. There she was in black and white — Delacroix's Liberté in dungarees. That gentle, resolute face, with short cropped hair, haunts me still.

We worry today about our youth. Why the violence, drugs, and alcohol?

Perhaps it's time not to talk but to look in their eyes. Do they sense that there is no longer a place for them upon the barricades? Is there no mission for their emerging humanity?

Día de los Muertos 2001

Today is for all of us who will never make it to the Hall of Fame. All Souls' Day has always struck me as the most democratic of feasts. While Halloween brings out the kid in us and All Saints Day pays respect to our ancestral all stars, All Souls' Day has the common smell and feel of earth. It is the day when our shoes get dirty, as we pick up the silent rhythms of feet rising and falling, feet long since under the earth.

In centuries past, untold numbers of priests would say masses for the dead. Relatives would offer desperate payments, too little and too late. Before that, the harvest moon was thought to be gathering the dead. The face of the moon was luminous with its passing throng.

Since September 11 the dead have been ever with us. Our adolescent nation has begun to grow up in the debris and dust. We're finding out how human memory works, detecting the real in those moments of loss and torment. Disregarding our dwindling portfolios, we have rediscovered in varied and surprising ways that the word "liturgy" truly means the "work of the people."

And so, let us celebrate *el Día de los Muertos*, the "Day of the Dead." Let us revel in what we would keep so far away — the fragile pulse of human life — and find it even in smoldering rubble. Touch what has broken out among us. Dance with the skeletons, see that they are kin, and kick up some dust to which we shall return.

The crèche of our lives 2001

I take issue with those who contend that Christmas is a religious holiday merely decked out in secular disguise. They would have Christmas confined within religious stocks. But I would suggest quite the contrary: Christmas may be our most secular holiday.

I say this not because the feast of Christmas was spawned from the Christians' competition for the ancient Roman audience. This is not about the hangovers from winter solstices or the cult of the Unconquered Sun. Nor am I worried about how commercialized the Christmas season has become in the hectic confidence game of today's feverish economy.

What I have in mind is subtler and more dangerous. I'm talking about stories being told in human terms.

Despite the frantic confirmations of the *National Inquirer*, we know that the birth stories of Jesus were not matters of historical record. They are confabulations of later communities. The myths that had sustained our religious flights have fallen like aging satellites. They have burned up in the atmosphere of reason and science.

Yet we can still detect in our cultural debris remarkable telltale signs. No longer are we captivated by gargantuan, heavenly armies, but we are moved by more modest lines, refugees from the grand and the grotesque, human beings groping for words and staggering from the wreckage of the cosmic Bastille. Life's meaning now toddles forward on two feet.

This is the time to recognize that humanity is coming out around the world. But we already know this. Our most endearing memories are the ones that have been reverently etched not in the heavens, nor on thrones, nor even in boardrooms, but in the fragility and finitude that mark the crèche of our lives.

If trees could talk ... 2001

By now most Christmas trees have been mulched, or dispatched in garbage trucks. Each year our house resists that automatic sloughing of the season. I am greatly to blame for this. While my wife worries about the fire hazard of a burning bush, I've been feeding the tree sugars and water to keep it green for the arrival of the three kings.

Actually it is the time after Christmas which means so much to me. After the glare and rush, after the gifts exchanged, the dinners cooked and eaten, after the phone calls, I treasure those moments when I simply stand or sit by the Christmas tree.

Many years ago a dear friend told me of the Lithuanian belief that at this time of year the trees would talk. Ever since I was a young child standing in awe of the shimmering tree, I thought it was so. Yet every year the tree stands mute.

In the corner of our living room space and time intersect. Memories run along the limbs, ornaments and angels, fragments of our lives elsewhere, gather and glimmer as the lights begin to bubble.

Then something deeper than sentiment is felt. An insistent sadness dissolves those incandescent memories. Is this not just a futile torch against the inevitable gloom?

Or is there more? A chance to learn how trees speak? Not in words, but in the silence, so touching, so palpably alive, not left behind on a Kentucky hillside, but invading, spreading, reaching out, right here in our living room …

O silent tree, holy tree.

Reading the Christmas skies   2001

It's beginning to look a lot like Christmas. No, I don't mean that unexpected snowstorm last week, which lingered longer than usual this time of year. Nor do I mean those unremitting waves of consumer frenzy, pulsating throughout the malls.

Call me nostalgic, but this Christmas season brings back haunting visions of the past. But not Dickens' romantic sprite. This is not a matter of leaping soot-covered roofs or stirring long lost bowls of wassail.

No, it's about looking up. About learning to read the heavens.

For some time I have been quite distressed sensing that things are running rapidly out of control. For a moment the Texas wildcatters are being forced to bide their time. Meanwhile military buildups continue at an uninterrupted pace. Virtual war games prep our sons and daughters for the clone of Desert Storm.

At home we are distracted by our Yuletide bonuses that now are gift wrapped in pink slips. Heads have rolled in the White

House over the economy. A presidential sleight of hand delivers only a snow job as the plutocrats prepare to make a bundle on our insecurities.

As I said, it's about learning to look up. A dear friend many years ago shared a poem he wrote soon after World War I. Amos Wilder, ambulance driver and winner of the Croix de Guerre, pastor and scholar, taught me not only to recognize when I was in a situation beyond my control but also to try to name the beast. He spoke of "march[ing] out on haunted battle-ground," for he had seen "daemons fighting in the sky/ And battle in aerial mirage." He realized that the troops in the trenches were "the shadows of celestial foes" and that the battle was a "mimicry of heaven's."

Whether from a desert bunker or the littered stock market floor, from a frozen cornfield of Iowa or the monotonous shopping mall, from an overcrowded drop-in center or a silent hospice room, this is the season to regain the habit of looking up.

It is time to name the forces that are distracting us from living human lives. These are not the usual gang of suspects, not the sensational news at eleven, the fifteen-second sound bite of agony.

It is time to look into the night sky and feel the chill of fear, to realize how much we've polluted the air, launching our desires into the atmosphere to keep from feeling the dread that nothing is out there. It is time to recognize that the music of the spheres is not static from the cosmos but the immature scratching from our political boom boxes.

'Tis the season to scan the skies like Londoners in the Blitz, to catch hints and glimmers of something more than night. I suspect that this is what the gospel writer had in mind when he invented an army of angels breaking out in song for a bunch of nobodies.

Shall we gather at the river? 2005

On Labor Day Cincinnati will gather at the river.

We've been doing this since 1977. It started as a ten-year anniversary party for WEBN, whose owner, Frank Wood, wanted to rock away the summer. The Rozzi family have aided and abetted with their fireworks, producing one spectacular after another.

Around a half-million people will be there, despite the constant attempts by City Council to childproof the event.

On Labor Day Cincinnati will gather at the river. Early on in the day Union workers will picnic at Coney Island. Their pale reflection of the sweaty, stubborn face of Labor recalls the cries for justice shouted in parades in 1882 in Providence and New York and two years later in Cincinnati.

In 1887 President Cleveland declared Labor Day a national holiday. No friend of labor, he was trying to put out some political fires. He recently had sent in federal troops to put down a railroad strike. Thirty-four workers were killed.

On Labor Day Cincinnati will gather at the river.

But rivers induce both memory and its loss. Before the fireworks launch us out of our minds, shall we take a moment?

Shall we recall the nameless ones who built this city with their sweat and bones? And, in this disconsolate summer, shall we remember where this river flows? Shall we follow it all the way down south where the dead float by and the living are numb beyond relief?

Shall we gather at the river,
The beautiful, the beautiful river?

▌ Peeling potatoes   2005

No word is necessary. The middle-aged woman, with her graying hair drawn back, does not notice the potato she peels on her lap. Her eyes linger on her son to her left as he briskly shaves the potato skin from the potato he's peeling. Sitting on a cane chair, with his feet drawn up on the second rung, he bends his head with a quiet smile on his lips. Still in his Army Air Force uniform, with a single service bar above his pocket, he has come home.

This is "Thanksgiving 1945." This is one of the images that crowd my memory whenever this most American of feasts returns.

Many people recall Norman Rockwell's famous "Freedom from Want" painting, featuring the archetypal Thanksgiving meal. Mother brings the bird to the table as father looks on approvingly. Each side of the table is filled with eager, bubbling faces.

But this is not the Rockwell that stays with me. Instead I return to that quiet scene before the hurly-burly of the table has begun. As a parent I know how much it costs to simply enjoy your child — now grown — beside you again.

You know the moment will not last. You hold your breath to keep it for a while. And in that interlude gratefulness — who knows from where? — gratefulness swells deep within.

As Americans we do our best to avoid such moments. We gorge ourselves with commercials, football games, family feuds, endless reports of airline delays, and cranberry sauce. We do our best to keep the racket going.

Nevertheless, those silent moments come; unexpectedly they linger. And we sense why we go through all those contortions to get home.

It's about those simple moments in which our hearts first opened. Moments half-remembered, much obscured.

And, now, sixty years from Rockwell's inter-session, again in a time of war, we wonder if our sons and daughters will ever sit beside us and peel potatoes again.

▌ The art of memory 2006

When I remember September 11 my mind returns to the sky. Everything that has followed comes out of that early autumn blue.

Media and politicians will continue to try to tell me how and what to remember. I resist that, resist what others would have me replay in my heart. There is something more insistent than a presidential bullhorn.

So I go back beyond a mayor who for the first time in his life became eloquent, precisely in his loss for words.

I go back through the months of reading in the Sunday Times stories of every single abbreviated life.

I go back to those firefighters and police when the world fell down on them.

I go back to that firehouse near Times Square, to the wall where I touched the names of the lost.

I have gone to ground zero. What did I see there at that nuclear metaphor in our midst? Bouquets of flowers on the chain link fence ringing the site.

I stood still and recalled not just the impact, the fire and the fall. I let things go deeper, deeper into my memory.

I recall a French artist who went back to his childhood village. As he walked along the street he could not recall his own past, could not recognize the place where he grew up. Then he stooped down, placed his fingers on a stone wall at the height where he would have stood at the age of four. All the memories came flooding back.

What do I recall when I stoop down? When I look up into that endless blue?

I see those acts of human decency, those moments of transcendence amid the debris. Why did so many go beyond themselves, beyond fear, beyond rage? Why did we sense that we were all in this together? When we discovered what the melting pot meant?

Am I embarrassed about recalling those moments, when I let myself go, when I realized that we all were so vulnerable?

Before our nation went on a five-year drunk, we had a moment when our people grew up, out of enforced adolescence. There was no time for militancy, for bravado, crusades or cowboy rhetoric. But it was a noble time.

It was a time when we got outside our little worlds, when we got dirty, caring for others. A time before politicians applied the spin cycle. I witnessed a horrible truth: the people could act on their own—without their leaders. Since then politicians have spent much to try to make sure we forget.

But I recall myself reaching out, not needing to go far to lend a hand, for whoever was beside me became delicate, became precious.

All the masks had fallen off and the world noticed, even in Teheran.

Dark matters   2007

Dickens got it right. No one wants to be at school at Christmas time. Neither the aching specter of the ninetheenth-century boarding school boy nor today's My Space coed wants to be around campus. I have often mused how, despite the seasonal protestations of good will and the fabricated attempts at merriment, no one really wants to be around a university at this time of year. Of course, students are working through both the onset of the flu and the last throes of exams, while professors regret the bulk of the assignments they must now read, and administrators lose track of time with end-of-the-year reports.

So, at this season, as the sun sharply descends, or when the afternoon moves from light gray to a harsher gun metal sky, I walk unnoticed around the campus. Already students are loading cars to make a fast getaway. They want to beat the coming ice storm that is forecast for Chicago. Others find friends to taxi them to the airport. The janitors get the floors done as quickly as they can and disappear into the night. Secretaries take off a few minutes early to get some shopping in at the malls, while a couple of the grounds crew hurriedly replace a burnt out Christmas bulb. Soon, only the basketball team will be here for the duration.

You can see it in their eyes. Everyone wants to be elsewhere.

Indeed, we are in the darkest time of the year. Long before Stonehenge, humans grappled with the loss of light, with the fear that it would slip away forever. They caught their breath as they sensed the inevitable descent into the dark. They sang and danced, hoping to wake the sun; they beat drums and made merry, desperate to believe that light would return.

On campus the lights are going out. The garlands of lights on lampposts futilely try to stave off the night. And it is only 6:00 p.m. The Library is shut down. A campus police car slowly turns away in patrol. I become a ghost as I walk about.

Where are we all going? The darkness so wonderfully concentrates the mind. We dart about like fireflies. Where are we going?

As we wait in airport security lines, or stare unthinkingly out a car window, as we lose our patience in a shopping mall, or try to find the perfect tree; where are we going? Are we not all going into the dark?

This is the terror that humans have ever faced. And now we can even see this in enormous proportions. The cosmos itself is predominantly dark matter and energy. Many try to be escape artists. But even Houdini left us in the dark.

Perhaps the universe is teaching us some wisdom. The mystics spoke of the dark night of the soul. Will we find something other than the face of fear in this dark night?

5

The Living & the Dead

Commentaries always border on the personal. Sometimes it is hidden and muted; sometimes it becomes quite evident. This section features people I have known or public figures that have affected my sense of life. It is fitting that I included some poetry I shared over the air. That seemed to be the most appropriate way of "giving sorrow words." In each case I was acknowledging someone who touched my life.

Good night, sweet priest 1996

My uncle never had the crooning charm of Bing Crosby nor the impish laugh of Barry Fitzgerald. Nor did he wear his priesthood in the solitary robes of Gregory Peck. Like hundreds of others who entered the seminary during the Depression, he looked upon his ordination as a way to do something in the face of that numbing terror.

He was a redheaded kid from Russell Street, a "good scout," as his brother, my father, used to say, who left college after two years, to learn enough Latin to get by at Mass, along with some Shakespeare to saffron up his preaching, so that he could be ordained and do some good.

Unlike the celluloid celibates of the thirties and forties, the parish priest led a pedestrian life—very much in the literal sense of that word. They knew their people from inside their kitchens, often leaving their meager salaries behind on the tables for those who "had their pride."

Whether counseling a pregnant girl at Catholic Charities, or worrying over Tuesday night bingo, he had a remarkable capacity to focus on people. It was never a matter of numbers or abstractions. "Kindness," he said, "Kindness is what people need, what they remember."

The Church my uncle served has changed greatly. And it will continue to change as it rushes into the next millennium. But there is a constant in the midst of this trek to glory deeper than dissent, more lasting than control: Loving "kindness is what the people need, what they remember."

Good night, sweet priest,
And flights of angels sing thee to thy rest!

A human touch 1996

Fourteen years ago Joseph Bernardin, the newly appointed archbishop of Chicago, greeted his fellow priests with the haunting biblical verse, "I am Joseph, your brother." What was meant as a felicitous introduction took on a somber tone in the last year. Beyond the possibilities of therapy, Bernardin faced his withering end with courage and candor.

Indeed, his honest response to the savagery of cancer produced remarkable results. No other hierarch in North America has had such a telling effect upon people. Bernardin achieved what pastoral letters only wave at; what doctrinal consternations largely evade; what televangelists never see—he chose to be human to the end.

In a society where the heroic is proportioned upon football fields, where celebrity lasts for fifteen minutes, and where image covers a multitude of sins, Bernardin walked with open eyes, ever more slowly among his fellow travelers. In fact, he caused us to slow down, to regain a modest pace, and to recognize the healing effect of a human touch.

Yes, Joseph truly became our brother. Not just the brother of priests, nor just the brother of Christians. He set foot on humanity's common ground.

And so, having walked with him to the edge of death, let us not forget that the story of Joseph did not end with his brothers' reconciliation, nor even with his death. Read on and learn that the people walked out of Egypt bearing the bones of their long dead brother Joseph to the promised land.

Out of South Africa 1997

It is almost twenty years now. No, I'm not thinking about the return of "Star Wars." News out of South Africa continues to startle the world. Five white security officers involved in the detention and killing of black leader Steve Biko are now petitioning the country's Truth and Reconciliation Commission in hope of receiving amnesty for their crimes.

For most Americans Steve Biko is an unknown. But in 1977 he was considered the most dangerous man in South Africa. Why? Because he believed that Blacks could no longer settle for life on someone else's terms. It was time to recognize the transformative possibilities inherent in every oppressed life, to build structures of community pride, and, thus, to turn the world upside down.

Then Steve Biko was jailed for the fourth time. Kept naked in a cell for 18 days, with his brain so severely damaged that he foamed at the mouth, he was driven naked in a Land Rover over 700 miles only to be dumped in another cell and left to die. All of this came out in the first investigation despite attempts to cover up the crime.

Inevitably his death became a pivotal point in the fight against Apartheid. But the story does not end there.

Now some, including Biko's family, would try his murderers. But if pardon is not given especially here, then is this not the real death of Steve Biko? Twenty years ago his dream of changing the deadly face of things did not die out in a prison cell, but now it could succumb to self-righteousness. How few of us today go beyond asserting our demands and attempt the most dangerous and subversive human experiment—forgiving one another?

▌ "Ah, but I do!" 1997

▌ Recently retired Archbishop Desmond Tutu, now heading the South African Truth and Reconciliation Commission, came to the United States for cancer therapy. After a lifetime of struggling to overturn the system of apartheid, Tutu took on a task that has engendered considerable criticism from both black and white South Africans. He is convinced, nevertheless, that for the South African experiment in freedom to continue there must be found ways of moving beyond the fruitless demands of reprisal.

Now cancer has entered the picture. No one knows whether Archbishop Tutu will be able to finish his work. But I have an inkling that he will face both the task of the Commission and his cancer with a singular courage.

Consider this. Once, during the days of apartheid, Bishop Tutu was walking down a sidewalk, until he came to a part where the cement gave way to a plank stretched over a muddy patch. As he stepped on the board, a white South African came from the opposite direction and was about to step on the same board. The man yelled at Tutu, "I don't give way to gorillas!"

Now what was Tutu to do? If he stepped back, he would give in to the oppression that he had long opposed. But, if he contested the right of way, he would quite likely have been arrested for disturbance of the peace. What to do?

With a twinkle in his eye, he stepped back gracefully from the plank, bowed and made a sweeping gesture with his right hand, "Ahh, but I do!"

Throughout his life Tutu has shown that turning the other cheek can be a shrewd, creative response to an oppressive situation. I wonder what further surprises he has in store for all of us.

The Book of Ruth 1998

Whoever imagined that the prophet Isaiah would have a soft Southern accent? Since 1974, when Sister Ruth Graf burst onto the Victory Parkway campus with a passion for truth and for teaching, students, faculty and administrators of Xavier University have known this to be so.

Despite her notorious reputation for being a stickler for attendance and a difficult grader, her classes were usually oversubscribed. A few years ago her Chair commented that her student evaluations sounded more like testimonials than ordinary assessments. Students knew from the outset that Sister Ruth cared; indeed, cared too much to let them off the hook.

Nor has Ruth Graf let her colleagues off the hook. With an uncanny capacity to assess character, she has, like the prophets of old, courageously warned of promises and pitfalls. On hindsight, many of her colleagues have admitted that they would have been better off if they had listened to her.

Her graduate experience at Hebrew Union College brought a radical insight to Ruth. When she saw up close how the New Testament was understood from a Jewish perspective, she was shocked. She resolved to do something. In 1987 Ruth co-developed the program "Healing Deadly Memories" which deals with the scriptural roots of Anti-Semitism. Since its initial grant from the American Jewish Committee, this unique program has continued to grow in national outreach.

Even Ruth's retirement from Xavier is not ordinary. There is a motto of the Mercy Sisters: "That others may follow." Last fall Ruth gave up her tenure track position to allow the Department to retain a promising young teacher and scholar.

Through it all Ruth remains a Kentucky wildcat: singular, feisty and free. While she has little regard for the pomp and pettiness of academe—especially unnecessary meetings—her honesty and affection have been the backbone of the Department. Everything for Ruth is personal. Indeed, it is so personal, that after taking her course on the Prophets, you come away quite convinced that Isaiah was a woman.

Fused into one   1998

Fastballs and fireflies were on my mind that Friday afternoon. I was looking to end the week with a game of catch with my sons. We would throw and throw until our arms tired among the glitterings of fireflies.

But it was not to be. My wife had been trying to reach me all afternoon. She had tickets to the May Festival. Jessye Norman was singing. The rest is a blur. Even our recalcitrant Nissan couldn't keep us from getting there.

Finally, after three excellent pieces, Ms. Norman, in a turquoise gown and turban, strode onto the stage. The Music Hall became electric. Each gesture and then each note revealed a woman centered and in harmony with the power that flowed so eloquently through her. Again and again I had the impression that she was holding something back, intimating the very strength of her soul.

Her final performance came from Strauss's opera "Capriccio." In the role of the countess who is torn between two lovers—a poet and composer— she asks which is more important: words or music.

The aria ends before the countess can overcome her indecision. Yet for those of us in that full house, with the air-conditioning shut off per Ms. Norman's request, there was no wavering. We knew in our bones, made radioactive by her luminous voice, the force of her song:

Words and Music are fused into one—joined in a new creation.
Mystery of the moment—one art set free by the other!

How memory matters   1998

It was March 1974 when I went to see John McCormack, then three years retired from being Speaker of the House. I had been to Washington the previous month attempting to find a job. Despite numerous applications and the best efforts of a congressional assistant, I left without prospects. Nothing was moving in that town distracted by the fateful Watergate developments.

So, I decided to take my grandmother's advice: "If you ever need help, go see John McCormack." Years before she had taken care of his sister. Never mentioning what she did, Nana would only say that John McCormack would remember.

And he did. When I mentioned Kate Logan's name, his eyes broke the long glacier of his face. He reassured his suspicious flunky, a throwback from the *Last Hurrah*, that he was quite happy to receive someone who didn't want a favor but only wanted to talk.

When he heard that I was of two minds—to go to law school and then into politics or to enter a program in scripture—he said, "If you want to have an effect on the present go into law, but if you want to work with the future, teach."

As we mused on things, he offered me a cigar. And, then, in that smoky back room in the Post Office that bore his name, he took two letters from his tailored coat. One was a yellowed note from Bishop Sheen, the other from Lady Bird Johnson, so touched that he would come to say farewell to her husband.

In that whirlwind year of Watergate I came to a decision. I found the future in the words of an old politician. I discovered how memory matters, and how men, old and young, can put their feet up on the desk, smoke cigars, and laugh as the sun goes down.

▌Enigma in pinstripes 1999

Yesterday there were private funeral services for the Yankee Clipper. Throughout his baseball career and even after it Joe DiMaggio, despite and probably because of his reticence, evoked in many a singular response. His passing brings us back full circle to consider once more the haunting question:

Where Have You Gone, Joe Dimaggio?
Joltin' Joe went home to San Francisco:
his funeral as modest as the man.
While cable networks chattered on and on,
splicing the void with highlights he was too
shy to turn into more than what they were,

while reporters kept digging, dogging him
to find some angle in his dying room,
while all the obits gushed about the tear
of fifty-six straight games in "forty-one,"
of thirteen seasons balanced on much pain,
of dirt kicked once, the only sign of strain,
of leaving roses for his Marilyn,
he left us speechless, humbly gliding past,
an enigma in pinstripes to the last.

A tale out of school 1999

Recently Harvard Divinity School announced that a Roman Catholic priest would lead the institution into the twenty-first century. Father J. Bryan Hehir, an eminent ethicist and the chief writer of the compelling Peace Pastoral of the American Bishops, took over as chair of the divinity school's executive committee.

Much was made of Harvard's original animus towards Catholics. The Dudleian Lectures, inaugurated in the eighteenth century, featured one talk devoted to "detecting, convicting, and exposing the idolatry, error, and superstitions of the Romish Church." Happily by the nineteenth century a Harvard President conceded that the idea of a "virtuous and devout Roman Catholic" was not a complete impossibility.

Yet amid all the applause and anecdotes, a footnote to the School's history was overlooked. For, in the spring of 1985, a Jesuit, George MacRae, served as acting dean until his sudden death in August of that year. I could run out of time listing George's academic accomplishments. But George was not one to boast.

Instead, I will tell a tale out of school. As an MDiv student I studied New Testament under George. After a second course with him, he took me out to the Acropolis, a Greek Restaurant. Somewhere between the moussaka and the Ouzo, he dropped a bomb on me. "What do you want to do with your life?" "You ought to consider going into New Testament."

George spoke words I never thought I'd hear. Secretly for years I yearned to do that. But all those languages! "You just sit down and learn!" He countered every fearful objection and left me with a future for the taking.

A week after his funeral, George surprised me one more time. His handwritten preface to my Gospel commentary was found amid an enormous pile of papers on his desk.

Nothing less than the future   2001

Yesterday Cincinnati said goodbye to a friend. Sister Jacinta Shay died last Sunday after a relentless struggle with cancer. She left at the end of the age.

Jacinta was a rarity. She was a genuine educator, never far from the source of her vision. Inspired by Maria Montessori, Jacinta was firmly convinced of the infinite worth of every child. She knew well that the child takes the lead in teaching if only the adults have the imagination and patience to detect the delicate clues right in front of them.

After founding a Montessori program in Louisville Jacinta returned home to establish Cincinnati's first Montessori preschool. Mercy Montessori became the first elementary Montessori school charted by the State of Ohio. About ten years ago the first Montessori Junior High in Cincinnati was begun. Jacinta was far from finished as she dreamed of a high school vastly different from the factory models prevalent today.

Jacinta would not want us to waste time enumerating her honors or her trips to bring the Montessori vision around the world. Adamant as always, she would want us to embrace the task and privilege of educating our children—to accept nothing less than the best for every child.

While we are learning this, we can't forget Monty, her Yorkshire terrier, puttering on the outskirts of the classrooms. Or the simple Christmas goodies she brought to each child.

Jacinta was at her best in ordinary moments. While today's educators fear human contact, Jacinta greeted her little ones as they were dropped off each morning. She leaves the memory of effortlessly coaxing reluctant children. Soon they would be hugging her and accompanying her inside.

She left us nothing less than the future.

"Buzz" 2001

Although classes don't begin until Monday, I've already been to school two weeks. A trip to Washington brought me back to Francis "Buzz" Corwin, that scrawny blond dreamer, whom I met in my first days of high school. He had lost a weekend early on in the semester as part of a search party for a plane that had gone off the radar. As a card-carrying member of the Junior Civil Air Patrol, he tramped for hours to find downed flights. Despite all odds, constant ingrown toenails, and poor eyes, he wanted simply to fly.

In his junior year, outfitting himself with a handmade costume, wings and a stinger, he became the bluejacket "Buzz." We all were stunned by this other side to our friend, who flew along the sidelines and opened us up to the frenzy of football.

Two years later Frank was finishing his tour of 'Nam. A specialist 4th class mechanic, he had worked on choppers the entire time. On his last day he talked a pilot into taking him up. They came back in body bags.

All this and more came flooding back to me as I walked down the path, past the stark, black granite panels of the Vietnam Memorial. I found Francis H. Corwin on line 6, 34th west panel. My fingers traced his name. I cried again for that doomed daydreamer, my brave, fragile friend. And I looked around and saw on both walls the enormity of our insane loss.

I left the Memorial as the skies over Washington delivered a steady rain. In the drenching downpour I looked back upon that chevron of remembrance and realized that Buzz had won his wings.

Jamal 2001

We met in the shadows two nights after our world had ended. I stopped at a local gas station to fill up, handing a twenty to the man behind the counter to hold while I tanked up.

By the time I finished, he met me at the door with my change. He was locking up for the night. This man I had noticed often behind the counter. A soft lilt of an Arabic accent was detectable. And so, when he handed me my change, I looked into his eyes and said simply, "How are you?"

Immediately he sensed my concern. His tightened shoulders relaxed, his tired face became animated. Out tumbled so much. Our names. Our anger. Our fear. In a gas station with its lights out two middle aged strangers talked of everything that counted: God, fragile human life, trust, our children.

Jamal had been in America for nine years. He had tried to make a go of it in Lebanon, his home, but the disastrous situation prevented him from making a decent living for his family. So he left his wife and three children to live in hope.

Next Tuesday was to be his citizenship exam. But now he saw his dreams of life here crashing down with the World Trade Center. Would they let this Muslim in?

On Tuesday afternoon I stopped for gas. I found Jamal in the garage. His smile told all. We embraced.

Today Jamal will pledge allegiance to our flag.

Arshaluis Arsenovich 2001

Gospodin Prezident Putin appeared live on NPR stations around the country last night. The president of Russia was taking calls.

In this topsy-turvy world we are now living in the watchword seems to be expect the unexpected. Both Bush and Putin dramatically declared their intention to eliminate two thirds of their countries' nuclear arsenals in the next ten years. Meanwhile the president of the United States was delighted to have Vladimir for an overnight and barbecue at his home in Crawford, Texas. Indeed, Barbara Walters in her recent interview with Putin contained her gushy up-close-and-personal style and actually let Putin reveal himself, even in his halting English.

It seems I've been waiting for these surprises most of my life. In fact, it goes back to Arshaluis Arsenovich Simenion. Five days a week, two hours a day, that little man taught the year-long intensive Russian course. He squirmed in his one good gray suit and almost leapt out of his shoes over the raised desk to flutter with his right hand: *tochnie, tochnie,* more exactly. When we got it right, he'd flash his monkey grin, gulping down repeated *da's*. Somehow he and his bear of a father, an Orthodox Bishop, escaped the Soviet Union, and Arshaluis was proud of his English accent acquired in London on the way to America. That nuance was always lost on us.

Now, as I strain to hear Putin's Russian under the English translator's drone, those wildly sad and dark eyes come back to life. The old Bishop buried his son only a few years after our class. But I still see Arshaluis Arsenovich in his half-lit office, hunched over our essays. And I hear his words again, untranslatable as his afternoon sips of *borshch*.

Out of the blue Northwest   2001

Her email startled me. The last time we talked Lisa was the Director of a Montessori School in Seattle. Her own artwork was maturing, despite the demands of her teaching schedule. She had had a number of successful exhibits. Now out of the blue Northwest she asked for a recommendation for law school.

Most recommendations are written this time of year. When the world is at its darkest, professors push aside their stacks of bluebooks and take up the art of soothsaying. Scribbled notes, wrinkled grade lists, and lingering memories become the tea leaves for our fortune telling. We offer what we can honestly, knowing full well the fragile prospect of our words.

I will write what I know. I will write of the third grader who crouched with her head between her knees to avoid bricks being hurled at her school bus. She grew up wondering what was fair as Louisville tried to desegregate. I'll remember that art student who held her own with pre-med scholars over questions of ethics and education. I'll keep in mind how she would not separate her art from the need to educate.

September 11 set its mark on her. That crater in New York sent tremors all the way to Puget Sound. The artist in her recognized that it was time to grow again. With her constant quest for fairness, her finely honed skills in conflict resolution, and an intellect that equals the finest students I have taught in over thirty years, she will bring to the practice of law what the world so desperately needs: an eye that sees justice stirring at the ground zero of our lives.

The Columbia Cascades   2003

Galileo from Pisa spies
the raw effects of gravity.
We see death streaming from the skies,

our dreams hard landing in debris.
Let's get it straight, right from the chart:
this was no tale of Icarus,
that featherbrained, teenage upstart,
who came down with high-wire hubris.
The seven boarded as a team,
(middle-aged eyes on a mission),
soberly suited up their dream,
aware that what goes up comes down.
We did not see what we had seen,
nor sense an errant blur of foam
could forecast damage on our screen,
an omen of their coming home.
Once out of sight, routine sets in.
We replay all our earthly dreads
from Baghdad to the Pentagon
as they somersault above our heads.
They take us in like gods of old
that ride the learning curve of earth.
Those distant landmarks they behold
spin out a transient, aching worth.
Their flight encapsulated life,
a suspended animation,
rocketed from this planet's strife
from a much conflicted nation.
Inside they train their eyes on moss,
detect in nature's nonchalance
what the proverbial ant does
to turn a life of work from chance.
One brought a sketch à la Chagall:
a moonscape from the Holocaust,
refusing to be held in thrall,
relic of a doomed young artist.
How can he keep Shabbat in space,
where sunsets never let him rest?
The Kiddush cup floats by a face,
the Torah scroll flies off his chest!
They finished their experiments,

went quickly through their last routine,
checked protocols, tied down the plants,
strapped in to ride out their decline.
We woke to replays from the blue.
Concussions from the atmosphere
inverted what we thought we knew.
Morning vaporized David's star.
So now we live with what remains.
That blue sky fades to Texas red,
fans out worldwide in bloody strains
and only promises more dead.
Is what they saw already lost?
Or shall we use our right to know
how meaning can be read in dust
and we can live like them below?

▌ Zardis lives! 2003

▌ "Zardis is alive!" So read my mother's note clipped to a news article. A few days before in Boston I had been sifting through the photographic remnants of my youth. I paused over a black and white trio, two altar boys flanking a young curate. With that ever-present smile, Stephen Zardis gazed slightly off to the left. I recalled something that young boys never admit: his quiet gentleness.

Then I began to mourn again. Stephen had served in 'Nam where Agent Orange was falling from the skies. In 1979, despite suffering from its effects, he led the fight against the chemical companies that concocted that vile poison. The news reported that he was doomed to an early death.

But Zardis lives. A quadriplegic and legally blind, living in a Veteran Affairs center for the last four years, he continues quietly to surprise. He has left his high school, brimming with minority students, a million dollar annuity in the memory of two cousins, one who died in Vietnam, the other on a plane that crashed into the World Trade Center.

Stephen still smiles. I learned that when I called him this week. What do you say to a man who keeps coming back from the dead? He joked about how the doctors and nurses have saved him countless times. My voice broke as we reached across the country, over forty years. That gentle one, from long ago, was on the line, reassuring an old friend that the courage to live is not dead.

Gandalf the wise

2003

Gandalf the wise has passed to the Western Isles.

On the morning, when the news of a tyrant's capture electrified the world, I was lost in a dream. I seemed to be walking away from a city. On the road to my left strode a man cloaked and gray. I thought him a friend I knew and called out. He looked over and then proceeded ahead. I turned back, then to my left, and saw a hill with wooden houses. Oddly one home attracted me and I felt a poignancy of a love, once so strong, so long ago.

The next day I read my emails. Al Folkard, who fought on North African sands and crossed the Rhine with the Allies' first reconnaissance unit, an English professor for fifty years, a man who opened the intellectual life to me by salting my imagination with Dante, Shakespeare and Eliot, died just after his beloved Emma reached his hospital room.

I remember another gray midwinter day. Distraught over my best friend's academic suicide, I could not find words to cope. Al sat down with me, throwing me lifelines of poetry through that late afternoon. Slowly I learned how to swim in words. By indirection Al found direction out.

I turn back to that dream and T. S. Eliot. Is life so wondrous that "I caught the look of some dead master," that when the dying "depart, ... we go with them," and join them in their unceasing "raid on the inarticulate"?

I, Asimov

2004

The new sci-fi flick *I, Robot* transported me recently not into the future but back to the past, to the Bread Loaf writers' conference where I met that most remarkable author whose novel has finally made it to movie multiplexes.

My first impression was not positive. Falling into a group of young writers, I sat down with them for our first dinner at Bread Loaf. A waitress, one of our group, working her way through the conference, complained that a guest writer had been hitting on her. It was Isaac Asimov. We sprang to her defense by writing a nasty limerick which she carried to him. Diverted by this challenge, Asimov immediately dropped his fork and took out a pen. Our war of words, stretching the outer limits of filthy limericks, went on throughout the conference.

Even in the breakfast line Asimov flirted. There he was—a stubby, eyeglassed toad, who magnetically attracted groupies. Nervous over his roving eye, wife number two-to-be dispatched her sister to chaperone.

There was no need to worry. Asimov's passion was not sweet young things; it was writing. He told of finally taking a vacation with wife number one and hacking out the days on a portable typewriter on the beach. Already he had written over two hundred books. He found he had a gift for gulping down and ordering data, which he promptly forgot as he jumped to another subject.

Somehow I grew fond of that brash, unbridled, yet loveable ego who spent his nights writing two more books.

The semicircle of saints 2004

As we wait in this uncertain summer for events to unfold, with so much beyond our control, many of us are bewildered. Is there any hope about?

It might, then, help to tell a story. Even better, a true one.

There my friend sat, holding his daughter's hand in the delivery room. She had not dilated enough to push. And so he sat. A labor coach by default. Her boyfriend was long gone. His wife, exhausted by her own chemotherapy, was waiting anxiously at home. The fifty-eight-year-old scholar was the only one left.

He was deeply troubled. What would happen to this child, born of a young woman, who was caught in a spiral of self-destruction? What good could he, the aging professor, be?

Between her contractions he fell briefly into a dream. There behind the head of her bed stood a group of figures from his entire life. He recognized teachers, colleagues, and friends. He felt a peace he had never known before. Was this heaven? All stood confidently, this semicircle of saints, signifying by their gaze that all would be well, that this child would grow and prosper.

That was four years ago. Grandma is in remission. And, despite creaking bones, she and grandpa are raising a girl that each day continues to surprise.

Lie fallow

2004

Not long ago I told the story of a colleague given to dreams. Recently he left me with another vision. David had been under stress for some time. Raising two grandchildren, tending to a wife apparently in remission, teaching scripture and finishing another book had taken a toll.

Fortunately David listens to his dreams. One night he dreamt what seemed at the outset to be a most frustrating situation. He appeared to be filling out a crossword puzzle. The clues along the side not only were vague, but, whenever he went back to check the clues, they had changed entirely! He was in the midst of a dream unable to escape the sensation that he would never get the puzzled solved. Sounds like a classic anxiety dream.

Or was it? As he sweated out this dream, David somehow decided to stand back from the puzzle. He then noticed that some boxes had been filled in despite the turmoil. What he read stayed with him. Just two words: "Lie fallow."

Wisdom embedded somewhere had spoken. He took those words to heart and let the energies of the earth assist him.

I wonder if this oracle has a wider audience? Especially at this time of year, with all the rush, what do we forget, as our hemisphere, so hard-worked, tilts into the dark?

Oh! Dass wat dat mean!

2005

In retrospect it was no way to deal with jetlag. But there I was in an all night restaurant, taking turns with my friend Ed, reading aloud the Hawaiian Pidgin translation of the New Testament. We went back and forth, becoming amazed at words we were hearing as if for the first time. Oh! Dass wat dat mean!

We then went back to my room and started reading our own words to each other. We wanted to catch that accent—that emphasis—the written text could not deliver. We even read aloud each other's work to see if there was something more to be savored.

Between readings we told each other how we had found our voices. How at some key moment in our lives someone was there to listen and to encourage our awkward attempts.

Such an interlude today seems out of place in a world of terror. The shock and noise ringing round the globe push aside such moments.

Yet, if we cannot continue to find out what we would say to one another, if we cannot hear another's voice, or detect a groping gesture, then we already are a captive nation.

Could it also be that such determined fury actually comes not from devils but from those who feel they truly never have been heard?

The company we keep 2008

Recently, on our way to a Jesus Seminar on the Road (JSOR) in Goshen, Indiana, Roy Hoover and I received a phone call that told us some startling news. One of the hosts of the JSOR had been dismissed from his position as interim pastor of a Mennonite community for his leadership in bringing the Jesus Seminar to College Mennonite Church. Don Blosser, a retired faculty member of Goshen College, and a retired Mennonite pastor, had further dismayed a couple of community members for his critical and compassionate reading of the New Testament in regard to the question of homosexuality. This vocal minority brought their concerns to the committee that originally had selected Blosser as interim pastor. Despite the fact that the committee thought he was doing excellent work in the church and had received high praise for both preaching and teaching, they reversed their own previous judgment and demanded his resignation on the chance that there might be some theological differences in the future.

This is not the first time that people have played the futures market in religious doctrine. Since Blosser's present service could not be used against him, the committee gazed into the future and could only envision potential discontent and division. It was better to sacrifice one man for the sake of the church. Besides, he was only a fill-in.

Decisions like this are made out of fear and the lack of imagination. The fear not only of religious division but of losing members (especially in a worsening economy) can weigh heavily on people who are responsible for a faith community. But it has been my experience that such fear often is based on the assumption that you know all you need to know about a situation. You already see the worst played out in your mind and you react to avoid that outcome.

When you decide out of such fear, you usually make your most profound mistakes. I have seen that in my own life; I had not waited long enough to be surprised by what I had not expected. I gave up too soon on a relationship, an opportunity, a project. Only later are you surprised by what you missed in making the decision.

So it is quite understandable that the committee acted in the way they did. It is sadly ironic that Don Blosser was the one involved. For his long teaching and pastoral careers, his training in conflict resolution, as well as his leadership of the New Perspectives on Faith Program, made him an ideal choice to handle any theological discontent and differences. In fact, the invitation of the New Perspectives on Faith Program to bring the Jesus Seminar on the Road to Goshen was given to demonstrate: that the very origins of Christianity could be approached in all their complexity, that different viewpoints were both possible and helpful, and that disputes could be carried out with civility and respect.

Indeed, this situation well illustrates the need for more, not less, information on the deepest traditions within Christianity. Sadly the churches (both Protestant and Roman) that emerged from the traumatic events of the Reformation have yet to come to grips fully with the demands and possibilities of historical consciousness. Churches have often retreated into pietism or ideological purity. They have yet to recognize the fragmentary nature of their knowledge or traditions. Moreover, they have yet to see that a complementary, critical approach allows people to envision better where they came from and where they are going. The long and the short of it is that we need each other, especially when we are at a loss for words or ideas.

Now what would happen if people became aware that the earliest communities did not all think alike, that disagreements were part of the growth of the Jesus Movement, that Jesus encouraged people to puzzle through his sayings, and that this itinerant would eat with anybody? What would happen if church committees factored these insights into their pastoral decisions?

Don Blosser was asked how he felt about this situation. He surprised everyone at the JSOR workshop. He said that while it was an important matter for him, his personal integrity was far more important. He spoke with great feeling. Then he added that he would be there on Sunday to preach his final sermon.

He would try to speak compassionately to their condition and model his vision for finding resurrection in these painful days.

As Roy and I drove south to Cincinnati on Sunday morning, we quietly and reverently imagined that tall and courageous son of Menno Simons calmly speaking with his people.

▌Bashir returns 2012

▌Bashir was back, sitting with me in a pizzeria, back after sixteen years. His craggy, gentle face was more relaxed; his hair graying on the sides. Long before George and Nick Clooney were alerting the world about Darfur, and even before Clarence Page (alone among American columnists) wrote searing editorial pieces on the crisis in Sudan, I was being schooled by a political exile from that tragic land, by a priest forced to flee through Egypt, who had somehow managed to end up in Cincinnati and apply for the Masters Program in Theology.

As Chair I had accepted his application and had numerous occasions to talk with him. Fortunately at the time our Department proved somewhat accommodating. One of our faculty refreshed her Swahili with him. And a visiting theologian from Tanzania kept him from getting overly homesick. But the shock of his last days in Sudan was still with him. Bashir would listen attentively in class. When asked a question he could respond well in English. But there seemed to be a lingering reluctance to offer more than what was required. He always seemed pensive, sadly so.

His final class was a readings course in the gospels with me. When we got to the saying "Do not resist evil," I asked him what he felt about such a remark. It was then that his shattered world was revealed. "I cannot do that," he said plaintively. "My brother was shot by soldiers right in front of me. They took me and I thought it was over. But somehow the trigger was not pulled. I escaped from what was left of my village and fled. My bishop told me to go to Egypt. Italian missionaries in Egypt helped me to get to the United States."

For the first time in almost two years Bashir was animated. The stolid patience he had exhibited had been washed away by a lingering, blistering vision. A stubborn resilience took hold of his speech. "I cannot let that happen. I cannot accept that saying." I attempted to explain that the original Greek did not support a simplistic endorsement of victimhood. But I sensed that this refinement was not being heard at the moment. Things were too raw. The pain was too close.

I remember a photo I took of Bashir just before he graduated. His face held an empty expression. From then on he kept sending occasional emails from various parts of the States. Twice I served as a reference.

He had spent some years in Nashville. Because the local bishop refused his services as a priest, he worked for over five years in the post office. Eventually a new bishop welcomed his offer to work. Bashir became engaged in the plight of many African refugees in the "Athens of America." He even became an American citizen. Two years ago, he shared plans of going to Canada to work on a joint program in law and economics. So I thought he was north of the border when he called me.

In fact, Bashir was back in Cincinnati. I offered to take him to lunch. And so it was at an Uno's on the east of Cincinnati, that we got a chance to talk and fill in the gap of sixteen years.

Instead of moving to Canada, Bashir had returned to Sudan. With an American passport, he was determined to discover what remained of his family that was living in the north, not in the recently independent Southern Sudan. Three aging sisters survived. Their only prayer had been to see their brother before they died. So Bashir traveled back home where Sunni radicals held sway and continued to reduce any pockets of Shia, Orthodox, Copts, or Catholics. To avoid any complications, he moved frequently, visiting various Christian communities. His message was clear: "No revenge. But don't be victims."

Bashir had learned something in exile. He had seen how Muslims coming to the States began to reread the Quran. Their experience of others had changed their reading of their sacred text. He saw that the Islamic radicals in Sudan and throughout Africa maintain a fundamentalist reading that screens out what is right in front of their faces. He also saw this in a number of the Christians in Sudan, a mirror image of the Islamic oppressors. He tried to explain to his countrymen that revenge would only trigger more violence. And yet, one must be wise enough to see that there is another way beyond reaction or submission. Walter Wink called this "the third way." I liken it as an imaginative jujitsu, where you anticipate and outmaneuver your opponent. It means taking an active, anticipatory role, where you imagine your enemy in ways he cannot imagine you.

Bashir returned to Sudan with more than what he had left with. He brought back over a decade of patient experience, a new way of reading an old text. He knows that his attempt was a modest one, that the oppressive regime still holds sway (and almost prevented him from leaving, but for a colonel from his tribe who waved him through at the last moment). But now he can read the Sermon on the Mount out of his exiled life; he can breathe freely, survey the land of terrible aspect, and understand what Jesus meant by "loving the enemy."

▌ In a very small room 2014

▌ The room always seems so small. You expect something much larger. But modern operating rooms are totally functional, designed to get things done *Stat*, appointed with only the necessary medical etcetera's. Then I saw an astounding video that reframed every experience I've had of operating rooms.

About to undergo a double mastectomy, Deborah Cohan, an Ob/Gyn and mother of two, enjoyed a dance with her medical team in the operating room at Mt. Zion Hospital in San Francisco. In her blog Deborah had invited family and friends to join her in creating a healing video montage. "I will be dancing in my little hospital gown and bouffant cap in the Mt. Zion operating room with the surgical and anesthesia teams," she declared. She asked others to join her in dancing to Beyoncé's "Get Me Bodied." She planned to watch how others joined in by watching their videos during her recovery. She asked, "Are you with me people?"

Her video is incredible. There is Deborah making some serious moves with her all female medical teams. The room was as electric as her smile. For about six minutes in that little room something quite wonderful happened. The women in the room, clad in a hospital gown and scrubs, kept the beat. With every wiggle and sway, Deborah delivered an unmistakable sense of joy. Given the prospect of her uncertain future, every gesture became a courageous epiphany.

This scene reverberated in my memory. Some time ago I had researched a much older dance scene in another small room. It comes from an ancient document entitled the *Acts of John*.

Situated within a number of tales about the legendary figure of John the disciple, there is a remarkable section that combines both hymn and dance. Instead of delineating Jesus' final meal with his disciples, this unexpected material details an unfolding round dance! Just before Jesus is to be seized, he gathers up his followers and says:

"Before I am handed over to them,
let us sing a hymn to the Father
and so go out to that which is set before."
Then he called us to make a circle as we grasped each other's hands,
he, being in the middle said, "Answer me, Amen."
　　　—Acts of John 94

There follows a series of antiphonal responses, a number of which are quite paradoxical. Among this curious series are the following:

I will to be born and I will to bear,
I will to eat and I will to be eaten up,
I will to hear and I will to be heard.
　　　—Acts of John 95

Indeed, there are also some telling words given to those involved circling around Jesus:

See yourself in me the one who speaks …
For yours is this the suffering of the Human One …
Recognize the suffering …
Learn how to suffer and you will be able not to suffer
I will be in rhythm with the holy souls before me …
　　　—Acts of John 96

By the eighth century the *Acts of John* was condemned as being docetic, that is, for considering that Jesus really did not suffer. He only appeared to suffer. The writing was denounced for evading the humanity of Jesus. However, I have always considered such a judgment to be a flat and unimaginative interpretation of the experience of that earlier community. Quite often theologians display a tin ear to the deeper registers of human experience. What those paradoxical lines were attempting was not a simplistic proposition but a complicated communication, where pain and insight crossed human boundaries. The combination of dance and song was a dramatic indication that something important was afoot. The words and the action invited participants into a radically democratic experience of shared insight. It is easy to see that later hierarchical perspectives would dismiss an image of Jesus and company moving all in rhythm on the same ground level. It is also apparent from this material that there were experimental moves within the developing Jesus traditions attempting to celebrate the experience of a transformative connection.

Such possibilities were not unknown to the ancient world. The cult of Dionysius was famous for its disruptive and shocking transformations. Euripides' *Bacchae* was only one instance of this movement that swept the ancient world. But it was the video of Deborah in the operating room that for me "repeated the sounding joy." The mingling of suffering and joy, courage and fear, hope and pain, was wonderfully embodied in that ecstatic woman. Indeed, it was infectious. She ignited the room. Through her eyes I gained a deeper glimpse into that ancient round dance. I caught the connection disclosed in the shifting shades of paradox. Real life was more than a sterile examination. For a brief moment, against the odds, the fragile beauty of our life beat wildly in our hearts.

▌ On the beach 2015

Once I saw him, I knew his image would never go away. That little body, tossed onto the Turkish shore, as if down for an afternoon nap. The left side of his head, his left arm and bent legs—all visible as he lies absorbed in the sand. The red shirt, blue shorts, and the tan soles of his blue shoes contrast against the incoming blue-gray of the waves, the dull steel colors of the wet sand. This was not a still life. Despite the ceaseless advance of the waves, it was a still death.

Everything stopped when that unknown child arrested me – and so many of us on this planet. Nothing was right in that familiar shape of a sleeping child. There was no crib, no tossed blankets, no necessary bear. Nor was there a slight lifting of his back to indicate all was well. Instead, the sad outrage of Lear howled through my brain: "Never, never, never, never, never."

Soon the news services began to attempt framing this lonesome image. But the more we learned the more our hearts broke.

Three-year old Aylan Kurdi, his five-year old brother Galip and their mother Rehan had all drowned, along with nine others, attempting to cross from Turkey to the Greek island of Cos. Two boats had set out and capsized in rough seas. Despite the efforts of Abdullah, the husband and father, his family was soon lost, eventually washing up on the tourist beach of Bodrum, Turkey. They had fled their home, Kobani in northern Syria, after it had been leveled in the fighting between Islamic State militants and Kurdish fighters. Their aunt Teema, living in Vancouver, had sent funds for their flight. They had applied for a Canadian visa but had been rejected because United Nations officials in Turkey did not give them "refugee" status. So the only avenue left was to pay the smugglers' price for an uncertain crossing. Abdullah had no funds left to purchase life jackets. Here was another family caught in the maelstrom of our violent, careless world.

I followed the newswires for the next week, catching the burial of the mother and boys back in their war-torn town. Abdullah's brief comments stung even in translation:

—"One by one they died"
—"I wish I could transfer my breath to them"
—"My kids were amazing ... What is more beautiful than this?"
—"Everything I was dreaming of is gone."
—"I will sit next to the grave of my family and relieve the pain I feel."

There have been and will be many responses to this trembling event. Abdullah got his wish to bury his family in their hometown. European officials have begun to imagine more humane ways to respond to this never-ending human crisis. Even in the States there is some movement for a compassionate response despite the neuralgic reaction of the know-nothings of the far Right.

Some Europeans have begun to see that the little body washed up on the beach speaks volumes in its tragic silence. The little one has become a question mark over the very identity of the European Union. Aylan has given depth and dimension to a crisis that often has been lost in smudged images of countless refugees, desperate, despondent, and dejected.

But that that little one cannot be reduced to a political beat, as he silently, paradoxically pulses, in ever-widening circles, the horror that each of us dreads: the terror of ultimate abandonment.

Augustine once described in his learned Latin the newborn babe of Nazareth as *infans*, the silent word who without a sound speaks to us. I suggest that Aylan Kurdi has gone beyond that theological play on words. Aylan brings Augustine and the rest of us back to the shore. Isn't that where Augustine himself encountered a little boy who stopped him in his tracks? Did he not remind Augustine that the rhetorician's entire mental effort was tantamount to trying to take in the entire sea? It was the voice of some unseen boy that admonished him, *Tolle, lege*, "Pick up and read" [the Bible]. Augustine did so and the rest is a very uneven history.

In our memory Aylan still lies on the shore. He no longer can babble. We ache to pick him up and read some signs of life. But there is no breath – only our own. We are on the shore, the place where millennia ago life crossed onto land, where things irrevocably changed for the earth. We are back on the shore. Nostalgia for old meanings will no longer work. Nor will bogus attempts to cover up our predicament. No blowhard whirlwind will satisfy the question of Job. No crucifix will assuage the horror of Auschwitz.

Is this not the real work of memory? We remember, not for some trivial pursuit, but to refuse to give up on the few and simple images in which our hearts open. Is this not how we begin to detect what it means to be human? Do we not see that the heart has places that are opened only through suffering? Do we not kneel down to pick up what remains and then, bearing what we hold, sing an unending lullaby:

> Sometimes I feel like a motherless child
> Sometimes I feel like a motherless child
> Sometimes I feel like a motherless child
> A long ways from home ...

6

Cultural
Asides

In this section my commentaries enter the lists of public discourse. How do we make sense of the bewildering interruptions in our lives? How are we to respond to the waves of cultural information? Often I entered at an unusual angle, ranging from Ronald Reagan to Howdy Doody. There was even some fun over the naming of hurricanes. On the other hand, I began to touch on the category of tragedy and our common experience. There are three pieces specifically on 9/11 and its aftermath. Even comedy became a serious subject.

Re-reading Thucydides brought back haunting memories. Our common discourse can be knitted up; the various items can be part of a larger quilt.

Heaven's Gate 1997

It has been almost a month since the first reports of Heaven's Gate streaked across our television sets. Each succeeding report would clarify and yet continue to baffle the public. What appeared to be a morbid roster of suicidal young men turned out to be, under the purple shrouds, a variety of intense people, more women than men, and many of them aging baby boomers.

The means of death, sleeping pills and vodka, soon was displaced in the public's imagination by the uncomfortable evidence of castration among some of the males, including the leader, Marshall Herff Applewhite. The group's web page was quickly discovered along with the seemingly bizarre exit scenario of their beaming up to a spaceship following in the wake of the Hale-Bopp comet.

Televised interviews with former Heaven's Gate members added a further dimension to their eschatology. They saw their actions not as suicide but as an exit, casting off the gross material body for the purer condition of mind.

But the most shocking element is the general puzzlement. Within America there are eight hundred to two thousand ongoing cults. The spaceship script has been around since the fifties, a variation of the Christian rapture game plan. The desire for a pure, androgynous existence above the material plane is the ancient gnostic dream.

Heaven's Gate itself comes right out of Genesis. Caught between a rock and a hard place, a bitter brother and a dysfunctional family, Jacob dreamed of contact with alien beings and woke up, frightened of the campground he then called Heaven's Gate.

It is time for us to wake up to the depths of our dreams, to wrestle with the terror within, to refuse to lose our heads for the sake of our hearts, so that we might not be mesmerized by madness but walk, at last, on our own two feet.

What sort of doctor? 1997

Perhaps I'm letting nostalgia get the best of me. But in the last few weeks I've become troubled over the future of medical care. This hasn't come from studying projected costs for the twenty-first century. It has come the old fashioned way: through people.

The ophthalmologist I've been seeing for some years hit me right between the eyes with her professional future. Unwilling to sacrifice the meticulous care she gives each patient, yet refusing to subject her medical art to the tyranny of numbers, she's decided to give up her practice.

Then a close friend mentioned that her trusted gynecologist is moving from this area to practice in a small town. That talented and patient physician, alert to the complex tapestry of an individual's medical history, no longer desires to wear the straightjacket designed by cost cutters and organizational form fitters.

Most troubling of all was a discussion with one of my students. Just back from an interview for medical school, this university scholar not only recounted the give-and-take of the conversation, but divulged the advice of her parents, themselves both physicians. They repeatedly urged: "Don't go into medicine."

My earliest memory of a doctor's office is that of a dark wooded waiting room and of Doctor Redmond waiting behind the office door to squirt me with a syringe of warm water. His office was a place where that old man listened long, and where I learned that medicine is not played according to the numbers, that treatment begins and ends in trust.

Some might immediately object to my anecdotal report. Nevertheless the questions keep coming: What will the doctor's office be like in twenty years? What sort of doctor will greet us in that room?

Our electronic hearth 1997

When you tune in tonight to your eleven o'clock news, consider this. Instead of just soaking in the news, notice how it grabs you.

A sensational story leads the way, exploding in urgent tones and frantic images. Whatever sadness swelled the TV screen for fifteen seconds is thrown into the background by breathless comments of a sober reporter. Then lesser tragedies spill out upon your screen, only to be interrupted by obligatory auto commercials. Often the barrage of pain starts up again until the talking heads must blithely turn aside to weather.

There another bombast blows. Backed by professional credentials and computer screens, the meteorologist casts an apocalyptic eye upon the earth. Whatever hints of hazard rides the weather balloon. Even a week of clear skies can be stretched like taffy to worry away the time.

All of this prepares us for the climax of the show: sports. Win or lose the hometown teams parade in quickly edited film. Numbers roll like ticker tape out of the sportscaster's mouth. The totals of the day are in. We can manage these wins and losses.

And, then, after a few playful moments, it is over. The liturgy of containment has come and gone.

The eleven o'clock news is very much our electronic hearth, that keeps the wildness of the world at bay. For half an hour disaster seems under our control. Familiar voices numb the pain.

I wonder if our news teams could handle the strangest news of all. A Zen monk put it well: "New Year's Day. Nothing special. Just human beings."

Shall we dance? 1997

Sumimasen. DAHN-su ni yu-ki mah-SHOH Kah? Forgive my fledgling Japanese. No, this isn't the Tokyo Morning News. It's just that the Japanese film *Shall We Dance?* which has been circulating for some time in Cincinnati deserves more than the customary movie review.

First of all, this film runs directly against the American grain. There is no high speed chase, no gratuitous violence, no frontal nudity. Indeed, it's about a middle aged man who dares to take up ballroom dancing. Yes, the Arthur Murray type of dancing. Except for the Lawrence Welk set, that should be enough to kill it for most American audiences.

And yet, from the film's growing popularity, there seems to be something there. A forty-year-old middle executive of a nondescript company looks out of a train window on his way home one night. Off in the distance he sees a young girl looking longingly from the window of a dance studio. Some days later he finally stumbles not only into the studio but into a rich and complicated set of relationships.

Therein lies the incredible beauty of this film. The man, who feels the unease of existence in the very flush of success, who risks the predictable pace of family and career for one dance with that girl, becomes a post modern Dante. Chastened by a

Beatrice, herself riddled by doubt, he discovers in dance a passion deeper than despair.

There is no mystical rose at the end. But there is a man and a woman dancing, swirling about one last time in a waltz, as the music turns on each one of us, "Shall we dance?"

▌Lady Luck   1998

▌In two days America will be exercising its religious devotion. Now I don't mean the usual Sunday practice of millions. I'm talking about something so "ultimate" that it has to be counted in Roman numerals.

Historians of religion know that a good way to discover the religious elements of the past is to consult that culture's calendar. This discloses the axial event, around which everything turns. Usually that day is New Year's Day. But, in America, the day that fixes our imagination more than any other is the last Sunday in January—Super Bowl Sunday.

Over the years we have come to recognize that what happens in the Super Bowl is not just a game. Nor is it an event that happens only on the playing field. The liturgy of the Super Bowl begins with a procession six months long. Sacrifices litter the fields as knees, ankles, arms, wrists, backs, and brains are given up in the heat and exhaustion of the games. The high priests dress in business suits and are found in luxury boxes.

There is, of course, constant commentary to the sacrificial scene, spelled out in the sacred patois of x's and o's. Survivors from the "olden days" in serious tones attempt to intensify the meaning of collision and pain.

Then there are the hymns, which punctuate the play. Fifteen and thirty-second interludes that, to the knowing eye, say more than their sponsors paid for.

For it all comes down to this—to that hyperbolic gamble where millions ride—where fame is fleetingly felt, where new product lines dangle and dance, where half-time lets heaven parachute down in sequins—it comes down to that "momentum" which everyone on the field, in the studio, at home, would control but which everyone knows belongs ultimately to what the Greeks named Tyche, the Romans Fortuna, and we, her modern devotees, call Lady Luck.

"Dwayne the 'Cane"   1998

Now it's "Earl." Just as we were getting used to "Bonnie," and "Charlie," and "Danielle," a new tropical storm was baptized. I don't know about you, but I think the way hurricanes are named is quite lame.

Way back in the fifties I remember Hazel came a-knockin' and left our basement filled with water. The name Diane also stirs memories wet and wild. Even then I never thought the name fit the storm.

Every hurricane season forecasters like to show us they know their ABC's. More recently, they've saddled those wild stallions from the deep with politically correct names right out of a Tupperware party.

Is it because the forecasters can't handle more than two syllables? That sound bites are at a premium? Why is it that we are at a loss in the face of terror, force, and the power of nature?

Hurricane season should be the time for poets to don their flight suits. At the first gust, our poet laureate should ride a hurricane hunter right into the eye of the storm. And in the midst of that tempest, in the natural holy of holies, let the poet conjure a name—

no Beth nor Fran, two spinster aunts, who stayed too long
no stick-on name tag for a cauldron of destruction: "Hello, I'm Andrew!"

Let the poet find the frenzy of words, just as the legendary Cuchulain "fought with the invulnerable tide."

And let us have a name we can mutter, as we brace for the worst, and shout out as the wind howls through our lives.

I cringe at the thought that "Dwayne the 'Cane" will be announced someday.

From time to time   1999

For the last few Sunday evenings I've been indulging myself. I've lost myself in the twelfth century world of Brother Cadfael, played so ably by Derek Jacobi. Like other whodunits this medieval mystery delivers a sense of order—at least for an hour.

But there is something else conveyed by the television performance. I do not find it in the books of Ellis Peters. For in them you get an inside view of the main characters. Peters deftly conveys the inner colors of that faraway world.

But the television version presents a more sobering vision. There is no avoiding the muck and mud, the iron and stone limits of that world. There is no getting around that peasants cannot imagine more than the next year's planting, that nobles are shackled to their castles, and that monks turn a jaundiced eye to this world.

Here is where a late twentieth-century viewer gets uncomfortable. There is no future in that world, except the eternal present found in death. There is no thought that things could be different, that revolutions are possible. In short, I felt claustrophobic.

And yet, why did I enter that imagined world in the first place? Wasn't it to find a moment's relief? From the flu that seems never to go away, from the Impeachment reports droning on and on like bagpipes, from the constant need to get some clarity in this murky world.

It seems I'm just as stuck as the medievals. But there is a difference. It's found in that imaginative move we make from one time to another. In that crossing we gain some breathing space. And every now and again we find the guts to imagine something else is possible.

▌The virtual empire   1999

So, the cat's out of the bag! Actually it's an eagle.

As 1999 continues to wind down, there is increasing talk about the American century. Since the fall of the Berlin Wall this has been the trend in political chatter. But, now with troops setting foot in Kosovo, commentators are more daring in the use of the word "Empire." The American colossus righteously stands astride the globe.

Americans traditionally have had problems with highfalutin phrases, especially those which smack of royalty or noble ranks. Usually we enter the international scene with initial reluctance and misgivings. But, once we're there, watch out!

We simply wanted to go home after kicking the stuffing out of Herr Hilter. But someone had to stand up to those Ruskies! We knew what we had to do. Whether we learned from Gary Cooper at High Noon or Dirty Harry on the streets of San Francisco, we knew how to make an heroic stand.

Why we even learned something from the quagmire of Vietnam. In the Gulf War and now in Serbia, we make war the way we prefer making love—mechanically, dispassionately, and at a distance. That way no one—no one we care about—gets hurt.

Let CNN bombard us with a continual feed of those barbaric horrors. Even those ruined towns cannot withstand the invisible hand which will bring ultimate prosperity: Pax Americana. So, why should we listen to those who would rain on our imperial parade? Don't they realize that our American enterprise is light years away from the debris of Mexico City, Rome or Babylon?

▌In "Dutch" 1999

▌Even before Edmund Morris' "memoir" of Ronald Reagan hit the bookstores, numerous preemptive strikes had been fired from op-ed pages, radio talk shows and television studios. Sober historians, predatory pundits, and Reagan clientele, taken aback at Morris' fictional insertions into this authorized account of the life of the former president, could not wait to read the book before they shot from the hip.

Morris has made it clear in the last few days that he tried to remain faithful to the facts of Reagan's life. Although in his initial dealings with Mr. Reagan, Morris found him "banal," "culturally a yahoo," and "unresponsive in conversation," he detected, nevertheless, in Reagan an elusive air. He began to see that Reagan lived inside his head, in an ideal world. His was a "totally interior" mentality. Reagan's long-standing engagement was in the theater of his own imagination.

Precisely because Morris felt that elusive pulse he despaired of being able to deliver an accurate rendering of the man in the Teflon mask.

And then he hit upon a way into Reagan's world—through fiction. He discovered that to get a sense of the former president he would have to do what Reagan constantly did. For Reagan's genius consisted in a confident capacity to believe and live in the fictions he had long constructed. Like a determined swimmer, Reagan moved forward in a cool, unhurried, and unreflective pace.

Many will be uncomfortable in pondering how a leader of the free world could thrive on fiction. But their uneasiness might disclose the disquieting source of Reagan's political success. Could it be that "Dutch" reflected the "airy nothingness" upon which their own lives depended?

No more seltzer 2000

This has been a bad month for cultural icons. Charlie Brown is in mourning. Cinderella married a millionaire and then, after a lost weekend, hit the morning news shows with her glass slipper still in her mouth. And, while the press was preoccupied with the republican shadow boxing of David versus Goliath, news leaked out about the custody battle over Howdy Doody, that freckle-faced puppet from the fifties.

"Say, kids, what time is it?" That's how Buffalo Bob Smith opened up *The Howdy Doody Show* from 1947 to 1960. The munchkins in the "peanut gallery" would chime in, "It's Howdy Doody time!" Puppets and people collided in song, silliness and seltzer. Despite the evil designs of Phineas T. Bluster, the naughtiness of Dilly Dally, and the cornball comedy of Clarabell the Clown, Howdy — with a freckle on his face for every state — would bob and weave with an air of innocence.

Right now the "Original Howdy" is locked in a bank vault, awaiting the disposition of the court. After barnstorming college campuses and shopping malls with Buffalo Bob, Howdy was returned to the children of his late puppeteer, Rufus Rose. It seems that NBC gave Mr. Rose custody with the understanding that Howdy would be eventually given to the Detroit Institute of Arts. Now the sons of Rufus, with a contract from a Manhattan auction house, want to pull some strings and turn Howdy into a golden goose.

There's no Indiana Jones on the horizon to rescue the big-eared boy, declaring, "He belongs in a museum!" But there is a melancholy realization that another memory is being itemized and turned into a commodity. There's no more seltzer to save the day. Has that cackling Phineas T. Bluster gotten the last laugh?

Beowulf and Bobby Knight 2000

The doom has come down for Bobby Knight. The president of Indiana University has issued a zero tolerance policy for the rough and rude coach. Columnists are already lining up to see who will win the pool on when the "General" will break out of his politically correct straightjacket. Mt. St. Helen's will seem like a popgun in contrast.

What is sadly not surprising is the way things were handled. In times past there was a chance, albeit a slim one, that a university president had an eye for more than a cultivated image and an ear that heard beyond the cautious mutterings of trustees. There was a chance that the traditions a president defended had been embedded in his life. Today it's a corporate patois, not poetry, that inflects a president's speech.

And yet it is the poets who give us a clue as to what is at stake. T. S. Eliot warns us not to seek "the wisdom of old men" but to learn "of their folly."

Indeed, administrators ought to go back to Beowulf. Read again (in the vivid translation of Seamus Heaney) the sage advice of Hrothgar, the old king, whom Beowulf saved from Grendel, the monster, and his mother:

> Sometimes God allows the mind of a man ... to follow its
> bent,
> grants his fulfillment and felicity on earth ...
> He permits him to lord it over many lands
> until the man in his unthinkingness
> forgets that it will ever end for him ...
> The whole world conforms to his will ...
> until an element of overweening
> enters him and takes hold.

In short, the Knight has become a dragon. This is a story for all of us, yesterday heroes who could turn tyrannical, unless we "winter into wisdom."

Bonfires of our
messianic vanities   2000

Every four years our country goes through the throes of a messianic spasm. Many pundits would object to this traditionally religious term. Yet historians of religion easily detect the same drives underlying our exercise in civic religion. Peoples' deepest dreams are stirred, conjured, and blown dry. We want to believe so passionately, so naively, that this candidate is "the one."

A number of knotted realities tug and pull on our political life. We grudgingly learn that we need each other to construct a life together. But our bombastic speech betrays us. We're in way out of our depths. "Power to the People" sounds catchy but we grimly realize that our lives are constantly entrusted to powers beyond our control. Technically we entrust the power to others. But listen to the sound bite rhetoric.

There the irony plays itself out. We are told we are a people who would live as they wish but we live as the spin-doctors prescribe: vicariously, as true believers, fans, and spectators. We are simply happy to bask in the presence of the likely winner.

Yet some observers have noted the lack of interest so far in this presidential run. It may not just be the prefab character of this race. There is the chance that some people have found their own lives and pursuits more interesting. This is not simple escapist isolation. Quite the opposite. People may be slowly coming alive, finding out what the human pursuit of liberty and happiness is really about.

Centuries ago the Buddha advised not to hover like moths around his light. "You are your own torches," he declared. How many of us can stand such heat instead of throwing ourselves onto the bonfires of our messianic vanities?

"More than words can say" 2001

The last three weeks have been very hard on us Americans. Overcome by those atrocious collapsing images, again and again we stumbled in our speech. We've found ourselves at a loss for words.

Long ago, when the world seemed to make sense, de Tocqueville observed Americans were not much given to poetry. We like our words plain and practical. We want them bustling on our streets, not hibernating in some garret.

But what happens when even the chattering of the tickertape comes to a halt?

In the debris of September 11 we stepped on the brittle edge of words. Surprises abounded. The hard-to-take mayor of New York City found a tempered eloquence at ground zero. When pressed by reporters about how many firefighters had been lost, Giuliani answered, "More than we can bear."

In the midst of a stunned nation even the diffident George Bush morphed into a laconic orator. The President's speechwriters spun gold from straw.

Then other words began to trickle in. We heard retellings of cell phone conversations, where words of love and courage held their own long after the savage shock.

We kept returning to the smoldering crime scenes. We hoped along with the rescue workers that some word would emerge from the rubble. As the number of stilled voices magnified, our horror grew. Never, never, never, never.

And then we looked around and saw each other. We took time to say even unimportant things, for we realized, however briefly, that every word weighs more than we can say.

▌We are not alone   2001

As the twin towers came crashing down, we found the devastation ever more terrible. In that hour when steel and flesh showered to earth we became sick at heart, realizing that we, seemingly so protected and innocent, had become like the rest of the world: disposable.

We recoil at the thought that we can be collateral damage, acceptable losses. All in the name of religious purity; for the sake of defending a cherished way of life against an invasive, barbaric culture.

Even our president has wondered why there are people who hate us so. We can no longer afford such naiveté.

It is time for us to grow up. Time to see what the rest of the world has seen for so long. Time to reflect on a haunting, planetary proposition: *We are not alone.*

It is time to realize that much of the world reacts out of hunger and hopelessness. Forty million will die this year from starvation or related diseases around the world. Half are children. That's 320 jumbo jets a day going down—no survivors!

It is time not for guilt but for wisdom. More stunning than any biological attack, a breakout has occurred and diffused throughout our human habitat. Terror itself disclosed something more seismic: *We are not alone!*

We can no longer hide in cubicles. For we, now forever vulnerable, have caught a whiff of freedom. We've found that we finally breathe, when we reach out without reserve. What the ancients called *holy* and kept at arm's length in sanctuaries has leaked now throughout the world. We touch it every time we look in the face of suffering and realize *we are not alone.*

Looking inside 2001

A few years ago William Langewiesche wrote an extended meditation on flight called *Inside the Sky.* He put into words what many of us have long felt. Flight's greatest gift is dramatically simple: it lets us look around. When we do, we discover a world larger than we have been told.

From then on my airline flights carried an extra dimension. I had always been amused at how passengers would focus on the trivial—peanuts or crackers—while flying six hundred miles an hour at thirty-three thousand feet. Langewiesche actually got me to ask again for a window seat despite the fact that my long legs cried out for an aisle. I would squeeze what I could from my small slice of the sky.

But things are not the same after September 11. I haven't had the energy to look beyond the wings. In fact, flying is no longer fun. With all the necessary delays and precautions, airline travel is no longer transparent. We now stare at what before we constantly and conveniently overlooked.

As long as I looked away I did not have to realize how inhuman it is. How unattractive, stale and unimaginative. How each seat is the equivalent of the "little ease," that medieval torture chamber.

It's not that the ambiguous food has morphed into granola snacks. Or that there are no more perks. It is that we now must be attentive to what we all simply agreed to overlook. What is revealed is what is there. And it was never really that good. Before we could dream around it.

I lost the sky in the smoke and debris of September 11. Perhaps it is time to look around inside and hear the uneasy drone of the passenger sitting next to me.

Enron in the eighth circle of hell 2002

Dante would have a spot for them all, all those high rollers at Enron, the slippery auditors from Anderson, the fawning

Washington pols, the Wall Street wizards, all of these would have a place in hell. Probably in the eighth circle of Hell, among the seducers and flatterers, the hypocrites and thieves, the fraudulent counselors, and, deepest of all, the traitorous.

This is the area Dante reserved for sins of the wolf. For unlike those who gave in to sins of ignorance or passion, lust or gluttony, those who ended in the eighth circle intended to pull the wool over others' eyes and then devour them. Of course, in Dante's hell the tables are turned, as those malicious souls are the ones eternally consumed.

But Dante is elsewhere. And we are in a hell of a mess.

The top executives of Enron bailed out as their corporate jet broke up, leaving workers and stockholders to crash and burn. For in America heaven and hell exist now, side by side. Golden parachutes and guaranteed retirements constitute our myopic paradise. And hell? All you need to do is visit the homes where the future has been ripped from the heart. Measure it in high blood pressure, sleepless nights, and overdue mortgages. Audit the real bottom line, where trust was deleted and the common good shredded.

Why bring up a dead poet when there are a dozen Congressional committees frothing over this? It is simply that Dante saw what we refuse to calculate. He understood that every number has a human face, that hope and fear accompany each business deal, and that heaven and hell are not far off but in every hand we offer to each other.

Pension plans are not a numbers game
2002

Thirty years ago my father staggered through our front door. His twenty-seven years of work for a middling milk company had been terminated by a terse notice on the loading dock. The company was bankrupt. The news got worse. The pension fund was gone. In just five years the new ownership, dissatisfied with peddling milk and cream, wanted to bring the business to a new level. They colluded with union officers to gamble the pension fund on new directions along with a fleet of state of the art trucks.

The enormity of it all hit home. A friend of my father, thirty-five years on the job, fell dead at my father's feet. The workers were told by their union leaders to keep quiet. They would get something. My father ended up with $4,000 in hush money.

You can understand, then, that I do not read about pension and retirement with an unwary eye. The Portman-Cardin Retirement Security and Pension Reform Act at first glance has much to recommend it. Certainly the major corporations, investment companies, and a vast number of well-heeled consulting firms think so.

But, just as history is usually written by the winners, tax and retirement laws are crafted by those who have the power to keep their money. While this legislation tries to allay middle class anxiety over retirement hopes, with provisions to increase 401(k)s and IRAs, grant portability of funds, and simplify provisions for small businesses, the fine print tells a familiar story.

The tax shelters of the wealthy will substantially increase as the benefits of the rank and file fall off. Ordinary workers can't even squirrel away savings. And half of American workers are not even covered by pension plans. Business owners now can shift workers still on more costly company pension plans to a new opportunity. Workers can fatten up their 401(k)s. But, since the bottom 60 percent of the work force can't put in much, the matching company contribution decreases. All the more compensation for executives and stockholders.

They say the devil is in the details. And they get more disturbing. The middle class will pay for these tax breaks. That's how it all trickles down.

❚ From the pages of Thucydides   2002

In what seems a lifetime away, one clear blue fall afternoon I sat reading on the library steps. Just a freshman, I looked up from the pages of Thucydides and understood why the Greek soldier and historian set down in writing the agony of war between Athens and Sparta. He wrote so that others might recognize the dramatic patterns of nations going to war. Thucydides demonstrated the tragic flaws in generals and in the empire of Athens itself. I looked up from the pages, saw the outline of Vietnam, and wept.

There is one section more than any other in *The Peloponnesian War* that continues to haunt me. While the war between Athens and Sparta continued to ebb and flow over a generation of lost lives, the empire of Athens became incensed over an island people, who tried to remain neutral for the duration. Thucydides describes how the Athenians sent a well-equipped force to convince the people of Melos to submit to Athens. Before the Athenians besieged the town, they met with representatives of the island. Thucydides constructed a dramatic dialogue that opened a window into the Athenian character.

From the outset the Athenians dispensed with the idea of justice. For them justice could only occur between two equal powers. The weak, such as the Melians, must learn to submit. The iron rule of the gods was Athen's creed: wherever you can rule, you will rule. The Melians should recognize their situation and take the expedient way out.

The Melians refused to submit. They hoped for relief from the Spartans, who never came to the aid of the besieged town. At the point of starvation, the people surrendered. The Athenian generals ordered the execution of all the males and sold the women and children into slavery.

You do not read Thucydides to predict a war's outcome. No, you read it to pick up more disturbing signs that show up in the speeches and gestures of a nation's gung-ho leaders. You note those telltale flaws reported in newspapers, on radio and television. You wonder how long that imperial arrogance will strut upon the stage. You look up from those ancient lines, gaze into a troubled autumn afternoon, and weep.

Begging the question   2004

Recently the Methodist Church in England ran a contest over what people would select as the eleventh commandment. The question was solicited nationwide on bar coasters in pubs. The cheeky winner, by the way, enjoined against turning celebrities into idols. If I had been there with a Guinness in my hand I know what my vote would have been: "Thou shalt not beg the question."

Most people today on both sides of the Atlantic must be forgiven for they know not what they do. Trying to sound intelligent, news anchors segue from a sensationalized report to a gratuitous editorial remark by saying, "This begs the question ..."

But they do not mean what they say. They presume that they are saying that this or that event "raises a new question," or "demands a further investigation." But that is not what "begging the question" means. "Begging the question" is a logical fallacy. Someone "begs the question" when that person asserts that something is proven when, if fact, it hasn't been. One can make all the claims one wants. But they do not constitute evidence.

You may immediately ask, "Why all the fuss? Shouldn't such logical niceties be reserved for the lecture hall?" "What does it matter if people forget about the nuances of argument?" "Whom will it hurt?"

Tell that to the thousands of Iraqis and nearly seven hundred Americans whose deaths rest on leaders' begging the question of the existence of weapons of mass destruction.

Imperial discomfort 2004

For some time I have wondered: why is America becoming more and more mean-spirited? Why are those, so sure, so certain, easily given to venomous declarations? Some would chalk this up to election year rants. But this nasty situation has been building for quite a while.

I suspect that it has to do, to a great extent, with Americans' discomfort with Empire. We know in our bones that an imperial America is a contradiction in terms. It runs against our deepest inclinations, our fundamental principles.

As a nation we were born with the conviction that no one would lord it over us. But now we stand as a worldwide colossus.

Past empires had no trouble with domination. Their social imagination prepared them to subject others. But we profess a fundamental equality of all.

So we have to justify our imperial moment. Our rhetoric heats up, dividing the world into good and evil, sane and mad. As long as we are on the side of the angels, we can feel good about ruling the world. We can relax with our supercilious leaders at the controls.

We needn't worry then over ghosts that threw a revolting tea party, nor try to imagine new ways of cooperating in a much-changed world, nor think that the billions of lives on this planet deserve more than our uncompromising gaze.

Liberté the librarian 2005

Have you seen the Librarian Action Figure? Dressed in an understated navy suit, she clutches a book in her left hand and raises her right with "amazing push-button shushing action." The 400,000 librarians around the country may take justified umbrage at this graying, conservative, three-inch plastic representation; but the recent rumbling in Congress over the Patriot Act brought this super heroine of the information highway to mind.

In a stunning vote this week the Congress, sending an overdue notice to the White House, finally has begun to discuss what should have been aired long before. A coalition of the willing voted to block the Patriot Act provision that would allow federal investigators to pry into the records of book lovers throughout the nation.

Their courage came from the example of librarians and bookstore owners throughout the country, who, from the outset, signaled the threat to our privacy and freedom. Who would have thought that the first line of our home defense would be behind stacks of books?

Librarians are used to working without fanfare, being overlooked. But that never stops them from being conscientious, from networking to get information into the hands of the people.

Take another look at that Action Figure, with a book cradled in her left arm, and a torch held aloft for all the world to see.

Between heaven and Charing Cross 2005

London went back to work. Despite the trauma and human loss from the senseless bombings, people made their way to work the next day.

Americans have a hard time understanding how this can be. Even at a distance we tend to become transfixed by disaster, endlessly rerunning gory film clips in our minds.

But London has been there before. Shock and debris go back generations.

Even in the worst of the Blitz something deeper was discovered. Behind the organ of All Hallows Church fragments fell out of a wall. They were parts of a noble Saxon cross, which once stood in defiance against the Norman invader.

There is something in the stereotype of a Londoner putting a kettle on in the face of chaos.

For the city has always been more than the sum of its parts. It carries forward visions and revisions, where the painter Turner found "angelic beings" in the squalor of the London docks.

Indeed, Londoners will muddle through their delays, circumventing the latest attack on this lasting experiment in universal living.

And as they finally get back to work, I should not be surprised that some might recall what the poet Francis Thompson saw:

> The traffic of Jacob's ladder
> Pitched between Heaven and Charing Cross.

▌The stuff of tragedy   2006

▌Not long after Arthur Miller's *Death of a Salesman* won the Pulitzer Prize in 1949 a debate ensued in our popular culture. *Life Magazine* weighed in, asking if the writing of tragedy was even possible in America. Surely "attention should be paid" to Willy Loman, as his weeping widow beseeched, but we know Willy and Willy is no Oedipus.

Would Americans be limited to the frequent patter and urban pathos of Neil Simon, or the depreciating narcissism of Woody Allen? Would we have to be content to reconstruct the Globe on western shores, replaying the Golden Oldies? Indeed, where would our writers find the stuff out of which tragedy is wrung?

Perhaps there is an historical clue to be found. The year 1599 was remarkable not only for Elizabethan England but also for William Shakespeare. Readers of Shakespeare often fail to consider the context in which he lived and wrote. But as the winter of 1598–99 wore on, it became perfectly clear to Elizabeth and her advisors that their attempt to keep the Spanish insurgents off English shores by fighting them or their allies in the Low Lands or in Ireland was proving disastrous. The treasury was almost empty. Word of military setbacks was constant from Ireland. Yet in this season of darkness the noble but foolish Essex took up the task to pacify the Irish and its wily Earl of Tyrone.

By the end of Lent in 1599 the banners of the playhouse announced the performance of *Henry V*. The buoyant scenario of a "band of brothers" matched the confident exodus of Essex to Ireland. But his unhesitant optimism met military and political reversal. His dreams of crushing the rebellion went up in the smoke of stalemate, uncertain treaties, and political intrigue.

As this disconsonant situation transpired in Ireland, Shakespeare began to draft *Julius Caesar*. Political complexity now trod the boards. No longer was it a matter of getting the guys together for a weekend bout on the continent. Now the struggle entailed the very heart of how a nation would be ruled. Patriots rebelled against a man who would be king. They feared rightly the demise of the Republic. But since this was Elizabethan England, and the Queen would see this play, those who rose up against Caesar would die.

Yet the play is not that simple. Caesar is dead before the action is resolved. In fact, Brutus emerges most nobly in his opposition and death. The audience is left contemplating the flawed and fearsome consequences of human action, where the best intentions are run through with a blade.

Before Vietnam many Americans were convinced that tragedy could never be an American product. But we have come to know that our leaders often wear blinders. And that thousands have fallen due to this.

The poet John Donne wrote from the royal court at the end of 1599. He writes hauntingly in his description of the clueless Essex:

He understood not his age ...
Such men want locks for themselves and keys for others ...

Sadly the stuff of tragedy is with us today.

▌The blasphemy of art   2007

Recently, far outside the gated community of theological discourse, a remarkable religious display went on international tour. Madonna, the pop diva and recent Kabbalah devotee, cut a triumphant swathe around the globe; and with it condemnations from every religious authority in her wake.

The Church of England worried aloud why such a talented person would need to offend so many people, while the Vatican spokesmen vented their spleen on such blasphemy. Even Danes and Russians agreed on someone to censure. Wherever Madonna went, from Los Angeles to London, from Rome to Düesseldorf, from Horsens to Moscow, religious leaders tried to pre-empt her arrival. But to no avail. Predictably, she played everywhere to sold-out venues.

What was the breach of religious decorum in her international *Confessions* tour? At one point in her show, Madonna re-emerged on a mammoth disco crucifix wearing a crown of thorns to perform the song "Live to Tell." Suspended on the giant cross encrusted with Swarovski crystals, she devoted her song to African victims of AIDS. It could have been more provocative but Madonna had no "wardrobe malfunction." A salmon blouse, with her blond hair down, black jeans and boots, cut a demure figure.

This was actually a tame image. Years ago Edwina Sandys sent her four-foot bronze statue of "Christa," a bare-breasted, wide-hipped woman, on a decades-long tour around the world. St. John's Cathedral in New York was only one among many locales that took a great amount of heat for displaying it.

Then there are the haunting words of Billie Holiday:

Black bodies swinging in the southern trees
Strange fruit hanging from poplar trees
Pastoral scene of the gallant south
The bulging eyes and the twisted mouth.
     — "Strange Fruit," Lewis Allen

Until she died in 1959 she continued to bring the reality of the crucified to the shadows of a segregated society.

Artists have understood — long before and better than theologians — that the crucified one has entered into the global domain. The memory of the death of Jesus has long since leaked out of the ecclesial ghettoes.

Artists have intuited that crucifixion was a primary metaphor — not to be written about since it was so degrading. It signified the dominating power of the Empire; an unspoken threat to those who would dare to rise up.

Throughout history artists have not settled for a factoid memory of the death of Jesus. The history of Western Art attests to the creative re-membering of the death of Jesus. This did not simply mean populating the death scene with friends and patrons. The varied tradition suggests that, just as the earlier Gospel writers, artists continued to inflect the death of Jesus in meaningful directions. We can see this already, for example, in a thirteenth-century corpus that sags under the weight of torture, or in Grünewald's stark figure that sums up much of his plagued and war-torn world.

More recently the *Ten Punching Bags* by Andy Warhol and Jean-Michel Basquiat carry on this tradition by delivering a telling exposé of the death-dealing effects surrounding the Jesus tradition.

Marc Chagall also was a self-conscious commentator on the crucifixion. He discounted neither his nor Jesus' Jewishness. Instead, the rising tide of anti-Semitism in Europe caused him to reframe that cultural memory. Chagall reclaimed the story of the death of Jesus, for it had originated out of Jewish concerns over the suffering of the innocent two centuries before the death of Jesus. With Chagall we see a re-membering in solidarity. Both in *White Crucifixion* and *Exodus* Chagall refuses to let the viewer forget the violence within the surreal situation.

Artists in their own ways continue to let us in on that dirty little secret of domination through controlled violence. And then they note the twist to the tale. The lost one, the zero, becomes a point of identification and solidarity. Something human is detected in the very midst of the forces of domination and dissolution. The voice considered silenced gains new strength and new legs.

Even the awkward appearance of Madonna plays upon this creative re-membering. But other artists and images prove to be more poignant. Remembering the dominating downbeat behind the death of Jesus can continue to expose the violence in a situation. It also can detect hints of humanity where none would be found. It can become a tool, an imaginative vehicle for reframing the human condition.

Consider what most of us have quickly consigned to oblivion: the cruciform, hooded figure standing helpless in the prison of Abu Ghraib. Why is this not an image of veneration? Tasteless? Unpleasant? Does it not bring us back to the breaking point of power?

So he goes ...   2007

For some time now theologians have played out their Christological speculations in two distinct theatres. The traditional venue of dogmatic theology never left the ancient house. Within the expected vertical sight lines, the meaning of Christ unfolded, brought down from the God-walk. More recently Christology from above has been countered by that from below. In this modern theatre-in-the round the "Man for Others" strides along horizontal, historical lines.

Oddly enough, the death of Kurt Vonnegut reminded me that Christological speculation is no longer confined to the usual settings. In his *Slaughterhouse-Five* Vonnegut interweaves within his retelling of the fire-bombing of Dresden glimpses of *The Gospel from Outer Space.* Such intercalations are part of Vonnegut's dark comedy. As he hides from the incendiary bombs, the narrator, Billy Pilgrim, recalls the science fiction of Kilgore Trout.

In Trout's *The Gospel from Outer Space* Jesus really was a "nobody," "a pain in the neck," who still said "lovely and puzzling things." The people amused themselves with lynching him because there would be no repercussions. Then it happened:

> And then, just before the nobody died, the heavens opened up, and there was thunder and lightning. The voice of God came crashing down. He told the people that he was adopting the bum as his son, giving him the full powers and privileges of the Son of the Creator of the Universe throughout all eternity. *God said this: From this moment on, He will punish horribly anybody who torments a bum who has no connections!*

Another Kilgore Trout book tells of a time-traveler who went back to the crucifixion of Jesus. As Jesus was taken down from the cross, he applied a stethoscope and listened:

> There wasn't a sound inside the emaciated chest cavity. The Son of God was as dead as a doornail.

Lance Corwin, the time traveler, also got to measure Jesus. He was five feet three and a half inches long.

What amazes me about these two fictional snippets is that they slip out in the midst of a devastating moment from World War II. Like Elie Wiesel, Vonnegut could never write a simple, factual account of the horror he lived through. Fiction provided the space for meaning to emerge. And in this free zone more fiction appears: a *Gospel from Outer Space* and a time-traveling account from the fictional Sci-fi writer Kilgore Trout. Indeed, the *Outer Space Gospel* stands in tension with the time-traveler's report. In the first, Jesus "the nobody" is vindicated by a God who can't take injustice anymore, while in the second Jesus is as "dead as a doornail." Fiction ricochets against fiction.

This tension actually continues in his last book *A Man Without A Country*. Vonnegut could not shake loose of Jesus. As he goes on a riff about Hoosier idealism, he recalls Powers Hapgood of Indianapolis. Upon graduating from Harvard, the middle-class Hapgood devoted his life to economic justice in this country. Brought into court over some picket line altercation, Hapgood was asked by the judge, "Why would anyone with your advantages choose to live as you have?" Hapgood answered, "Why, because of the Sermon on the Mount, sir." Vonnegut simply comments: "Hooray for our team."

The humanist Vonnegut later admits: "But if Christ hadn't delivered the Sermon on the Mount, with its message of mercy and pity, I wouldn't want to be a human being. I'd just as soon be a rattlesnake."

Vonnegut spent a lifetime looking into the absurdity of the twentieth century. The only way he could survive was through comic relief. As he described his work, he spun out each section of his books like a cartoon, ending each with a punch line. Then he went on. "So it goes."

Vonnegut can teach theologians many things. The arguments of High and Low Christologies look rather parochial when seen from the end of the universe. When we begin to catch the planetary drift of our lives, we find that not only has the God-walk tumbled into ruins, but the dinner theatre often plays to an empty house. Indeed, we have a responsibility to carry our past into the future. That is the human trek. But what do we bring with us?

Vonnegut would remind us that reality is too important and too complicated to be taken seriously. His work echoes the earlier artisanship of Jesus, whose wit and wisdom thrived on the unexpected in the midst of the mundane.

What would happen if theologians admitted their fictions, their fragile attempts at making sense of the debris and fragments in this ever-awesome universe? What can we wittily detect out of the corners of our eyes?

7

Political
Soundings

My commentaries span three presidential administrations. They move from Clinton to Bush to
Obama. I received significant positive response
when they were aired. I tried to present a position
beyond the simple reactions of the parties. Gaining
perspective was a difficult endeavor, but it was
aided by historical memory that expanded my horizon of comparison. Sadly much of what I wrote
still has bite today. To continue to push the enve-
lope of reflection I have concluded with an uncomfortable piece on "Jesus of Nazareth – Presidential
Timber."

Imagining the real   1997

Over a hundred and sixty years ago, the great commentator on America Alexis de Tocqueville worried about poetry in our young republic. He feared that poets, attempting to avoid the meanness of the common citizen, would lose themselves in the clouds, settling for bombastic creations instead of coming to grips with reality.

Such a fear reasserts itself at every presidential inauguration. Next Monday, with its blare of bands and media hype, will be no exception. For a presidential inauguration is an archetypal event, a rehearsal of the ancient enthronement scene, where the people's leader receives divine legitimacy. Whether it was Babylon under a stern Marduk, Rome under its implacable Mother, Paris under an imperial will, or Washington under a civil God, the assumption of power is always dramatically and necessarily expressed.

But there may be more than a raw play of power next Monday. And if so, it will be because of a striking confluence of dreams. We celebrate not only—what has become to politicians a rhetorical cliche—"a rebirth of freedom," but also the memory of Martin Luther King, Jr., a man who refused to let the dream of freedom die. His vision continues to march into the American psyche. He took the American dream out of the clouds and put it on the streets, into the lunch counters, and deep within our soul.

In fact, my hope that the American dream will continue to find a voice rests not in Bill Clinton's prose but in the poetry of Miller Williams, who has been chosen to say a few words. Miller is a poet who takes on the banalities and terrors of a world that is coming apart and transfigures it. He does not avoid but imagines reality. After listening to him, you can see the ordinary as strange and open to surprising depths.

Perhaps next Monday he will speak in that honest Arkansas accent a few words that will keep our dream alive and walking steadily into the next century.

The mother of battles   1998

Before we go to war again, let me tell a very old story. Hints of this tale have slipped out in remarks by Saddam Hussein as he alluded long ago to "the mother of battles."

The phrase comes from the ancient Babylonian creation story, the Enuma Elish. Originally two primordial beings Apsu and Tiamat, male and female, engender the divine elements. But these gods rebel against their begetters and succeed in killing Apsu.

Tiamat, however, escapes the revolt, creates a slew of monsters, marries the chief one, Kingu, and initiates a war of revenge upon her offspring. Tiamat spawns "enormous serpents, chockfull of venom...." Cowed by her power, the gods quake in their divine boots until a younger god, Marduk, declares himself their champion and takes on "the Mother of all." Mounting the storm, his terrible chariot, Marduk confronts her: "Why did you have to mother war?"

Quickly capturing Tiamat in a net of the four winds, he shoots an arrow in her belly, cuts her womb, smashes her skull. Her blood streams to ends of the universe. The world is fashioned from her carcass and from her consort's bloody body human beings are formed.

This story was sung on New Year's Day in Babylon to honor Marduk's victory. Civilized order is preserved by violence. Whoever conquers has the favor of the gods. Life is combat. Since our very origin is violent, killing is in our blood. Unrelenting control is the condition of human existence, the price for order.

One might conclude that this is Saddam Hussein's script. But it is not his alone. The "new world order" was proclaimed by an American president, after the fertile crescent was ripped apart by a "Desert Storm." And now we may once more unwittingly prove that we are caught in the same violent net.

Saving face 1999

How long will the United States wander in the desert? Will it take a generation before we rethink our dealing with Iraq?

It took us forty years before we allowed a baseball team to play in Cuba, before we could imagine a long-suffering people distinct from a demonized dictator. Fidel is no longer a major threat to us. The visit of an aging pope exposed the cracks in that island bunker.

But, after a war, eight years of sanctions, and a recent bombardment, Saddam is still glowering from Baghdad's billboards.

America has been relentless in pursuing its righteous cause. But at what price? We have conveniently forgotten who originally armed Saddam to the teeth. We claim that the sanctions in place will punish Saddam by destabilizing his following.

Instead, the Iraqi middle class is being wiped out, while an elite beholden to Saddam has grown up. In the last two years alone over 200,000 Iraqis have died. Malnutrition harms everyone but Saddam. The crippled school system has over a 30 percent drop-out rate. Books and even pencils are kept out of the country. If the situation continues an entire generation of surviving Iraqis will have grown up knowing nothing but the devastation of sanctions.

Is there another way? George Marshall knew of one. Bombard the people with goods. Increase UN monitoring to insure the transport. Show a power stronger than vengeance. Remind them of the Merciful One they know from the Koran. Hit Saddam where it really hurts. If he cannot provide for his people, he will lose what it's all about: saving face.

Election nightmare 2000

Things are getting pretty scary as we near Election Day. It's somehow fitting that it comes exactly a week after Halloween. Two political hobgoblins have been trick-or-treating the American people for some months now.

These beggars are not satisfied with one visit. They go home and change costumes to come back again and again. They've even haunted our televisions. Their sighs and sneers have coalesced into a paralyzing form of speech that can only be called "Boregush." Yet, despite their flame retardant personalities, you can still get a glimpse of the façade behind the mask.

We've seen these kids before. In black and white: Gore as Wally, Beaver Cleaver's older brother, always anxious of his peers; Bush as Eddie Haskell, snidely conning his way around family values; and the voters, sadly, as the Beaver, helplessly looking on.

Bush and Gore. A professor's nightmare. Gore is the student who tries too hard, who gives you everything covered in the course except the precise answer to the question. Bush is the frat boy who hasn't studied a lick for his final. Right in the middle of the exam it dawns on him that he is getting away with murder.

But there is another empty pumpkin on the stoop. While Gore strides mechanically and Bush looks in vain for a math crib sheet, are we any better suited than the tin man and the scarecrow? As Americans, we are impatient with displays of intelligence. But why do we discourage genuine cross-examination, serious and sustained argument? Could it be that we fear that there is nothing inside, as our flickering thoughts go out?

The chill along the spine 2000

Where is Alexander Haig when you need him? Pundits have been falling off their horses ever since the TV networks twice reversed themselves over the electoral status of Florida. A delicious irony seems to be unfolding. The candidate whose strongest suit was popularity, running against the Washington establishment, might eventually eke out a victory through an established technicality, despite the techno candidate's winning the popular vote.

Not since Benjamin Harrison snatched electoral victory from the jaws of popular defeat has this happened. Republican Harrison lost the popular contest by little over ninety-eight thousand ballots but substantially defeated the Democrat Grover Cleveland in electoral votes. Democrats suffered this twice before in 1876 and in 1824.

Before we get lost in lawsuits, let's stop this political blather. Instead of focusing on the numbers game, let's go against our insistent inclinations. Our society wants things right now. We avoid genuine risk like the plague. The so-called rational market shudders at the mere whiff of uncertainty. Both candidates desperately attempted to give us precisely that: an effortless choice. Yet what stands before us and those stuttering commentators is quite the opposite.

For a few moments sense the haunting feeling that things are not in our control. None of this was part of anyone's game plan. Don't trot out the cliché that the system is working to avoid this.

Instead allow yourself the chill along the spine that comes on realizing that we are in way over our heads. It may be that for many of us Americans such unexpected resistance to our scheduled success is the closest we shall come to detecting the dark hands of Reality.

Beyond the banality   2001

For less than a majority of Americans Saturday's inauguration of George W. Bush signals a restoration of decency and business sense. "America Inc." will mark its return with modest gray. The shenanigans of the Clinton era will be—barring further legal hiccups—just an embarrassing hangover. The White House will run with the cool efficiency of a Harvard MBA test case, as Alan Greenspan leads the country towards the ever-receding horizon of a soft economic landing.

Now there are some who will miss a president speaking in complex sentences without having to strap himself to a script. They will wince at the inevitable verbal monkeyshines of Dubious George. Yet they cannot forget that the Bubba of effortless prose had a hard time keeping his copulatives buttoned up. Nor can they deny that President Dubyah brings a boyish honesty to Washington. Truly a man without pretensions, he has never disguised his awkward ambition. Indeed, he styled himself after his masterful predecessor, campaigning as Clinton-lite.

We owe George W. a round of thanks for reminding us how truly mediocre our leaders can be. If this was not already exposed in the Florida Triangle, the matter-of-fact inaugural will bring us face to face with the banality of power.

As de Tocqueville reminds us, Americans exercise their sense of equality by cutting pretenders down to size. We love our presidents served up on the platter of daily opinion. There is, in fact, a fundamental wisdom to this democratic feeding frenzy. Every now and then we realize that America is not a beltway entertainment industry but a hazardous human experiment. More than adolescent ambition is at stake; for our true business is freedom, patiently divined in our common good.

A corruptor of youth?   2001

President Bush wants us to become a nation of readers. He is determined not to leave one child behind. I wonder if the President knows where this will lead. For if he supports education that values critical thinking, then we are hardly at the level of playing the simplistic numbers game of required testing.

Critical readers ask questions. They will inquire not only about the dubious grounds upon which our educational assessments are made but also into the very stories we tell ourselves to keep our fragile empire together.

What will happen when young minds begin to see a pattern in the way we would go to war or in preventing a rogue missile attack? Will they recognize the variations upon a familiar cowboy theme? A threatened frontier town is saved by a stranger, who violently restores order and then rides off righteously into the sunset. Eden—whether in Kuwait or in America—is preserved at the high cost of technically improved, surgical violence.

Will they begin to put two and two together when they read the financial news? They'll do the math that adults are reluctant to admit. They'll weigh short-term stock profits against thousands of layoffs and speculate on how inhuman our calculations have become. They'll detect the desperate fear that keeps us at our jobs.

Critical reading learns from silences, from what has not been delivered. A critical reader will do more than simply read a President's lips. Indeed, if students catch on to it, President Bush will end up like Socrates, condemned for corrupting the youth of the nation!

▌A jailhouse rock   2003

▌ As thousands of American troops move into position to encircle Iraq, as North Korea plays out the coldhearted role typecast some months ago by our president, as thirty-five thousand more are laid off by K-Mart, as Palestinian and Israeli leaders sway back and forth in their suicidal dance of death, as Republicans ready legislation that will keep the plutocrats prosperous and make sure that every child in America will be left behind to shoulder the mushrooming debt, as millions contemplate longer life and suffering without medical support, as the numbers of AIDS victims from Africa mount without end and without any sustained relief, as reports of violence and terror punctuate our waking hours, let us stop on Monday to remember a man who created a life out of the tensions of his time.

It will do us no good to treat Dr. Martin Luther King, Jr. as some cultural icon. We do not have the luxury of collecting his bobblehead doll. Nor do we have the time to waste by packaging his memory in order to keep it out of Trent Lott's sight.

Some people remember by putting things into a museum. Others enter the past to get a taste of the future. If you can in the next week, read something of King. If you have the courage, go beyond the stirring, but too familiar, cadences of his "I Have a Dream" speech. Read those words written in down time, written behind bars: his Letter from a Birmingham Jail.

There he sat writing a longhand response to eight Southern white religious leaders who considered his nonviolent activities untimely and unhelpful. And so, with time on his hands, he wrote a reasoned and compelling reply.

But reading this Letter will not be enough to see where King was going. You won't get it, until you see that King wrote the Letter from a jail cell because of his conviction that "We are caught in an inescapable network of mutuality, tied in a single garment of destiny. Whatever affects one directly affects all indirectly." He could not let his people go.

For many of us 9/11 seemed to bring home that sense.

But King did more than allow us a comfortable review from our La-Z-Boys. He took a nonviolent stand against the violence of the American system. It was quite fitting that he cited the story of the three youths thrown into a fiery furnace by King Nebuchadnezzar for their civil disobedience.

King's words are still back there in the heat of a Birmingham jail, trusting that others will join him "in the kitchen."

Despite the forces of violence that geometrically increase each day, his words declare love of enemies a matter of planetary sanity and survival. In the suffocating oven of our lives he would lead us with a jailhouse rock, singing, "We are not alone."

No doubt 2004

Almost four hundred years ago the English poet John Donne decried the new wave of thought that was building throughout Europe. "The new philosophy calls all in doubt, the element of fire is quite put out."

Donne could not build a firewall of words against that trend; actually he contributed to it by his own self-critical poetry and sermons.

I was reminded of that nugget from the past by the recent comments of the president. Despite the surge of reports from think tanks and weapons inspectors that the "weapons of mass destruction" probably did not even exist when we preemptively attacked Iraq, the president still assures us that "There is no doubt in his mind."

Such confidence at first sounds comforting. Isn't a good thing that the Commander-in-Chief has such certainty?

But wasn't Kennedy also confident before the Bay of Pigs?

The hard lessons learned on the blood-soaked Cuban beaches sobered Kennedy considerably. He later maneuvered through the Cuban Missile Crisis because he brought a tempered skepticism to information and the urgings of his military advisors.

What worked for him was his ability to doubt, especially his own rash rush to judgment. He even dared to think that his enemy was more complicated than the stereotypes of evil our nation had constructed. Indeed, Reagan also was big enough to see more in Gorbachev than what his speechwriters scripted.

But last year things were different. Who would be so unpatriotic as to doubt our intelligence?

Leave no Beaver behind 2004

Have you ever felt that you've seen this all before? That you have been caught in some time warp, some endless black and white re-run?

The recent events in Iraq don't bring me back to the protest-laden days of Vietnam.

No, the images that shoot through my brain come from *Leave It to Beaver*.

"Let us return to the days of yesteryear." Is this some neocon mind control, causing me to seek the "good old days," where streets were tidy and mothers stayed at home wearing pearls?

Then I realized that *Leave It to Beaver* may be a way of penetrating the controlled artifice of Bush.

As I listened to the president's recent campaign remarks, the smirking figure of Eddie Haskell seemed to nod behind the podium. If you remember, Eddie was that cynical gambler, who had a knack of getting away with it. He was willfully ignorant, socially shortsighted and subversive, using any relationship as an opportunity to keep the con going. The Beaver was the only one who always saw through Eddie but had to stand by helplessly as Eddie pulled the wool over June's and Ward's eyes. The adults who should have known better never did.

Here in 2004 the world is still in black and white for many Americans. We prefer to keep our lawns manicured and not dwell upon the body bags proliferating in the garage. And if it comes to a draft to keep this world intact, we shall leave no Beaver behind.

The other side of empire   2004

Despite protestations of Defense Secretary Rumsfeld that the atrocities committed against Iraqi prisoners were "not the way America does business," the photos catapulted over the Internet, cable TV and print media have unleashed hell in Washington and around the world.

The president, sounding very much like Claude Rains in Casablanca was shocked and disgusted. Senators predictably are holding hearings on this ugly display. Inevitably military heads will roll.

What staggers me is the feigned innocence of our leadership. If they wish America to dominate in the world, what do they think an empire looks like?

All you have to do is visit a museum or two. Look at the Akkadian king, forty-three centuries ago, who ascends a mountain in victory while crushing his enemies under his feet. Or that Assyrian bas-relief from the seventh century before Christ where prisoners-of-war and captured civilians are roasted and flayed alive. Then there is the artful Gemma Augustea, an onyx carving in bluish white, where Caesar Augustus, now a heavenly god, sits enthroned over a scene below where naked captives—men and women—are about to be impaled on poles as Roman trophies.

Of course, this Administration is not overly concerned about museums. But they do read the Bible and evidently endorse a God who delights in blood and body bags as he puts all in subjection under the feet of the lion of Judah.

American makeover   2004

The countdown has begun. For the next five weeks we shall hold our breath to see the results of the American Makeover. What should have been a simple technical affair—lipo-suctioning evil from Iraq's body politic—has turned into major surgery.

Even Doctors Nip and Tuck, Rumsfeld and Wolfowitz, have begun to hedge on their well-rehearsed protocols. They will no longer underwrite the Botox regimen recommended by specialist Chalabi, whom they once considered a quick fixer but now a quack.

Other cosmetic consultants have begun to repent of their naïve neocon prescriptions. They realize it is not possible to save face unless they put an entirely different expression on this monumental malpractice.

Meanwhile Mr. Bush has reiterated his will to stay the course of treatment. Assuming the plenipotentiary powers of Plastic Surgeon General, he refuses to allow any mirrors in the oval office. What could reflection bring to the operation? Would it not only show what we cannot possibly be?

So why worry?

Folks, this is not Reality TV. Of course, it would have been so nice to turn the ugly duckling into a swan—Miss Iraq, liberated from her burqa and modeling a swimsuit, cut from the same mold as Miss America.

But, despite new surgical procedures, the stitches are coming apart and infection is spreading. No matter that the bandaged patient staggers like a zombie.

This is not reality coming into our living rooms but Mad TV, where the imperial eagle rapidly metastasizes into a ravenous buzzard.

▌ Like good ol' boys   2004

Over two thousand years ago Octavian, the new ruler of Rome and avenger of Caesar's murder, faced a dilemma. If he claimed to be king, he would end up like his departed uncle. So, he portrayed himself as the first citizen of Rome, modestly clad and circumspect in behavior. Under that cover, he turned a republic into an Empire.

This historical nugget helps me understand recent Republican rallies. They seem very much like company picnics, where only faithful employees get in, as the corporate stars make their appearance, mingling like good ol' boys. Somehow an ice cream cone with the folks keeps minds off astronomical salary disparities and inevitable pink slips. Aren't those silk suits just like us?

At other times the rallies take on the aspect of an annual shareholders meeting, where the executive board calmly report in button down voices. Since everything has been fixed in the back room, they can face any objection with bemused disdain.

And what about those true believers who identify with their Chief Executive? By sporting the brand W, they wear their symbol of ownership around their necks. Madison Avenue brings back what the propertied classes of Rome so long ago knew how to apply on the bodies of slaves. Of course, Texans also know where a brand belongs—on cattle.

Presidential epithets 2004

One thing you can learn from the British is that in the long run people somehow muddle through the follies of their leaders. In fact, when you run through the list of what is actually the longest effective monarchy in the world, the American presidency, you discover how unremarkable most of our leaders have been.

Just deck out our presidents with what would be royal epithets and you may discover some perspective in this unbalanced election year.

Let's hail the chiefs:

Virtuous George the Unsmiling, Difficult John, Red Haired Thomas, Little Jemmy, Mediocre James, John Quincy the Congressman, Old Hickory, Martin the Little Magician, William of Tippecanoe, Long Face John, James the Pious, Rough and Ready Zachary, Millard the Stout, Franklin the Handsome, Bachelor James, Honest Abe, Andrew the Grim, Ulysses the General, Rutherford the Unblemished, Left-Handed James, Chester the Bottom-Feeder, Grover the Beast of Buffalo, Iceberg Benjamin, Grover the Beast Returned, William the Nice, Rough Rider Teddy, William the Large, Woodrow the Pure, Warren the Unfit, Silent Cal, Herbert the Inept, Franklin the Fearless, Give 'em Hell Harry, Dwight the Bald, John the Undone, Tragic Lyndon, Richard the Unshaven, Pardoner Gerald, Jimmy the Timid, Ronald the Actor, George the Follower, Shameless Bill, Incurious George.

A consuming mandate   2004

It is quite clear to the religious right that Mr. Bush has been given a mandate from heaven. And why not? Isn't he a man of faith, who walks humbly in the shadow of the presidential jet? Does he not demonstrate his compassionate side to the TV cameras, even recently to the White House press corps?

You know where Mr. Bush stands. His campaign litany never wavered. He reiterated the fears deep within the American soul. The conservative elect knew that he had tapped into their hearts, where sex, security, and salvation hung on dangling chads.

But now the gloves are off for the true believers. It is time to capitalize on this moral majority. There is no need for litmus tests for Supreme Court judges. Just read the Constitution as you read the Bible. Isn't all so simple?

Now is the time for the nation to know the fear of the lord. It is time to remember that we are perpetually at war; time to keep stoking the images of our demonic enemies; time to wrap ourselves with the fetish of the flag; time to straighten out our family values; time to keep the wolves of the world away from our homes.

Time, at last, to detect what keeps stirring the angry abyss of the neocon soul—the invisible hand of a consuming god.

Distinctly reptilian   2004

The Rorschach pattern of Election Day is finally beginning to make some sense.

I see neither a trumpeting elephant nor a dejected donkey. Instead, the emerging pattern is distinctly reptilian.

Clotaire Rapaille, a onetime child psychiatrist turned Fortune 500 marketing consultant, helps us crack the code.

Why did many people in Ohio, long out of work, vote for morality over their own economic hope? How could they support candidates who consistently return their devotion by delivering a country that is poorer, dirtier, meaner, and more polarized? Why do so many vote directly counter to their own best interests?

Rapaille would point out that it is not a matter of logic. No, the staccato stump speech of Bush and Cheney spoke to a deeper level.

They spoke not to the reasoning sectors of our brains, but to the reptilian core—to that primordial part of us that worries over our survival. In brief, they elicited our deepest fears. Sex and security trumped any reasonable appraisal of life in America.

No need to worry over math, or problems multiplying on this planet. Simply close your eyes, click your heels and you'll feel safe at home. Just take no notice of that growing, ragged shadow, as ancient as oil, lumbering like Godzilla through the wreckage of our lives.

City of the dead   2005

It has often been observed that Washington DC is a city of the dead. Monuments and museums tend to give that lingering effect. Especially, as you look down on the city from John Kennedy's grave, you begin to see how the avenues of Washington become as silent as the nearby rows in Arlington National Cemetery.

Such morbid thoughts seem out of place during Inauguration week. But I've been someplace else for some time. I've been in Petra, the lost city of stone. No, I've not had the chance to get to the Middle East. Petra has come to Cincinnati. The Art Museum pulled off a cultural coup by bringing a civilization of sandstone and silence to the banks of the Ohio.

What dramatically remains are the graves, literally carved from the multicolored shoulders of that desert land. There was once so much more. Indeed, Petra once was very green. They had solved the water problem. But now there are so few words. The fractured limestone figures hint of a life balanced at the crossroads of trade and cultures. Columns were variously topped off with Indian elephants and Roman eagles.

So my mind has been going in and out of centuries. As the fife and drums make their way down Pennsylvania Avenue, why do they echo down the colonnaded street of a long-dead city?

Gulag, American style   2005

The Administration's response to the recent Amnesty International report was predictably swift and condescending. Mr. Bush dismissed it as "absurd," while Mr. Cheney was personally "offended." Mr. Rumsfeld doubted that any objectivity could come from ex-inmates. Indeed, their entire response fixated on the word "Gulag."

How dare anyone compare the endeavors of freedom's beacon with the despised prison system of the Soviets?

For some years I read with students Alexander Solzhenitsyn's *Gulag Archipelago*. Solzhenitsyn experimented in "a literary investigation." He went beyond a simple indictment of what he called the Soviet "sewage disposal system." He wrote not only to remember the victims and the terror but also to interrogate his readers.

He stops short of simply throwing the villains into the pit. Instead, he reminds us that "the line dividing good and evil cuts through the heart of every human being." We hover throughout our lives close at times to being demons, at other times to saints. But sadly we live mostly like scared rabbits, only making a sound at our execution.

He leaves, not only for our leaders, a disturbing proverb:

"Don't dig up the past! Dwell on it, you'll lose an eye!
Forget the past, you'll lose both eyes!"

A spark of Socrates 2005

The battle lines behind the confirmation hearings of John Roberts have been formed for nearly two and a half millennia. Teams of word wizards and image mongers from both sides of the aisle are ready to ply their trade as assiduously as their ancient predecessors.

In ancient Athens the Sophists represented a new trend in the experiment of democracy. They claimed they could teach men how to use words in winning over others. What counted was the result: a man could defend himself in law court or win the assembly to his opinion. Words well used would bring success.

There was only one flaw in all of this. One man found it out. He did this by simply asking those rhetoricians what they meant in their flurry of words. He would not let them go with a glib rejoinder. Instead, he doggedly cross-examined them, until they realized that they really did not know what they were saying.

I wonder if there is a spark of Socrates left in Washington. Is there someone courageous enough to ask an honest question and to keep pursuing it until the truth is reached?

But if it is business as usual, then we shall never find out if there is any more to John Roberts than acolyte good looks and a buttoned-down portfolio.

Shadowboxing 2006

Were you taken in by the recent tag-team kabuki play, where Alito played dumb and the senators dumber? Or, did you keep up your I-pod firewall, maintaining some distance from that beltway bizarro world?

Despite attempts by FOX and CNN to dignify their autopsies, the residue left resembled the shabby burlesque halls of the fifties, when all the talent had fled to TV, leaving tired strippers on their own.

The initial launching of hot air balloons by senators on each side of the aisle probably eliminated the later use of a filibuster. Even for those windbags there is only so much hot air to go around.

As for Alito, he succeeded in saying nothing. After so many grilling hours you would think this a remarkable feat until you realized that this is the standard modus operandi of Washington.

Perhaps you were amused by this latest version of high stakes Texas hold 'em, where bluff, calculation, and not giving yourself away are all part of the show.

But there is a tragic aspect to the judicial committee's episode of Survivor.

The law and the Constitution are not a card game. Nor were our founding leaders godfathers. They did not envision their descendants hobbled by cement shoes.

Instead they inspired a conversation. And, if the Constitution is still to make sense, we have to keep the discussion going.

But to do that means that we cannot simply ask someone to endorse our convictions. That is the game the senators played. Nor can we refrain from speaking our mind because it might prejudice a later judicial decision.

Both sides never engaged in real thought, in genuine discussion, where truth is detected in the give and take. Why? Apparently because neither the senators nor Alito want to risk changing their minds.

Everyone has a position. That is no surprise. But what makes for human growth is when a person actually can admit arguments and evidence into consideration. An open mind is not an empty head. Nor is a conviction the end of the discussion; it is a contributing side to the conversation.

However, the reluctance to show your cards may indicate a deeper intent. It may mask an elitist worldview that does not see the need for change, only the application of an over-arching vision that the masses need never know.

The shadowboxing in that senate room may signify that we have crossed a Rubicon, leaving far behind the democratic mime, as we sit numbly, locked down in Plato's cave.

▌Rosetta Stone 2006

▌Perhaps you missed it. With the Super Bowl dripping over in advertisements and now the Winter Olympics' hallucinogenic effect on us, there was little chance to notice that the Pharaohs defeated the Elephants 4-2, in penalty shots, beyond overtime play.

Yes, Egypt defeated the Ivory Coast for the All Africa Soccer Title.

The President of Egypt along with his Prime Minister and select officials cheered on the Pharaohs.

It was a welcome relief for everyone. Especially after the recent boat disaster claiming over a thousand lives.

Relatives rioted, burning the offices of the boat company, whose officials had told the captain of that burning vessel to sail on, despite the cries of passengers. Now the ship company's owner had been recently appointed by the Egyptian president to a post in parliament. The president himself turned the tragedy into a public relations coup by visiting with the grieving families. Meanwhile, Egyptian papers fanned the flames of the Danish blasphemy. But the Soccer Championship restored balance to the ship of state.

Once again people simmered in agony while an incompetent government, controlling all branches, stumbled on with impunity. Not matter how bumbling, how feckless, those responsible remained unaffected.

Meanwhile, the media helped displace the anger. External enemies were provided to let the people blow off steam. Another national spin cycle. When those in charge are no longer held accountable, it leads people to think things are inevitable, that there's some sort of intelligent design—only beyond our ken.

To make some sense of this I turned to Aslan—not the movie lion—but the Egyptian writer Ibrahim Aslan. He wisely points out that all of this careless governance "creates a bewildered citizen who is addicted to sorrow and suffering." He adds, "It has reached to the point where Egyptians do not feel entitled to anything. And all they want is justice. Across history, in literature, Egyptians peasants asked for justice, not freedom or democracy, just justice, social justice."

Perhaps it is just a mirage, caused by spending too much time wandering about in heated Egyptian affairs, but this story sounds so familiar, so close to home. It seems to take on a familiar shape, as suggestive as a cipher, perhaps our own Rosetta Stone.

Sage advice 2006

Before we go to war again, before our martial arteries harden beyond repair, before we let leaders draw another line in the sand, let's take a time out.

Let's go back to that moment just before things went wrong, when a president was reading the children's book *My Pet Goat*.

If I had a moment with the president I would recommend another children's book for his pre-bellum reading. It is a comic book memoir of an Iranian girl, detailing her life from her sixth to fourteenth years, as she lives from the days surrounding the fall of the Shah, the Iranian revolution and the Iran-Iraqi War.

Persepolis: the Story of a Childhood, crafted in black and white illustrations by Marjane Satrapi, delivers with its simple narrative a picture of Iran far more complex than anything the media has been offering.

This story, told through the eyes and words of a child, says something that we do not want to recognize—that there are human beings, long-suffering and limited, frightened, wanting to live decent lives, with a marked sense of honor, not seen on cable, but on the ground in Iran.

Through the eyes of a child we see the relentless series of horrors that besieged her family. We learn along with her how her grandfather was imprisoned and eventually destroyed by the Shah, and how her uncles were tortured by the Shah and then executed by the revolutionaries.

The illustrations are stark. A movie theatre bombed by the Shah's men takes on the fluidity of a Chagall painting, as four hundred lives flame out in agony from the burning building. Then there are the thousands of boys, each given a painted plastic key to Paradise, fodder in the Iraqi War. Satrapi shows them advancing, unprotected in a suicide attack. A white blast turns them into shadowy bits blown violently apart.

And the words. A mother about to lose her son to such madness says: "All my life I've been faithful to religion; if it's come to this, I can't believe in anything anymore."

Marjane's sane and resilient parents finally decide to send their daughter out of the country. They worry not only for her life but for her chance at an education. The night before she leaves Teheran, her grandmother comes to visit. As her grandmother holds her for the last time, Marjane catches the scent of jasmine from her grandmother's breasts and the words from a woman whose husband died years earlier from political intrigue:

> You'll meet a lot of jerks. If they hurt you, tell yourself, it is because they're stupid. That will keep you from reacting to their cruelty, because there is nothing worse than bitterness and vengeance. Always keep your dignity and be true to yourself.

I wonder: could an American president take such sage advice from a children's book, from a grandmother, from an enemy?

Border crossing   2006

The setting: A time of War.
The place: our country.

For decades this nation had been flooded with foreigners, almost none speaking English, yet they remained invisible, necessary cogs in the American economy, until the pressures of war forced patriotic Americans to view with alarm the uncertainties within. The debate over the wisdom of America's going to war was now shifted to what was perceived as a threat to the security of the homeland. People began to realize that, around the country, in cities and in towns, there were places where English was not heard on the street.

A number of Americans, not serving in the armed forces, formed nationwide movements to do something to stem this perilous tide. They began to police the borders of their communities. The fear of crime and the additional costs to the state by these foreigners brought calls for legislative reform. Indeed, many of these immigrants became political agitators, calling for boycotts and strikes, demonstrating in public for rights. The agenda for the upcoming election registered the concern over immigration issues. Finally Congress ended its debate and passed measures that would severely cut into the invasion of these foreigners.

A parable for our time? Not quite. It is a resume of America in the early 1920s. The non-English speaking immigrants were the faceless multitudes of Italians and Eastern Europeans who provided the backbreaking labor that fueled our industrial progress. It was a time when we wanted to throw off the entangling alliances with the rest of the world. Just wanted to keep to our selves, preserve our American way.

But the Depression and World War II burst that illusory bubble. Certainly 9/11 has knocked away any residual doubts that we are part of this complicated world.

Still, when it comes to borders, there is that primordial instinct. We all draw lines of identity and safety. Thus far and no more! Border crossings beget deep and unseen fears. Who moves there in the shadow lands? Stop or I'll ... What will I do? What will we do?

Shall we give into our fears and let politicians and political handlers have their way again with us? Shall we turn those desperately poor into national nightmares? Since Osama continues to elude the American eagle, why not turn to more tractable prey? Indeed, it is much easier to magnify our national exuberance, enfolding all these immigrants in the wavering flag of our fear. Let's turn the continental United States into a gated community! Why should the Chinese have the only Great Wall?

Or should we be more than repeaters of history? It is time to stop all the games with people's lives. Time for Mexico to do more for their people than simply sending the expendables north through the desert with a cynical *con Dios*. Time to get beyond the shouts of American business concerned to keep the profit margin climbing. Time for us to acknowledge those invisible millions who shore up the base of our economic boom.

What do you say to a woman, tired beyond her years, who, with her five children, survived four days and nights in the

Sonoran Desert with not even a hat in order to reach her husband, as she turns down your bed covers in your hotel room?

Dream time   2006

The campaign walkabout is almost over. Shenanigans from the right and innuendoes from the left are plummeting like leaves upon the wind. Lawn signs and billboards suddenly will lose their raucous intensity. And photographs of well-coifed candidates already mingle in the gutters with the debris of Halloween.

It is fitting that our elections come so close to the Day of the Dead. At that time when the earth turns towards the darkest part of the year, the thought of mortality sobers you up.

For on Election Day there is no more carnival. There are no more funhouse mirrors, where distortion dictates the unending order of the day. Spin and hype give way to the pedestrian: checking off names, waiting in line, and entering alone for a few moments into a closed space.

And we in Ohio are once again in the heart of it all. Even Jon Stewart agrees. Our voting site snafus in the last presidential election kept the country careening towards becoming a banana republic. The recent voting registration maneuvers have only underscored the continuing farce. Meanwhile the dominating political party of the state tiptoes around our convicted governor, and wishes they never heard of coin collections and golf junkets to St. Andrews.

As we enter the computerized voting booths, not a few of us wonder if our votes will even be counted. Around here Diebold has become a punch line to an uneasy joke.

All this sounds rather grim. But, in a state where much of our jobs and brains have been leaking out, it is grim. As our population falls we are greeted with rising statistics in crime and poverty. Our state legislature spends more time trying to provide us with holsters than health care.

Yes, we are in the heart of it all. Daily we take back the remains of our sons and daughters, as the specious hope for democracy blows to bits in Iraq. We board planes from one of the most expensive hubs in the country, not feeling any more secure than we did on September 12. And if our imagination follows the Ohio all the way to the Gulf we cannot avoid the catastrophic message of Katrina.

We bring all this and so much more into the voting booth. We know that Lincoln was right. Politicians can fool us some of the time. But we continue to vote because they cannot fool all of us all of the time.

When we enter the booth, we make an American Passover. Jews remind us, from their Passover Haggadah, that every generation needs to enact their founding pilgrimage. This is a journey where we keep faith with those who have walked before us, with those who have fallen so that their children's children may continue to make this journey.

Next Tuesday we Americans will enter our dreamtime. Dreamtime is an aboriginal word meaning the time of beginning, when things were joined together. Each of us enters alone into the company of our country. As slogans stop whirling around our heads, dreams of what we hope our life together can be crowd in.

For a few moments, we shall demonstrate that democracy comes not in power plays but in the fragile act of human choice.

▌ A daredevil performance   2007

▌ If I did not know better, I would have thought Evel Knievel was still launching himself across buses. Despite the gravitas of the setting in the Bush Presidential Library, Mitt Romney's speech on religion had all the trappings of a daredevil event. So much was riding on his performance.

There he was, revving his rhetoric, poised to soar between the ghosts of John Kennedy and Brigham Young. With his lead in the Iowa polls lost in the dust of Mike Huckabee's pickup, he had no choice but to make this leap of faith.

Indeed, like the aphoristic camel Romney was straining to slip through the needle's eye. This was his challenge: while playing off the Kennedy appeal to the separation of Church and State, he had to prove to the Evangelical Right that he could be trusted. Despite the fact that many of those conservative ministers had long considered Mormonism a cult, he had to convince them that he, like they, put his sandals on, one foot at a time. He would show them that he was not afraid of answering the media's altar call. By confessing that Jesus was divinely dominant, the one great hope of mankind, Romney gave the dramatic impression that he could be one of the good ol' boys.

But, to paraphrase the Greek philosopher Thales, you can't jump over the same river canyon twice.

Even those who were not around to hear Jack Kennedy's speech in Houston can listen to it on YouTube. And, when you compare both speeches and their particular contexts, it is not hard to conclude that Mitt is not Jack Kennedy.

In fact, Mitt is much more like the Roman Emperor Augustus.

Augustus had an enormous problem. The Roman Republic was gone; an Empire now stood, a Colossus over the world. Augustus' military victories left him alone on top of the Seven Hills. Since the Romans hated kings he had to construct the fiction that he was merely the first citizen among equals. And, to demonstrate that nothing had changed, he became a model of state religion. To the Romans religion was a re-connecting, a binding back, to the ancient gods. Augustus was simply enabling this conservative process.

And that is what Mitt Romney was attempting. He would "preserve American leadership" by being true to his sense of religious liberty. He hoped that the voters would see in him the same religious type with which they had become so comfortable. He wanted to convince his audience that the faith of his fathers would find a place alongside McCain's *Faith of My Fathers*. He wanted to reassure all who would soon caucus that if this were Iowa it must be heaven and that America's God was still on the coin of the realm.

Yet, before he cowboyed up with his confession of faith—right on the edge of the cliff—he threw me for a loop by saying, "Americans tire of those who would jettison their beliefs, even to gain the world." It is hard for me to erase apparently another Mitt Romney who ran for governor of Massachusetts. Somehow he had jettisoned his New England convictions. But then I realized he was not ditching those beliefs to gain just the world, he was gunning for the presidency.

"The mystic chords of memory"
2009

Two months ago I was in tears. It started the day before the presidential election. A rally on the campus of my university featured hip hop stars campaigning for Obama. As I looked around it was impossible not to notice that I was a minority: white, middle-aged, male. Then the MC urged us all to look around, to our right, to our left. He said to see the new world where diversity was staring you in the face. Universities in recent years have taken great pains to enlighten students on the ideas and challenges of diversity. Courses have been designed, programs initiated. But, here on a soccer field, where the surrounding working class neighborhood invaded the campus, diversity became real.

The crowd was urged not to worry about standing in line to vote, for most had experience in waiting in line for the latest music release or video game. I realized I was in another generation, for "standing in line" had other associations for me: the silent lines of protest in the sixties as well as the separate lines for "colored" water fountains. There were some in the crowd, black and white, who remembered those other lines. As I began to hum "We shall overcome" the tears began.

The next day, as I waited in line to vote, that haunting protest song returned. I looked at the packed voting place and tears again welled up. Later that night, when Ohio turned blue and soon thereafter electoral victory was announced, my tears resumed. Visual reports from Grant Park in Chicago and then from Europe and Africa echoed the refrain world-wide: "Yes, we can!'

In the midst of a world-crippling financial disaster, where trust appeared no longer bankable, where greed has been supersized and valued and the common good reduced to a pipedream, the American people chose once again to become a people of promise and rejected the established politics of fear.

But that was two months ago.

Once again we are at the beginning. The Romans had a word for it: *revolutio.* This does not mean what modern listeners assume. It meant a return to the beginning. The wheel has turned once more. It could mean the recapturing of a golden age. Inevitably, however, even that golden period would morph to lead. Indeed, there was a religious cast to all of this. For *religio* meant a tying back, a return to the past. The religious Roman tried to link the present to the past, forging a chain of tradition that sustained the momentum of the world. The first Roman emperor Augustus understood all this, and, while he transformed a debilitated republic into a functioning empire, he kept up the appearances that things had hardly changed. Indeed, his propaganda factory (including Virgil) worked overtime, declaring that the gods and destiny had long ago ordained this happy situation.

Of course there was a price for all of this. The *Pax Romana* came at a cost. Order and harmony were purchased through controlled violence. The "way things were" assumed a pyramid of power, where 15 percent of the population were serviced by the other 85 percent. If people had problems with this, the legions were poised to strike, moving on well-kept roads. Torture and crucifixion were the standard response to any "uppity" ones.

But there were alternate voices. One of which was Paul. In his letter to the Romans Paul begins by identifying himself an "an envoy appointed to announce God's world-changing news." He then mentions an "anointed lord" who has been enthroned "as a son of God." This Jesus was executed by the empire. In effect, Paul is saying that a counter regime existed, since the God of Israel refused to forget that shamed nobody and elevated him to a status of power. No longer was the news of Rome the only story about how the world worked. It is not surprising that later legend tells of Paul losing his head over such treasonous thoughts. Indeed, we really do not know what actually happened to Paul. He disappeared as many have done under a dominating regime.

But the die had been cast. Another model of governing had been inserted into the imagination of the Mediterranean. Jesus had been "chosen" not because he conquered but because he trusted that God was reliable. Or, to put it more bluntly, God was no longer hovering above the apex of the pyramid of power. Rather, the divine had become mixed up with the refuse of the empire. Where could one look to find the holy? No longer in the heavens, the hall of fame of heroes and superstars; rather, look where those are being crushed by the very weight of the pyramid.

Paul remained true to his Jewish roots, especially that radical memory "Let my people go!" He discovered that the God of Israel joins in solidarity with the lost, the abandoned, and the crushed.

It is that long distant echo that I heard ricocheting across the world two months ago. Unless such "mystic cords" of liberation are taken up anew, unless we reinvent and enact the promise of the common good, the hope that people felt will be sorely disappointed. And then we shall simply reinvent the wheel, where domination and torture are the order of the day.

▌ Into the dark 2009

▌ It is ironic that both supporters and opponents of the economist John Maynard Keynes have in their own way endorsed his pithy remark: "In the long run, we're all dead." Supporters have noted that economic disasters will not resolve themselves and that without government intervention over the long run the economy will inevitably flat-line. But opponents to Keynes's ideas of economic stimulus also have curiously labored under his maxim. Since there was no necessity to look to the long run, they went on a feckless short-term binge, attempting to squeeze as much profit before the bubble burst. A sense of fate seems to enclose either option.

Such considerations take on added urgency in these times. Speculation seems out of place when your neighborhood is on the block, when your retirement has vanished and when you hold a pink slip in your hand. The tickertape parade of the Dow Jones Average has transmogrified into some ancient augury of regret. T. S. Eliot's words poignantly apply:

> They all go into the dark,
> The vacant interstellar spaces, the vacant into the vacant,
> The captains, merchant bankers, eminent men of letters,
> The generous patrons of art, the statesmen and the rulers,
> Distinguished civil servants, chairmen of many committees,
> Industrial lords and petty contractors, all go into the dark …
> And we all go with them, into the silent funeral.
> —*Four Quartets* 2.3

Indeed, if it is appalling for our economic reality, what is in store for the epiphenomena of our culture? Critics have begun again to raise the question of the worth and value of the "nonproductive elements" of our society. What good, for instance, are the liberal arts in a foundering economy? In fact, can't we assess the real worth of such disciplines and studies? Are they not parasites on the body economic? Indeed, as intellectual Ponzi schemes, they hold on for dear life, demanding higher tuitions, until their worthlessness is exposed. With the fat cut out, it's time to gnaw on bones.

Of course, some people have started to play the religion card along with the inevitable blame game. Have we not as a nation forgotten the true meaning, the true purpose and worth of religion? How could we forget that the primary task of religion is to provide a moral break on human waywardness?

But both the simplistic reduction of our intellectual enterprise and the return to "old time religion" still play the zero sum game of fate.

Critics of the intellectual life would lobotomize the brain to keep the rest of the body alive in some sort of vegetative state. Meanwhile religious stalwarts would have us check our freedom at the vestry door. Both would bring us back to "the basics" where control is their uppermost concern in such uncertain times. But neither would emancipate.

I can't speak for you, but I can hardly catch my breath, trying to inhale within this claustrophobic atmosphere. How can we find some room to breathe?

At the risk of being economic parasites, let's spend some time among the dead. The ancients, when faced with situations beyond their control, fell into mythic speech. Myths were hardly what we now consider them. They were fundamental stories that provided orientation and identity. People found out where they came from, where they were going and who they were. To speak (or dance) in myths meant that you were involved in something greater than you knew.

There is one myth that may speak to our condition: the tale of Orpheus and Eurydice. Orpheus was renowned as a singer and musician; with his voice and lyre he enchanted animals and birds, even inspired trees and rocks to dance. But with the sudden death of his wife, Eurydice, he attempted the impossible: a journey to the underworld to retrieve his love. Hades and Persephone were won over by his song. They permitted Eurydice to return to earth on the condition that Orpheus not look back at her until they both were on earth. Of course, Orpheus looks back too soon and Eurydice vanishes forever. Nothing remains but his lament.

We, too, sit at the edge of a world gone to hell. And we would go literally through hell to rescue all that we have lost. And yet, at the very verge of coming out of it, Eurydice is still lost. Here is where the tale can turn into something unexpected. If we follow the mythic script to hell and back, we wind up repeating the damn thing over and over again. But what if we did the unthinkable? What if we abandoned the script? What if we let go of what we were used to, of what we thought the world was made of, of how we thought things work? What if we faced our fear of abandonment and, instead, abandoned what we have been so desperately trying to hang onto?

What would happen? There still is grieving to do. Orpheus laments. But is that all? What if we found transformation in the very moment of abandonment, of letting go? I contend that this is how religious consciousness genuinely provides a breathing space. It is the parabolic strategy employed by Jesus when he turned his mythic world upside down and left his listeners with more than they had bargained for. Paul experienced this when his cherished notion of God was lost on the cross of Jesus. It is time not to reduce our minds to mush or to turn back the religious clock. For that simply consigns us to a living hell. It is time for courage; time to maneuver in ways we never dreamed of; time for surprise.

A new Adam (Smith) 2011

Some days ago I asked one of my colleagues in Economics what he thought about our University's Divinity School. He looked at me as if I were daft. There is no Divinity School on campus. I added that I was talking about his school, our celebrated Business School. "Now I know you're joking," he responded. But I could not be more serious.

Indeed, while it is not news to observe that the economic situations both in this country and throughout the world have been tottering on the brink for much too long, it might be useful nevertheless to gain a different perspective. And, because of my habitual forays into the ancient world, I would suggest framing matters from that long-ago viewpoint. What would happen if we saw things from that far-off time? How would an ancient inhabitant of Alexandria, for example, discover clues of divinity? And what connection would all that have to economics?

For the ancients religious matters were not a cerebral exercise or a creedal litmus test. They would simply observe your behavior and ask: to what are you devoted? What have you spent your time on? What has consumed your interest? If you follow those lines of behavior then you will locate your god/goddess. This is the one that keeps things going for you. This is the one who feeds your dreams. This is the object of your devotion. I often ask my students to map out their times, noting how and why they have spent their days. Rarely does the God of Abraham and of Jesus show up as the abiding object of devotion. Students even abbreviate their focus of attention with the standard $.

I then explore how the ancients thought their economy operated. How did the market of the Hellenistic world work? How did it move successfully from an agricultural economy to an urban experiment? While economic historians bluntly describe the ancient situation as an extractive economy, where the elites took from those under and around them, the ancients saw things from a justifying theological perspective: the surplus which drove their economic engine came from the gods as favors and benefits. One responded to such benefits with ritual sacrifice which would, in turn, elicit more favors from the divine. Entrepreneurial success was not due to marketing genius or random factors; it was brought about through cultivating favor from the divine. The ancient economy was in effect a divine *oikonomia* (the term by which the Greeks referred to the divine management of the world).

Such observations have led me to declare that my university has a Divinity School. Our Business School provides the rationale, the content, the tools, and the social cues to negotiate the forces and currents of life in our world. The Business School suffers, however, from the assumption that its subject matter does not entail a theological component. If it does, many would argue, then, let the Theology Department in Arts and Sciences deal with it (because anything theological is inconsequential and immaterial). And yet I observe how seriously devoted the School's administrators, professors and students are in their pursuit of learning to do business. I see my marketing students in business suits only for real-life interviews (they know what to wear for liturgical functions); otherwise shorts, sandals and tees are fine for the classroom. If they would only ask: "where and how do you devote yourselves?" they would find that they are as religiously obsessed as any ancient follower of Isis. In fact, if that ancient observer would describe how these modern students see capitalism working today, he would go beyond contemporary criticism that capitalism has been transformed into high stakes casino gambling, where the elite bet the house with others' money. He would see in their devotion a divinity which ever shapes their end: *Tyche, Fortuna,* or in the vernacular, *"Lady Luck."* And he would be well aware that she is a fickle goddess.

But there is something even more disturbing about this Divinity School. It does not recognize the major insight of one of its founding theologians: Adam Smith. We often hear of Smith's metaphor of the "invisible hand" guiding the market despite the limited self-interest of the players. But few, if any, read his *Theory of Moral Sentiments* where he lays the intellectual basis for modern capitalism. The "invisible hand" of the market was set within Smith's moral matrix of compassion and imagination. Sympathy with others undergirded the entire enterprise. A lingering Presbyterian sense of justice lies at the heart of it all. The invisible hand is not some mechanical zombie but the deeper impulse of our compassion and imagination of the other. It is precisely the human factors of imagination and compassion that carry us through our business with one another.

The tragedy is that we have left that insight long ago. We have exiled compassion and imagination from our balance sheets and board rooms. We have allowed the bankrupt ideology of social Darwinism to justify the terror and fecklessness of market behavior. We ride the roller coaster of the tickertape with greed and fear as our only companions.

We have forgotten that the capitalistic enterprise does not consist in simply hedging bets but in constantly building for a future in which we all share. To fail to notice the interconnection of all of us in this country, on this planet, is actually a failure to see new marketing possibilities and resources. Moreover, we have failed to use our imagination to envision the consequences of our short-term gains. In sum, we failed to realize that a human face haunts the bottom line.

We have been told again and again that at the heart of our economic woes lies a crisis of confidence. We do not trust one another, do not trust the system, do not trust those who would regulate affairs, and we do not trust those who, behind the scenes, keep the game going.

There is, therefore, a real task for theology in the marketplace (and for a business school to be more than an unconscious enabler): to name the forces that dominate and determine our existence; to gain some distance and some breathing room to assess what is going on and to respond creatively and critically. It is time to expose the fundamental stories that we keep repeating to ourselves without success and which disintegrate our life together in this country and on this planet. It is time to act responsibly; not to react and continue to fuel our addictions. It is time to see if there is anything in our religious heritage that can throw a different light on our troubling situation. This is the work of *oikonomia*, of managing our world.

Where did our futures go? 2012

As the presidential campaigns continue inexorably, and as both parties declare that nothing less than the future is at stake, I have been struck by the meagerness of the futures offered to us. Of course, we are slowly extricating ourselves from the financial catastrophe visited on us only a few years ago. Yet, the prospects for our children and our grandchildren look rather grim. In contrast, I think of an earlier time, when the future looked open. There was talk not only of reducing the labor week but of a culture of leisure. We even played with the possibility of transporting ourselves in flying vehicles, not dependent on oil. As the space race heated up, we began to imagine life in three and four dimensions, populating space stations, and going "where no one had gone before."

But, to steal from that rascal poet François Villon: *ou sont les Jetsons d'antan?* Even our futuristic cartoon dreams have been transmogrified into teenage vampire soap operas. The prospect of a life of leisure, like a limping satellite, has fallen back to earth under the gravitational pull of a dog-eat-dog world. Where we thought people would work less, we find that their jobs have been outsourced and performed by others in even worse labor conditions. Those who still have jobs have been asked to redouble their productivity. Even the advent of the computer and the internet has not reduced but intensified work, so that we find ourselves hunched over our computers responding to insistent and unending email. For those employed, there is even less time to step back and ask whether any of this is what we truly want. Is this the future that we dreamed of?

One could say that there are moments in time when opportunities existed to consider our options. Certainly after the fall of the Berlin Wall in 1989 there was the time to ask what sort of a world we would have. But that conversation was soon drowned out by those who declared that Capitalism had carried the day. Indeed, subsequent American administrations have continued to proclaim this victory of neo-liberalism. And that doctrine has continued to be applied strenuously in various national economic straits such as in Chile, Russia, Poland, and now Greece, Ireland, Portugal, Italy and Spain. In order to settle the books, more than social services have to be cut; everyone involved must get a "haircut" trimmed to the stipulations of the banking experts. There is apparently no other way of envisioning a way through.

Such reflection brought me back to an ancient inscription, where the future also was dictated according to a singular world view. The *Priene Inscription* (9 BCE) presents what the Greeks in the province of Asia (now Turkey) thought of the Emperor Augustus. The emperor was sent by divine Providence to "order all things" and set life "in the most perfect order." As a savior (*soter*) he brings peace to a war-weary world and delivers benefactions that posterity can never outdo. All of this is part of the "world-transforming message" (*euaggelion*). Indeed, they even rearranged their calendar by setting his birthday as the beginning of their year.

In effect, this inscription, as with other pieces of Roman propaganda, was intent on declaring that this was where the future was going for Rome and for those within the Roman orbit. If you wanted to be part of this successful enterprise, all you needed to do was to submit to the Roman message and occupation. As we learn from the Roman pacification of Spain (which took two hundred years from the end of Punic Wars), completed during the reign of Augustus, submission meant nothing less than everything. As Strabo notes, even the native tongues of Spain were lost. All came under the influence of the Roman gravitational pull. There was to be no other world-wide message.

And yet history indicates that there were other dreamers— even as the Augustan revolution was being secured by his successors. We know of an artisan from Galilee who crafted parables and aphorisms about an alternate vision of life. His healings and eating practices embedded his vision in concrete reality. His performance evidently was infectious and this alternative way of imagining life together survived the catastrophe of his death. Moreover, that Messianic Jew, Paul, in his letters challenged the Roman Gospel with a counter proposal. Indeed, his vision came from re-imagining how the God of Israel could accept a crucified, godless one. Both Jesus and Paul went in directions where the angels of the establishment feared to tread. Each offered to his listeners a life different from the prescribed outcome.

What do these historical observations mean for us? First, we gain some degree of maneuverability. We gain space and time to think about our own situation. We can realize that history is not a simple story of one inevitable future, but a contested field. This should sharpen our ears and eyes to be on the alert for indications of alternative possibilities even within our seemingly predictable situation. Secondly, it means that theology is embedded in this very debate of where we want to go on this planet. It is not an other-worldly affair. Rather, it is an intensive reflection of how we envision the depth of our life together here and now. What kind of life do we cherish and wish to transmit to our descendants? What, then, are those "Gospels" that prevent this from happening? Can we name those dominating visions and see through their suffocating control? Are we afraid that we have too long ascribed to those dominating visions and would lose whatever we have? Would we rather hang on to an ever-declining world and lose our chance to live?

▌ Right under their noses   2013

▌ Before we become caught up with the latest divine enthronement ceremony, commonly known in this country as a presidential inauguration, and before we consign to oblivion the last presidential campaigns and election, it would be good to consider the underlying theological yield from the November ballot boxes.

Conservative comments on the 2012 election have ranged from the initial shock of Rush Limbaugh ("I went to bed last night thinking we've lost the country") to the caution not to gloat over the victory, thinking that God has spoken through the people. Rather the liberal coalition should consider the harsh reality underlying the reason for their vote: a disintegrating social and religious reality (manifested already by the "moochers and takers"). Keep in mind what Han Solo said to Luke, "Don't get too cocky, kid!"

Such reactions and proffered advice come not simply from a stunned cadre of conservative pundits. They arise from assumptions that many Americans have been making since the time of the Great Communicator and the emergence of the self-styled Moral Majority. An individualistic, if not literal, reading of the Gospels, coupled with insouciance to fact and history, reinforcing the idolatry of American exceptionalism, found full-throated testimony in the electronic personae of Jerry Falwell and Pat Robertson.

We should not forget that the Jesus Seminar began its work within that national atmosphere. At a time when a Secretary of the Interior was intent on selling millions of acres of national forests since they did not matter with the End Time so near and when some officers in the Pentagon were conducting weekly prayer sessions to be ready for Armageddon, Bob Funk typically went against that apocalyptic grain and invited scholars to try two outrageous courses of action: to take history seriously by reopening the quest for the historical Jesus and to make a public report of the findings of the seminar in order to redress the national conversation on religion.

Part of the initial success of the Jesus Seminar was precisely the stimulation of a critical discussion on religion. But it was not simply this public report that must be noted. My experience with the Jesus Seminars on the Road throughout North America has confirmed again and again what has been flying under the media radar. It is not just a band of scholars that must be taken seriously. There is a significant portion of the population in North America that refuses to give up on religious questions, while at the same time rejecting the conventional ways of expressing and embodying religious traditions.

But don't take my word alone on this. The Pew Forum on Religion and Public Life has been observing for some time significant trends in religion in America ("U.S. Religious Landscape Survey). Not only is the group entitled "Unaffiliated" becoming the group experiencing the largest increase in numbers, but the established Protestant churches have seen marked declines. Even the Catholic Church would have suffered a significant decrease if it were not for population growth of Hispanic Catholics. What is also telling is that while the numbers of the "Unaffiliated" are increasing, this does not indicate that there has been a concomitant drop in people asking religious questions.

Certainly this agrees with my experience "on the Road." People are loath to sacrifice their heads at the expense of their hearts. Yes, increasing numbers have been leaving established churches for some time. But the reasons are not simple. Certainly what must be taken into account are the various ways in which the established churches have discredited the cause of religion. The continued cover-up of the lingering sex scandal by church leaders has gravely damaged the Catholic Church. Nor has the attempt to control women in the various denominations been lost to most. The knee-jerk interpretation of 9/11 (among other social and political events) by purveyors of the electronic gospel has become the locus classicus of biblical errancy.

The election of 2012 brings further evidence to the fore. Despite the attempts of conservative Catholic bishops to steer the faithful in a definite direction about abortion, same-sex marriage and religious liberty, more Catholics voted for Obama than Romney. The "Nuns-on-the-bus" delivered quite a counterpunch to the Catholic Vice Presidential candidate who had discarded the common good of Aquinas for the selfish angle of Ayn Rand. The aged Billy Graham was roused to remind Evangelicals of supporting a Bible-based value platform, while Ralph Reed's Faith and Freedom Coalition alarmed the faithful in churches, on the phone and through televised commercials to maintain their long-standing moral commitment. Yet despite these and enormous financial inputs from political action committees what was once the Moral Majority lost the battle against same sex marriage in all fours states where it was on the ballot, saw marijuana legalized in two states and witnessed the loss of Senate candidates who avowed anti-abortion rights. R. Albert Mohler, Jr., the president of Southern Baptist Theological Seminary, ruefully concluded that "the entire moral landscape has changed. An increasing secularized America understands our positions, and rejects them."

Sadly such a reading of the situation stills plays out of the tired dualism favored by conservative churches. Science still does not enter into the inner sanctum. Not only did the Republican campaign fail to see the ground game of the Democratic organizers, but conservative supporters have been blind to the seismic shifts in religious sensibility across the nation. The Obama campaign took into consideration what the other side could not imagine, did not deem important enough to be worried about. While conservatives nervously focused on the country's borders, another migration had long been underway right under their noses, on the streets, in cities and towns, on farms, factories, mountains, and sea coasts—a polychrome coalition that refused to let that fragile exodus, that extended tissue of human trust, disappear from the face of the earth.

Jesus of Nazareth: Presidential timber? 2014

There is a prevailing truism in American politics: with a black man having been elected president, it will be only a matter of time before a woman and even a gay person is elected; but America will never accept an atheist. The most recent polls seem to support this as they continue to describe this country as extremely religious, even though the major Christian denominations are experiencing steady decline. Presidents invariably end their speeches by invoking the blessing of God on the United States of America. Indeed, George W. Bush declared that Jesus was his favorite philosopher. And, as the next presidential election season begins to heat up, no candidate will be asking Richard Dawkins or Daniel Dennett to be part of the team of advisors.

America is a Christian nation, a godly people. This is as certain as our dollar bills. Just look on the back of one. "In God We Trust" rests underneath the guarantee of the United States of America, above the "ONE" and between two circular mandalas. The left mandala features a solid masonic pyramid surrounded by vegetation, with the divine eye hovering over all. A new world order is declared in Latin under the divine nod. Meanwhile on the right an imperial eagle, carrying an American shield and under a magical Solomonic seal of thirteen stars, extends its wings and holds in its talons an olive branch of peace and the arrows of war.

We don't need to go beyond the back of a dollar bill to discover America's theology. It is quite clear that we have a sense of the divine, articulated in symbols that have rumbled through time from the empires of Egypt and Rome. This theology rests on the recognition of power. Pyramid and eagle forcefully display this. And that is, as it should be, for the ancients (far more realistic than many of us) understood that the divine world was all about power. The ancients would invoke the divine whenever they recognized that they were in situations beyond their control. Their myths gave them a coherent frame in which to cope with the damage and uncertainty of living in this world. These myths also gave them a rationale for justifying why the few were dominant and the many expendable. But, most of all, such mythic language gave them access to power—to invoke, to save, and to thrive. How fitting, then, are these symbols to support our currency, our economy and our class structure. Each of our transactions sustains and encourages this desirable flow of power. Presidential candidates will be seeking to siphon this flow in their direction. How else will our exceptional enterprise survive?

Before getting too carried away with this potential circulation of power, it might be telling to ask what is missing from this symbolic assembly. Since many of us consider America a Christian land, should we not ask if there is any hint of Jesus of Nazareth around these national avatars of power? In fact, if these images intimate what the divine means for us—prosperity and power—where would Jesus fit in? If we remove the fourth century imperial do-over from the earliest fragments of Jesus' words and deeds, we find a peasant crushed by a pyramid of power. His crucifixion was confirmation that the Empire's gods had him in their clutches.

To make matters worse, his followers were considered atheists, for they did not support the economic and political system sustained by the gods. Indeed, if you listen to what he had to say, you would never see him as imperial or presidential timber. How could anyone imagine falling into the arms of an enemy and coming out the better for it? Who would dare think that the marginal and socially misfit could be worth anything? Why would anyone waste time on losers or eat with just anybody? To operate on the conviction that life has depth and is ultimately reliable flies in the face of any realistic assessment of the world. In fact, the god Jesus envisioned is no god at all. In terms of our own currency, Jesus had no god. Today he would be seen as an atheist. His god did not play then nor does it play now to the way power works. To imagine a god showering benefits on the "makers and takers," the "workers and wasters," indiscriminately and without the fear of ultimate retribution is simply a recipe for social chaos and disaster. There has to be a clutching talon of control as well as the eternally vigilant eye, maintaining security and surveillance. No one wants to risk losing "a good thing."

But isn't that what that peasant proposed in paradox, about preserving life by losing it? Wasn't that a platform of nonsense? How can one expect more from reality, more than our predicted earnings? Could we ever think that there was something more, that our deepest desires might come true? How could we run an economy without determining everyone's dreams in advance? Why would anyone dare to go beyond the reptilian reactions of our brainstem: is life more than fight or flight? It is folly to forgive others unless they grovel before us first, isn't it? Can we really ever expect to be truly surprised? Who can count on the compassion of others? No, such are the pipedreams of someone who does not know what the power plays of a god are all about. Indeed, that godless one even had the gall to suggest that we are missing something, as if we were blind, with a massive timber in our eye!

8

Theological Maneuvers

This section directly engages the explicitly theological issues that emerged in the public forum. In each I have tried to take an unusual angle of response. Even Buffy the vampire slayer takes on a different role! The rituals of our civic religion come up from critique, such as the apotheosis of departed President Reagan. Indeed, the Super Bowl is "outed" as a national cultic event with "A Super Bowl Prayer." The *Da Vinci Code*, Reza Aslan's *Zealot*, and the Gospel of Mel Gibson come under review. Despite some comic relief, each commentary tried to get underneath the glare and hype to a deeper magic. Sadly this entails recognizing the tragic power games that undermine our life on this planet. At the same time, the vision of the Canadian Astronaut Steve MacLean produced an unexpected golden glint to this discussion.

The missing links 1997

I must confess that all the scholastic arguments for the existence of God, despite the elegance of their mental gymnastics, leave me unmoved. If you lived only in your head, then you might be satisfied. But there is something missing in all that metaphysical sound and fury.

Likewise, the infinitive gaze of modern science into the cold reaches of the galaxies or into the quirky realms of the subatomic keeps this observer wishing for something more.

What shivers my timbers is a thought more earthly. I begin by considering the odds of my existence. I suspect that the delirium surrounding the pennant drive of the Boston Red Sox set my father in motion; at least, I calculate this backwards from my premature birth. Then there is the fact that neither of my parents wished to attend the dance where they improbably met.

Now I do not assign Cupid or Destiny to that chance meeting. I simply am struck by the odds. Then I run through my grandparents' tales and discover the ever-growing field of unlikelihood. I keep untangling my genealogical lines, imagining how each generation hazarded long enough to produce, willy-nilly, an offspring.

Face it, each of us is a tottering survivor, a preposterous happenstance that boggles the mind all the way back to the bones of Lucy in that African gorge.

The emptiness of interstellar space is nothing compared to those silences of thousands of years, when our ancestors went about finding a way to be human. The bonding energies of subnuclear particles are not as compelling as the dreams that kept our ancestors staggering into the future. And the eloquent arguments for God stammer before the incredible cry of a newborn.

Buffy the theologian 1999

Recently hell has been in the headlines. I'm not talking about Kosovo, or the mass killings in Atlanta, or even the relentless heat wave in the eastern United States. A papal lecture on the nature of hell has raised some theological hackles. What, no fire, no brimstone! What do you mean hell is some sort of extreme loneliness?

Before anyone accuses the Pope of being a liberal theologian, just consult Dante's Inferno. There you can find the imaginative basis for the papal remarks. Frozen in the sea of self-centeredness, the triple-headed Satan gnaws on the traitorous spirits of Judas, Brutus, and Cassius. Dante icily notes: "This was not life and yet it was not death." In short, the Pope is as orthodox as Dante.

But for Americans, allergic to Thomistic hairsplitting and light years away from the medieval cosmos, there is another way to see hell.

An image has been long with us: in the movies, in recent best selling novels, and now, in the teenie bopper exploits of TV's *Buffy the Vampire Slayer*. We know the script. The vampire with no reflection in a mirror but a rabid and endless thirst for blood.

Mirror, mirror, on the wall. Images emerge when nations teeter and egos fall. They reflect us in twisted and refracted ways.

But vampires? Could they be close to home? What does it mean when we can't sit still and look within? What happens when we're driven by an endless desire to consume? How often at 2:00 a.m. are we awake but feeling neither alive nor dead? Buffy the theologian would call that hell.

Good Friday's dirty little secret 2000

Once again Jewish and Christian memories coincide this week. Passover began at sundown on Wednesday. Today is Good Friday. For two millennia the double helix of Jewish-Christian relations has revolved, too often fraught with tragic misunderstanding and terrible consequences.

Rabbinic Judaism and Christianity emerged from the smoke and debris of the fall of Second Temple Judaism. When Jews and Christians today attempt to find out what caused the breakup, like so many other feuding families, no one can exactly recall what precipitated the divorce.

Now is not the time to try to sort out sore points. It is a time for memory.

In 1905 Antokolsky, a Jewish sculptor in St. Petersburg, wrote:

For several weeks now I have been working on "Christ," or as I call him "Great Isaiah." Jews may have renounced him, but I solemnly admit that he was and died a Jew. The Jews think I'm Christian and the Christians curse me for being a dirty Jew.

In 1938 Marc Chagall painted the White Crucifixion. Thrown in still, white light at the center was a crucified Jesus, wrapped in a Jewish prayer shawl, surrounded by a riot of images. Soldiers attack from the upper left, just above collapsing Jewish houses. A synagogue burns to the right, as Jews flee in the lower right hand corner. Above the cross Jewish spirits hover in shock and distress. On the bottom left an old Jew stands with a plaque on his chest. Before repainting the plaque read "Ich bin Jude. I am a Jew."

Good Friday carries for Christians a dirty little secret. It is a memory that Christians forget at their peril. There is that innocent one on the cross, who never stops saying, "Ich bin Jude. I am a Jew."

Virtual images   2000

Recently an odd thought struck me. In fact, it made me down right uncomfortable—even claustrophobic. Before the advent of the photograph you could never see yourself as others saw you. No matter what efforts you went through, the only way you could approach what others saw of you was through the contortions of your own imagination.

Today we presume so much in our lives, including what we look like. But before the camera the common person had to rely on virtual images in mirrors and hints supplied by others. Only the rich could afford a portrait.

The tale of Narcissus was very much our story. Here was a boy who fell hopelessly in love with his reflection in the water. He drowned trying to reach what he thought was another beautiful boy.

For the ancients there was a way out of this imaginative straightjacket. They saw themselves in the eyes of the gods. They assessed themselves and their world from the standpoint of eternity. In other words, they bounced their consciousness off the screen of the heavens. The divine world was their virtual reality. The mystic Meister Eckhart summed it up nicely by saying that the eye with which we look at God is the same eye with which God looks at us.

Then Matthew Brady and others brought us back to earth. Things became up close and very personal. No need to rearrange our faces. A picture became worth a thousand words. A haunting one could stagger Shakespeare. We see what countless generations before us could only hope to craft in their mind's eye.

Yet, some would say that we have lost that eternal gaze. Or, have we finally begun to see as human beings?

Theology at thirty miles an hour 2001

There is a war of biblical proportions going on out there. And, if you're driving in your car right now, it might be directly in front of you.

The rear bumpers of numerous cars display symbolic fish. Some of these rudimentary signs are filled with the Greek word for fish: ΙΧΘΥΣ. This was a code word for the early Jesus believers. Each letter of the Greek term stood for a word in an ancient confession: Jesus Christ, God's Son, Savior. Hastily sketched in the dust, the fish served as a signal of recognition for Christians, considered dangerous atheists by Roman officials.

Now drivers of a more rational cast could not resist an evolutionary improvement. The fish has grown legs and wears DARWIN, a new school name, on its side.

But the bumper debate is hardly over. Right before your eyes you can see how far people will go in a theological dispute. Another symbol swims through the exhaust. A larger fish, with mouth agape, is on the verge of consuming that Darwinian mutation. Match point and game for the righteous.

But is that all to this fish tale? Don't the triumphal ones see that the joke is ultimately on them? For their big-mouthed behemoth proves their opposition's point: the survival of the fittest!

Perhaps an older sea yarn might help us here. You know, the one about Jonah. He fled what he knew to be devastatingly true:

that even the godless were worth a visit. In a godforsaken land that humorless man stood with his mouth open, surprised by a Reality more uproarious than he could stomach.

▮ A designer universe? 2002

▮ When Galileo peered into his telescope and spied the moons of Jupiter, the world, as people knew it, began to implode. John Donne, the seventeenth-century poet, decried how science, "called all in doubt, the element of fire is quite put out."

The shock waves of the scientific revolution are still felt today even in "the heart of it all"—Ohio. In response to a draft of the Ohio Department of Education science standards, some state lawmakers have introduced bills mandating the teaching of "intelligent design." They would address what they see as an imbalance in the teaching of evolution. They want students to get a chance to consider that a higher power might have played a role in the creation of life.

If such legislation passes it will prove that the politicians know a lot about gerrymandering, little about science, and even less about theology.

The argument of intelligent design is a new, improved version of creationism that had been dismissed by the courts as science. This is creationism in academic tweeds.

Proponents of intelligent design essentially beg the question, that is, they assume what they must prove. But what they want to prove—"the divinity that shapes our ends"—cannot be empirically proven. Their expressed concern for complexity is not wide enough. They fail to deal with chaos, randomness, and the unexpected. Tornadoes and teenagers shatter any attempt at design.

The issue is not about science; nor is it about truth. It is about design, not God's design, but the intent to use the language of science to maintain an ancient worldview. It is actually outdated theology in a lab coat.

What proponents of intelligent design do not want to face is what caused Copernicus to keep his findings quiet until his death. They do not want to face a universe uncomfortable and ever perplexing. Such a response is quite understandable. But it is no excuse to legislate a pseudo-solution.

Is it not time to grow up and recognize how strange reality is, to perform the humbler task of piecing together the fragments of our universe, to realize, along with Dorothy, that we're not in Kansas anymore?

▌That gnawing emptiness 2002

▌ This is a most difficult, painful time for those whose trust has been betrayed. This is not simply about the journalistic feeding frenzy that has absorbed the Vatican for the last few days. Nor is it about a group of celibate seniors, closeted among artworks, and fetishizing over the niceties of embroidered distinctions. Nor is it about the hand wringing communiqués of administrators, who would deflect accountability by doling out updated protocols. Nor is it about statistics on pedophiles, nor the number of gay clergy.

What stares us in the face is the Church's dirty little secret. It is the rank abuse of power. This is not limited to the sexual abuse of boys. It certainly includes what seems to be avoided in all this uproar: the victimization of women by priests.

But there is more. The abuse of power is not simply physical. The Church has known how to wield a psychological mace for years. We can see it in how both clergy and laity have been reared, how much their education in the faith has been a sadly disguised intellectual abuse.

Only in recent times have courageous voices spoken of this dysfunctional situation, where humiliation, emasculation, and silence are the rules of the game. The present crisis has allowed people within and outside of the Church to see the disastrous condition. Even conservatives are expressing their anger and dismay. Liberals are once again stirring the pot of reform.

But this goes deeper than any conservative call to discipline. It shatters the superficial solutions of progressives. We can glimpse both in the staggering reports of abuse and the official minuet of control and perceive that the abuse of power can take many forms. We can hear the echoes of this from one of the victims of abuse. A young priest, who was both inspired and molested by a priest, declares:

> I saw that priests were given power. And it is power over people, although I never wanted to become that kind of priest. I was looking for power within myself—strength within myself, which I never felt.

Indeed, this tortured young man has put his finger on the lie that is the abuse of power. Why does this happen again and again? Because of that gnawing emptiness in the heart. What we so desperately want, what we never feel, energizes our power plays over others.

Such a hunger can turn our fundamental images awry. Even the scene of Jesus with the children takes on a haunted aspect. As the children look up trustingly, the face of the Nazarene grows vampire teeth.

Because I can, I will 2002

I know it sounds daffy to those who think theologians should maintain their irrelevance by staying within their gated religious communities. But I can't overlook the theological attempts by the administration's spokespeople as they try to justify bushwhacking Iraq.

From its earliest beginnings, America has been embedded in theological speculation. We try to avoid any smattering of theology today by repeating ad nauseam the Jeffersonian distinction between church and state. We say we want to avoid the religious warfare of the seventeenth and eighteenth centuries, yet we smolder with religious fanaticism at school board meetings. All the while genuine theological reflection is shut within the choir stall.

It is time for Americans to realize that theology is a human enterprise. Every time we try to make sense of the depths of our lives, we are theologically daring. Each time we struggle for words to dance on the emptiness of our nights, we are in the company of a long tradition of pioneers. We need to come out of the theological closet.

This brings me back to the theological basis for the attack on Iraq. Actually it rests upon a simple theological assumption: "Because I can, I will do it." This position is hardly new in the history of theology, although it has been updated in desert fatigues. Because Saddam can wage war of unbelievable proportion, he will. And because we can use our arsenal of freedom, we will.

If such a position looks rather simplistic and childish, theologians from various traditions have long thought so. Paul in his letter to Rome explored that human flaw. The Greek dramatists called it by the name of hubris. Buddha saw through that immature posture.

The fundamental isolation of this position fails to imagine that we are all together on this globe. Even our own bitter experience tells us of the folly of presuming that we can will our success. Indeed, such lockbox certainty misses what makes our life so rich: surprise, complexity, and comedy. There are other scripts besides a puritan rerun at the OK Corral.

▌ An experiment in truth   2003

▌ Recently Mr. Joseph Loconte, fellow of the Heritage Foundation, observed on NPR and in the *New York Times* that in the rush to war everyone seems to want Jesus in his camp. He quickly points out that the liberals' reading of the Bible, their version of the Sermon on the Mount, is simplistic at best.

His reading suggests that the biblical picture is much more complicated. Jesus is no naïve flower child but a deliverer of tough love. Thus, while everyone wants Jesus on his bench, the discerning reader of scripture knows that Jesus would not compromise with any axis of evil.

In a final rhetorical flourish Mr. Loconte concludes with an image from the Scroll of Revelation. How could those well-intentioned do-gooders have missed that rampaging Lion of Judah?

His interpretive rope-a-dope is well designed. While he stands for complexity against the single-minded rants of radicals, the image of Jesus he broadly paints nevertheless resembles a predictable projection of the fears and hopes of our nation. He also never mentions that the Lion of Judah turns into a lamb, slaughtered by the imperial system. Only a Vince Lombardi Trophy is missing from the robust account of Loconte's Son of God.

Luther warned long ago that scripture has a wax nose. You can bend it any way you want. How do we know that the profile Loconte offers is historically accurate? Or is he really worried about history?

Why does Mr. Loconte never deal with that uncomfortable aphorism "Love your enemies"? Certainly he is not alone in avoiding a saying that critical biblical scholars contend comes from the historical Jesus. Augustine, for one, twisted it inside out, using it to justify putting our enemies to death in order to show them how much we loved their souls.

But what was Jesus thinking when he delivered such a wild-eyed saying? How do those words square with the violent redeemer that Mr. Loconte champions? Could it be possible that Jesus imagined that reality was not segregated by an iron curtain into good and evil, just and unjust?

Would Mr. Loconte risk contaminating his image of Jesus? Would he join in a critical reading experiment of a much too familiar tale that mingles terror and surprise? Would he dare take a second look at a fragment that seems to fill out the aphorism on enemies? "A fellow went on his way from Jerusalem down to Jericho...."

The gospel of Mad Max 2004

In a few days the season of Lent begins. But the delicate gesture of mortality, etched in ashes on people's foreheads, will undoubtedly be swept aside by the Technicolor gore of the latest version of the gospel of Mel Gibson.

Considering himself inspired, Mel the evangelist works in a medium that truly is the Bible for most Americans. Scholars and preachers might protest, but even they know where people go to discover their deepest dreams. Since we no longer can populate the heavens with our hopes and fears, we project on the silver screen the possibilities of our lives.

Isn't that the hook on which moviemakers depend? The dream industry gambles millions on our living our lives vicariously. Mel the producer is banking on our virtual lifestyle.

Gibson will show us nothing but what we believe to be true. Isn't it a violent world out there that persecutes the last great hope of humanity? Isn't even Mel a martyr as he dares—against all liberal nonsense—to bring the truth to everyone in Aramaic and Latin?

But there is something Mel cannot reveal. For that would bring the Thunderdome down. A story originally crafted by Jews to make sense of the death of an innocent one has been turned inside out. The imperial system that killed Jesus continues to thrive in the telling of his story. Uncomfortable with those who disappear in death, we gaze desperately at the standard version, which casts good news into a lethal weapon.

In what do we trust? 2004

Recently the Supreme Court heard arguments over the phrase "under God." An avowed atheist boldly presented his case before the Justices. I wondered if anyone there had been interested in asking what sort of God is this country assumed to be "under"?

If this were an ancient history question there would be a way to an answer: look at the money in circulation. For in the ancient world coinage betrayed the religious proclivities of dynasties.

So I inspected our common tender: the dollar bill. Turn it over. There is a confession right above the "O" "N" "E": "In God We Trust." To the left there is one side of the Great Seal of the United States. Thanks to the founding fathers' Masonic influence a triangular eye hovers over a pyramid with thirteen rows of bricks. The Latin phrase "He favors things begun" reinforces the divine approval. Below the pyramid a banner proclaims a "New World Order" over a fertile land.

To the right an eagle reiterates the theme of thirteen colonies in its nimbus of clouds and Davidic star, its tail feathers, and in the leaves of an olive branch and arrows, clutched by menacing talons.

The Eagle did not start out as Ben Franklin's wild turkey. It has flown all the way from ancient Rome. The pyramid and the "eye" predate Moses. Everything intimates a divinity at home in Empire, defined by power and pride. Do we trust this God in which there is no hint of compassion?

Neglected again 2004

For fourteen months *The Da Vinci Code* has been on the New York Times bestseller list with over six million copies sold. This becomes even more remarkable when you finish this quick paced murder mystery and realize that it reads like the first draft of a movie script. Despite the meager characterization that never gets beyond stereotype, readers refuse to put the book down, as they leap from one mechanical puzzle to the next.

But if you talk with someone who has read it, the discussion turns from brainteasers to question. Has the church perpetrated a cover-up? Was Mary Magdalene not a repentant prostitute but the companion of Jesus and a major figure in the Jesus movement? Could the royal bloodline of Jesus and Mary continue to this day? *The Da Vinci Code* throws into question what most Bible-readers would see as the master story of Christianity.

Has the heretical camel by this fictive ruse gotten more than a nose under the ecclesial tent? Already a panoply of neo-conservative books has been published to defuse this puzzlement by "cracking" *The Code* before the movie comes out.

Curiously both author Dan Brown and his neocon critics have been taken in by their own fictions. Critical scholarship has dissolved the dynastic fantasies of the French far-right as well as the simplistic version of Christian origins.

What does seem to be the case is that Sophia, Lady Wisdom, continues to be missed. Who dares to think when church and state prefer the party line?

▌Becoming a god 2004

▌Centuries ago a Roman emperor lay dying. He mocked his own demise by whispering, "I believe I'm becoming a god." Despite his skepticism in the face of death, the emperor had already been deified in various parts of the Empire. Statues, temples, and associations had been set up to maintain the supply of benefits that would come from the imperial cult. The emperor's funeral confirmed this devotion. After a magnificent parade, as the body of the emperor was set ablaze, an eagle was released, signifying the emperor's ascent to the heavenly throne room.

The weeklong funeral rites of Ronald Reagan gave students of religion evidence that the god business is still a going concern. A man, who discovered that he could craft his myopia into a mask reflecting American optimism, entered the imperial pantheon. Even before death the former president had been translated into a congenial icon. Indeed, Mr. Reagan for many years had been fashioning the role of a lifetime. He had refined his voice through B movies, TV hosting, and radio commentary. This was a part he could perform with relaxed sincerity, without thinking, for he truly became his script.

Now, more than ever, he belongs to the airwaves.

Like the gods of old, his engaging image and likeable likeness will be found everywhere and nowhere. Through the mass production of the media his face will shine in the electronic firmament, offering all a virtual reality. The sun will never set on his sunny persona as long as cable TV runs 24/7.

An ancient reprise 2004

Believe it or not there is something older being replayed than the current thirty-year old bushwhacking over Vietnam. The standoff in Najaf between the militia of Moqtada al-Sadr and the combined Iraqi-American forces is not a simple "problem," as an American general termed it. It reprises an ancient story.

It begins in the late seventh century, when Ali, Muhammad's closest relative, finally became Imam, that is, leader. This pious advocate of justice was assassinated after only five years as the Prophet's successor. Some years later Ali's second son Husayn decided to take a stand against the injustice and tyranny of the caliphate throne. Accompanied by fifty followers, their wives and children, Husayn marched in opposition to tyranny to bring the Muslim community back to its authentic practice.

But on the sacred fast day of Ashura the Caliph's troops surrounded Husayn's little band on the plain of Karbala. All were slaughtered. Husayn was the last to die, with his infant son in his arms.

For Shia Muslims Najaf is holy because the story of Ali and Husayn has become enshrined there. As Moqtada al-Sadr declares that the Mahdi, the Shiite Messiah, the last Imam, is about to arrive, he and his messianic army have taken their script from that old story. Their defeat will mean not the end but a confirmation of this tragic tale.

The crucible 2005

There won't be any neon signs with the flashing words "No Gays Need Apply," no Gay Buster sign across the Beechmont Avenue threshold, but according to advance notices from Rome, the Vatican's righteous sword will be swift and telling.

In response to the enormous priest scandal, along with its devastating financial effects, the Vatican not only will issue a paper on Priests and Seminaries but also has appointed official inspectors to ensure that there will be no gays in the formation ranks.

Despite the hope of many to return to the innocent patter of Fr. O'Malley, to a time when things were clear and distinct, in black and white, collar and cassock, this heavy-handed approach will not solve what is eating at the heart of seminaries.

Fear and loneliness have haunted the corridors long before Vatican II. Edwin O'Connor in his novel *The Edge of Sadness* decades ago detailed the sad, slow descent of an idealistic young man into emotional solitary confinement and alcoholism. Henri Nouwen over thirty years ago did not mince words over the depression in pre- and post-Vatican II seminaries.

The question lingers: How to provide the structure for those who would serve God's People? Young, and now not so young, students need a fighting chance of finding the best ways of selfless service. But no giving of self comes without trust. And trust is not guaranteed by fiat or containment policies. It begins when students learn to live through shattered ideals and grow up able to sense the awesome complexity of our life together.

A deeper magic? 2006

Within the last month there has been another British invasion. Not Redcoats, nor a Beatles' reprise. No, it's kids' stuff. Or, so we think.

Harry Potter returns for another installment, while Aslan and the land of Narnia finally leap from C. S. Lewis' book to the screen.

Again and again advertisements and reviews speak of "magic returning." It is curious that the various Christian coalitions, formerly so up in arms over the magical properties of J. K. Rowling's books, never blink at the enchantment of *The Lion, the Witch and the Wardrobe.*

Evidently there is some magic that is religiously correct — especially when witches meet their maker.

But all this bother about magic spins me about. These films are not simply children's fare. Adults flock to them. For some the films bring back childhood feelings. For others the screen's magic once more works its spell. And it is a strong bewitchment. It has kept us in thrall since the earliest days of motion pictures.

Film has become the American bible. We find our visions and revisions, our hopes and fears, our cues and exits, on celluloid.

We live vicariously through celebrities. We ingest the scripts for our lives along with buttered popcorn.

But there is a deeper magic at play. Or, more precisely, a sense that there is no magic in our lives. Particularly at the end of this most exhausting year, when there seems to be no end to the beating we are receiving. Nature and politics, winds from the sea and the beltway, have taken a severe toll.

As things fall apart we cast about for some way to make a connection, to give some sense to what appears to be relentless horrors and hazards. We wonder if there is, as Tolkien would put it, "some inner consistency to reality."

Most of the time, we settle for some virtual reality to keep ourselves anaesthetized.

But there are moments when the spell is broken, when we can see through the fog of war, cut through the mist of fear. There are those unexpected and fragile moments when we detect the generous power of the human heart.

Out of the theological closet 2006

Limbo has come out of the theological closet. Recently a papal advisory panel, trying to tidy up some theological loose ends, has recommended jettisoning the whole idea of limbo.

Although many associate the term with a sprightly West Indian dance, and others recall the literary escapades of Dante and Milton, few people realize that the notion of limbo arose from the lingering sense that something was rotten in the system.

For Medieval Europe Christendom was the world. Baptism was the ticket for the greatest show on or off the earth. In this universe the long arm of the law reached into eternity. What you did here was accounted for in the eternal regions. Everything fit neatly in the universal scheme of things, except for that nagging issue of innocence. What happens to infants who die without baptism, or those noble pagans who never had a chance of enlisting?

Thomas Aquinas tried to plug what appeared to be the black hole in the universe of justice. He imagined a borderland, a legal fiction on the very edge of hell. He doctored up Augustine's black and white tale of two cities with unexpected shades of gray.

The good news: your lost child is not suffering in hell; the bad, your child has no enjoyment of God.

When parents hear this bottom line, they smell not just the sulfur of hell. They detect the distinctive stench of an institutional cover-up. For the theological spin-doctor avoided the deeper issue—whether such an arrangement, built upon the traditional assumptions of justice, adequately meets the complexity of death and life.

Limbo was a testament to empire building even in the afterlife, despite the fact that the apostle Paul saw the God of Jesus as ending systems of boundary construction, legal exclusiveness and self-importance. Indeed, what happens to those ironclad certainties when God joins the enemy, links up with the losers, the condemned, the socially outcast and cursed?

What happens to any success story that tries to tidy up reality, to reduce the mess, to keep the dread of loss and the hope for belonging at arms' length?

So now the whole pre-emptive house of cards falls. I suspect there was no way around facing that annoying memory of Jesus who long ago told his frowning followers to lighten up and let those messy kids in.

▌A Superbowl prayer   2006

Ladies and Gentlemen,
  Moms and Dads,
    Sons and Daughters;
  all those in the stadium
  and all those watching around the world,
  in pubs and at tailgates,
  at parties and online,
    in hospitals and in Baghdad bunkers,
  let us raise our eyes
  to the end zone screen
    and watch
        as cameras in the Superbowl blimp
        catch the vapor trails of NORAD angels
            patrolling our skies,

keeping us safe and secure
so that we may avert our gaze
from all that troubles us
or causes us to doubt anything
and consign any civil disturbances to oblivion.
Let it not be as it was
in Sumer,
in Babylon,
or in Rome.
Let it not be thus with us—
an Empire whose time has come
proclaiming Bud and Tostitos
with Liberty for all
around the world.
So let us gird up our loins,
by pre-emptying our bladders,
icing our beer,
and stocking our snack trays,
so that we might be ready
upon our couches,
or beside our barbeques.
to enjoy our commercial antiphons,
revel in their special effects
and resolve to wear out our plastic
to keep our economy bullish.
Let our half-time show provide wisdom
teaching our young
that irrational exuberance can be co-opted
by seven figure contracts;
encouraging our middle aged
that they may still be enhanced
to continue to get satisfaction;
reminding our elderly
that this is what they worked for all their lives.
Let us see what it means
to know our place
on the sidelines
or on the couch,

whether in halter tops and pompoms
or holding mics
or munching popcorn.
Oh yes, let us learn
how the few, the proud and the strong
those with influence and money
or a cousin on the team
can get to join the heavenly chorus of fans
robed in yellow, black and blue.
Above all, yes, above all,
let us replay the face of our warrior god,
again and again,
arising from the pileup
from the testosterone spaghetti of arms and legs
So that we may know what our virtual life is all about,
as we stay tuned to
"The Greatest Show on Earth,"
where the beatific vision
comes in HDTV.
Amen.

A matter of fiction 2006

It's coming! The international best seller *The Da Vinci Code* arrives this week transmuted to a screen near you. Right before your eyes you'll detect a secret kept hidden for centuries. Indeed, if you believe the hyperbolic movie trailer, "the course of history will be changed forever."

Tom Hanks will help us all break out of our religious braces while wooing a comely French cryptologist in a breathless race to Truth.

Everything seems to be falling out as planned. Even the Vatican has provided the best publicity by urging the faithful to forego this film. Opus Dei has set up a website fortress to counter the novel's offensive version of that religious group. Conservative Christian authors have launched an armada of volumes against this pulp fiction. The producers could not have gotten any better press. Nothing sells better than the forbidden.

But what exactly makes this novel so fascinating? Why does this quick paced murder mystery, a transparent first draft of a movie script, with characterization that never gets beyond the stereotype, nevertheless captivate millions of readers?

It is not so much the book but the questions the book raises that have sustained the novel's remarkable success. Has the church perpetuated a cover-up? Were Magdalene and Jesus an item? Does the royal bloodline of Jesus and Mary continue to this day? Has the heretical camel finally gotten more than a nose under the ecclesial tent, undermining the entire fabric of faith?

What is actually at stake is not this drawn out romantic fiction. Critical scholarship sometime ago has dissolved this monarchical fairy tale.

But what is truly unsettling is this: for many readers it is the first time they have ever imagined that the master story of the origin of Christianity might itself be a fiction. Of course, *The Da Vinci Code* opens up this possibility by planting another master myth.

The Da Vinci Code, however, can provide an occasion for a deeper and more complex discussion. It has become evident that religious questions are no longer confined to theologically gated communities. For over three centuries biblical scholarship has made the case that the Christian tradition had no simple origin. Indeed, with the publication of the Gospels of Thomas, Mary, Peter, and, most recently, Judas, the public is beginning to realize that Christianity was a variety of responses to the vision and fate of Joshua, the son of Miriam.

In fact, we can say that the historical Jesus, that Jewish artisan, has leaked out, no longer the private property of the churches.

If we would get to the heart of things, we shall have to face the fact that the origins of the Jesus tradition are murky and meager.

In the midst of the extant fragments we shall come upon a politically charged murder story—a peasant liquidated by an Empire. We shall also detect a vision of a God, offering benefits indiscriminately to bad and good, just and unjust. We shall see how Jesus' followers had to make things up as they continued to live in that vision. And we shall note how inevitably people began to fall back into the default patterns of domination and how women, so briefly taken seriously, were cast once again as second class humans.

Do we have the courage and desire to become such critical searchers or shall we settle once more for a virtual reality?

Seeing things

For the last few weeks I've been seeing things. Sort of a double vision. My friends and colleagues would be amused, but not surprised, since I'm usually dangling at least a leg in the murky pool of the past.

It started with a poem by Seamus Heaney. In a collection of poems entitled *Squarings*, named after the various ways a boy sizes up how to shoot a marble, there is an extraordinary piece. It retells the tale of some ancient Irish monks. While they were at prayer a ship appeared to them in the air. Its anchor caught on the altar rail, and a crewman climbed down a rope to try to free the ship. But his struggles were to no avail. Then the abbot spoke, "This man can't bear our life here and will drown, unless we help him." With the monks' assistance the ship resumed its course, as the man—in Heaney's words—"climbed back out of the marvelous as he had known it."

Such a vision left me topsy-turvy. How was it that the man from the flying ship could not bear the life on earth, indeed, was leaving the marvelous?

Then I met the Canadian astronaut Dr. Steve MacLean, a crew member of the Atlantis Shuttle Mission. He had mentioned in his lecture a most incredible sight. Later I asked him privately to tell me again what he had seen. He spoke of one of his extravehicular activities. From the shuttle the largest object is the looming earth. Now, when the shuttle flies over the Pacific or, to convey the sense from space, under it, at night, things get very, very black. But if you look up, over the horizon of the earth, you can see golden particles of light. This is space dust, primordial debris from the initial explosions and collisions of our universe. As your eyes focus, you begin to see that it is like a giant river of light, flowing directly to and around you, tethered to the shuttle. For him it was a moment of wonder; as a scientist he recognized his ancestors. He was surrounded by this light, which caught the reflection of the coming sun. We both recalled the lyric from a song, "We are stardust; we are golden."

Now you have both sides of my stereopticon, my magic lantern. An astronaut brought a vision back to earth. A poet tethers briefly a vision in the air. MacLean has seen what very few have had the opportunity to witness; and fewer still to sense the pregnant enormity of dust particles. Heaney has mucked about in long forgotten legends to catch a glimpse of what it means to live on Spaceship Earth.

Past and future bounce about my brain. Synapses fire, lifting off into unknown trajectories. At a time when our nation careens from calamity into catastrophe, when there is not a glimmer at the end of the tunnel, I found hope in unexpected places.

Whether by words or rocket fuel we hover over our lives. Each one of us can do it—if only in our dreams. Each one of us can catch a glint from that blue marble as it revolves with everything so dear.

What's in the box?   2007

He's back! The self-proclaimed "king of the world" James Cameron has made another titanic splash. But this time we don't even have to go to the theatre.

This Sunday night the Discovery Channel will air a documentary on tales from a crypt. The buzz is that the "lost tomb" of Jesus has been found. Since the bone boxes, known as ossuaries, found twenty-seven years ago in Jerusalem, are inscribed with what appears to be "Yeshua bar Yosef," "Maria," and "Mariamene," Cameron has gone out on the proverbial limb to contend that this cluster of burial boxes quite likely held not only the bones of Jesus and his mother, but also those of Mary Magdala, presumably Jesus' wife—and Judah, the son of Jesus.

Already conservative scholars and pastors are mounting a counter offensive. There will be a rebuttal, thousands of calls and emails will see to it.

Meanwhile, out of Africa the story of the Anglican death spiral has been headline news for days. Nigerian Bishop Peter Akinola has been throwing his ecclesiastical weight around, reducing the Archbishop of Canterbury to the mumbling prospect of a church where some believers are more equal than others. For quite some time the Anglican Communion has been performing a theological high-wire act, allowing various perspectives to worship side by side. But, with the shunning of Bishop Katherine Jefferts Schori, the elected leader of the American Episcopal Church, a dramatic turn has been made. Biblical literalism at the service of an undaunted self-righteousness has returned. The Roundheads are about to strike the field again. How many heads will fall this time?

Many people hearing these stories will simply file them under religious madness. Who cares if the bone box of Jesus shows up? Why would anyone worry about trying to hold a group so diverse together? Why waste all that energy? Don't we have enough problems with the quagmire in Iraq and our tenuous society at home?

Like it or not, both stories have to do with memory. The memory of Jesus has infiltrated our culture, our world. Cameron's production will jolt what has been long sedimented in the minds of many Americans. Meanwhile, Bishop Akinola makes a blistering defense against the inroads of the Enlightenment. How can tradition stay tradition in this whirlwind of modernity?

Indeed, there is a problem with keeping our memories of Jesus airtight.

Consider what seems to be a simple scene. People are bringing their children to Jesus so he can touch them. But the disciples scold the adults. Jesus then reminds his followers that God's empire is populated with such.

Most of us glow in the nostalgia of the story. But there was no smiley face on Jesus' tunic. The disciples acted appropriately for the period. Children, until their reached their legal majority, were not considered fully human. Moreover, since you never knew where they had been they would have been considered impure.

Nevertheless Jesus would associate with those dirty nobodies. When I consider those in whose presence my skin would crawl today and imagine Jesus touching them, I shudder.

Unlike an ossuary or a political pose, this memory—when you turn it over—is a jack-in-the-box!

▌ Sweet Jesus! 2007

It seems to be a Catholic thing. Whether the medium is animal dung or Cadbury chocolate some Catholics take great umbrage at how their sacred icons are constructed. If this were a matter of the moon and stars of Proctor and Gamble, the parties involved would end up in court. But there was no need for legal action when the latest artistic brouhaha hit New York New York.

A midtown Manhattan gallery was about to exhibit during Holy Week an anatomically correct, nude, crucified Jesus, made from over 200 pounds of milk chocolate. The artist, Cosimo

Cavallaro, is somewhat notorious for his fascination with food. He once covered a room of a New York hotel in melted mozzarella cheese, sprayed five tons of pepper jack cheese on a Wyoming home, and festooned a four-poster bed with 312 pounds of processed ham.

But his latest edible endeavor never made it out of the refrigerator. The show entitled "My Sweet Lord" was cancelled even before it began. A flurry of emails, phone calls, and statements from outraged Catholics had their effect. Cardinal Edward Egan considered this "a sickening display," while Bill Donohue, the pit bull president of the Catholic League, declared it to be "one of the worst assaults on Christian sensibilities ever."

New York, for the time being, has been saved from the junk food Jesus. But it was not the prospect of those 480,000 calories, or 32,000 grams of fat (enough to insulate you for over a year) that occasioned such dignified wrath.

No. It has to do with the body of Christ. The image of the crucified Jesus is embedded deep in the psyches of Christians. It has become an unspoken metaphor of their identity and belief. Moreover, the Catholic tradition has been built on and encouraged the use of images and rituals to express the depths of this faith tradition. So it is no wonder that Catholics would have a neuralgic reaction to this exhibition.

But it was a reaction; not an intelligent response.

Our society has been trigger happy for some time. Whenever something odd or uncomfortable confronts us, we tend to react with cries of outrage. Even to chocolate figures.

Some Catholics were up in arms over the frivolity of the piece. Is Jesus just some chocolate bunny? Many more could not take their eyes off the totally nude Jesus. How dare that artist remind us of Jesus' sex?

There is an old proverb: "The devil can never take a joke." When it comes to matters of religion in America it seems that we are possessed by many demons.

And we also have lost our sense of history. We have forgotten what crucifixion meant in the ancient world. Jesus was liquidated by the state. He was tortured, humiliated, condemned. There were no loin cloths, no Mel Gibson outtakes. No one thought of turning a crucified image into a silver neckpiece.

Can Christians today come close to an image of the crucified? Shall they settle, instead, for their own religious confections?

Would anyone dare gaze at the outstretched arms of that hooded prisoner in Abu Ghraib?

A terrible irony 2002

There is a terrible irony before our eyes this Good Friday. Christians around the world are still haunted by the final agonizing image of Jesus of Nazareth. But this year American Catholics are having a hard time focusing on that ancient memory.

Daily news stories uncover layer upon layer of clerical betrayal and episcopal cover-up. Reluctant diocese after diocese surrenders to legal authorities names of those who have abused the trust of the innocent. What many thought was being adroitly kept at bay through carefully crafted policy statements has broken through in ghastly headlines. The more that comes out the worse it gets.

Some have decried all this publicity as another example of the media's anti-Catholicism. The Protestant prejudice of the nineteenth century is rehearsed—the Know Nothings are brought to life again as the Ursuline convent in Boston burns away in bitter memory. But not even conservative Catholics are buying that spin.

Then there are the talking heads. They tutor us in what we already know: that child molesters can be found anywhere; that celibacy does not necessarily lead to pedophilia; that church reform may not address the immediate problem.

In the midst of this deflection we do learn some telling historical tidbits. A second century letter, disguised as advice of Paul to Timothy, declares how you could tell whether a bishop is genuine: is he able to keep his children in check? Don't choose anyone, moreover, for the overseer's position if he has more than one wife. Evidently the question of control was around almost from the start. Then there's that medieval nugget: celibacy was made a church discipline to keep priests from deeding church property to their children. Centuries of subsequent spiritual havoc have attempted to buttress that calculated policy.

What is clear is that the laity are light years beyond "being scandalized." Adamant Knights of Columbus, disaffected liberals, and even alienated church alums agree in their outrage at the incompetence of church leaders and the lack of personal accountability. They sadly see that honesty has not been an organizational trait.

But something else has been dislodged. Impromptu meetings throughout the US have revealed not just the seething anger of the people. It is as if there has been some sort of time warp and Vatican II was still fresh with the hopeful voice of that fat, Italian peasant; for speaker after speaker in these listening sessions easily distinguished the Church as the community of the people from the self-absorbed governing structure.

The situation goes far beyond the Sunday collection plate. The threat to the economic viability of an archdiocese is no longer the bottom line. From bingo halls to late night TV the unimaginable is heard. Calls for accountability are spelled out: princes of the church should act like men and, if warranted, should resign. Yet even an Episcopal resignation or two will not stop the waves of revulsion.

Many ask aloud how could such an institution attract and even foster such inadequate candidates. Could it be that the very flaws of the organized structure draw them?

This goes to what many in the church have long feared would come to light. There is no "mystery of evil" here, as the Pope would label it. The people's eyes are open. They see what is tawdry and quite familiar. It is the dysfunctional situation of the abuse of power, where humiliation, emasculation, and silence are the rules of the game. This is the institution's original sin.

Yet there is more here. Today we remember a subversive scene. The image of Jesus comes down through time neither in sacerdotal splendor nor with the benefit of sanctuary.

This sad occasion may well provide us with a clue as to where Jesus left a lasting mark. There is no more time to waste with those unending power plays where only boys can meet the predetermined gender requirement. Rather it is time to cast our eyes upon a truly revolting image. The death of Jesus exposed what the Roman system would bring home to anyone uttering a dissident word. He died humiliated, helpless, and reduced to silence. He died in solidarity with the untold victims of coercive power.

Biblical literacy: The art of going to hell

2006

Most Americans prefer their religion straight up. We'd fly Southwest Airlines to heaven rather than get tangled up in the main-line mumble jumble, those theological ticket games. Isn't that what's happening with the Episcopalians and Presbyterians? Why bother with what scholars produce? Conservative Catholics and Baptists appreciate a bottom line approach. Whether it's the Pope or the Bible, we know that God sounds a lot like Harry Truman.

But things don't always stay that simple. We don't even have to sit in a pew to find this out. Whether on canvas or on a page, artists have made our life more complicated. In fact, America has been plagued by writers who often throw a monkey wrench into the religion machine.

In the Post Bellum era Mark Twain lobbed a grenade through the proper window of piety with *The Adventures of Huckleberry Finn*. Even today there is still residual uproar over its un-PC use of the N-word. But that is not what makes Twain religiously dangerous.

Twain brought Huckleberry to a critical point. Was Huckleberry ready to be good, renounce his wild ways, and turn the runaway slave Jim in to his owners? For Huck this was not a simple decision. It became an everlasting matter. "Doing the right thing," "the clean thing," meant writing to Jim's owner and telling him where his slave was.

But this good, clean feeling did not last. For Huck got to thinking. He remembered his experience on the river with Jim, with a friend who cared for him. And Huck realized he was the only one Jim had left to count on. So, he tore up the letter and uttered, "All right, then, I'll go to hell."

With those words the dam of American religious tradition broke. The experience of genuine relationship rewrote the way we look at being religious. The secular adventure of a vagrant boy would trouble us all the way to Selma and Memphis.

Even today this subversive re-reading of religion continues. John Updike's *The Terrorist* follows in the footsteps of those who would imagine the mind of the alienated. Updike pushes our religious imagination into the world and hopes of Islam through the eighteen-year-old Ahmad Ashmawy Mulloy.

This son of an Irish-American mother and an Egyptian father, who disappears when he was three, pursues the purity of
divine transcendence. His adoption of Islam at eleven, his repulsion at American materialism, hedonism and consumerism,
and his growing desire to give his young life meaning, lead him
eventually into becoming the driver of a nitrate-filled truck, des-
tined to blow up the Lincoln Tunnel.

In fact, during the final ride to the Tunnel, Ahmad and Jack
Levy, his former high school counselor, engage in a desperate
conversation that brings Ahmad right back to the Qur'an. At the
critical moment Ahmad, reacting to Levy's death wish, makes
a breakthrough by rethinking the sacred text. He realizes that
God does not side with all those who would seek death. "God
does not want to destroy: it was He who made the world." This
insight comes against and over his romantic literalism of the
Quran. Because a faithless, Jewish sixty-year-old, depressed and
thinking his own life of little note, nevertheless sticks by him,
Ahmad can see the world differently, even if the "devils have
taken away" his cherished God.

Updike, like Twain, refuses to let Americans off easily. He
will not let us use 9/11 as an excuse to configure templates of
prejudice. Instead, he reminds us that experience and relationship carve new avenues of insight, especially where we would
only turn away from the useless, the lost, and the alienated.
Updike also signals how a sacred text can be revisited. Through
his fiction he breaks up the precious certainty of the literal imagination. He does not do this with a scholarly dissertation but
through richness and depth of character. Ahmad finally intuits
what critical readers of sacred texts eventually discover: that we
are as complex as the books we read.

Both Updike and Twain would bid us to go to hell and find
there what we thought impossible with other people.

▌A declaration of independence   2007

▌ Out of Africa the story of the Anglican death spiral has
made headline news. Nigerian Bishop Peter Akinola has thrown
his ecclesiastical weight around, reducing the Archbishop of
Canterbury to mumbling about the prospect of a church where
some believers are more equal than others.

For quite some time the Anglican Communion has been performing a theological high-wire act, allowing various perspectives to worship side by side. But, with the shunning of Bishop Katherine Jefferts Schori, the elected leader of the American Episcopal Church, a dramatic turn was made. Biblical literalism at the service of an undaunted self-righteousness has returned in earnest. Are the Roundheads about to strike the field again? How many heads will fall this time?

Perhaps these images are a bit strong. But I must confess that I have become involved in this debate—albeit from the sidelines. The last three Jesus Seminars on the Road I have given have been at Episcopal communities. In Philadelphia, Kansas City, and Washington DC, I have experienced thriving and socially committed communities. Their challenging conversation during each session proved that intelligence and genuine trust were not unrelated. Yet, there was an undeniable downbeat throughout each Seminar. The specter of an international schism haunted our time together.

This ecclesial matter has become personal. Many good people of whom I have become fond nudge me to ask: what can I contribute from my competence to this dismaying situation? What can a critical scholarly perspective bring? What has been learned of the early Jesus traditions that might throw light on this discussion? Can we, in fact, learn something from the history of our ancestors?

"Suffered under Pontius Pilate" is more than a creedal catch-phrase. That Jesus was executed by the state was voted red by the Seminar. Indeed, Jesus' Roman liquidation is confirmed by extra-biblical evidence. We also know that within a few years of his death some followers of Jesus attempted to make sense of this public humiliation. His death was not shunned but reconstructed along heroic lines. He died like the Jewish heroes of old. Paul later would see in his death the surprising solidarity of the God of Israel with the nobodies of the world. The Gospels of Peter and Mark recast his death story upon the Jewish template of the tale of the suffering and persecuted one. Matthew, Luke and John continued this creative tradition.

But all of this tradition tempts us to steer clear of the original datum. Roman crucifixion was not for anyone. Slaves and those who raised a sandal against the Empire received this fate. Such a death was meant to send a signal to all who would undermine Rome's authority.

As a miniscule blip on history's screen, the death of Jesus was indeed revelatory. It exposed the Empire's dirty secret: Rome's domination was maintained through violence. The elite, who mentioned crucifixion only in euphemisms, held onto their divine status at the expense of tortured human life. The condemned were humiliated in a variety of ways—flogging and mockery were merely amusing interludes. They were to be liquidated, rubbed out of human memory. Lime pits would devour what was left after dogs and birds had a bloody feast. To stand against imperial Rome meant nothing less than annihilation.

It is this brute fact of history that it usually overlooked when Christians invoke their mythic memories. Because Christians have often served the advances of imperial designs, we forget that Jesus died at the hands of a colonial power.

Now is the moment for the American Episcopal Church to declare their independence from the colonialism that runs through ecclesial veins. It is not simply a matter for committees to work their backroom magic. This is not just an accommodating moment. It is, rather, a moment of revelation. The Archbishop of Canterbury has already been outflanked by a bishop who has learned well the lessons of colonization on how to achieve mastery. There is, moreover, a great temptation to return the threat in kind. But that will only perpetuate the cycle of ecclesial reprisal.

It is time for all sides to consider the human cost, to see how the behavior of dominance is at play, to discern how Empire is still at work in creedal guise. How long will Christians maintain their righteousness at the expense of others? Who will dare look up and see that their cross is still flying an imperialist flag?

▌Aftershock 2011

"One damn thing after another," I often hear in conversation these days. Such a cliché seems to be an apt description of life throughout the world. Recession, bankruptcies, revolution, counter-revolution, earthquake, tsunami; all run starkly across the tickertape of our televisions. It's enough to get out the Book of Revelation and start tweeting that the "End Time" is near. Yet, even that frantic reaction has been tried again and again since the first millennium without much result, except for the financial gains of those who construct flowcharts and game plans for the Final Days.

Mainline Christian denominations have usually tried to fly their apologetic hovercrafts over such "contingencies." They have been content within their apostolic command posts to observe, comment, disapprove, and warn, but they have stayed aloof from "the thousand natural shocks that flesh is heir to" (*Hamlet* 3,1). But two World Wars, the Holocaust, and the suicidal competition of the Cold War have taken their toll. The architectural synthesis of the Medieval mind long ago fell into "bare ruined choirs," while the rational wager of modern theological systems, like their financial siblings, has come up bust.

Yet, because of, not despite, these tremors, some things have opened up. The aftershocks of war and Holocaust caused scholars to reimagine their traditions. It became clear amid the debris of the twentieth century's disasters that the Jewish tradition was not simply a lead-in to the Christian success story. In fact, the experience of shock actually threw light on what they were investigating. Christian scholars began reminding their churches that the God of Israel was a disturbing God who remembered slaves, those nameless ones who would have disappeared into the sands of history. Indeed, the prophet Amos could not get over the shock of that image and upset the wealthy, gathered at worship sites to insure their fortune. That non-professional prophet was cheeky enough to declare that genuine worship was tied in with justice to widows and orphans, to those overlooked by the insouciant rich. Moreover, we find among the stories of Jesus a continuation of this distressing trend. Unfortunately, his uncomfortable tale of "a man who journeys from Jerusalem" (as preserved in Luke 10:30–35) has been cushioned by Luke's reframing and by centuries of "nice guy" interpretations (see the context Luke created for Jesus' parable in Luke 10:25–29 and 36–37). But, if you imagine the tale as that of a man who falls into the hands of his enemy and comes out the better for it, then your world is in for a staggering moment.

Even Paul, that wild-eyed apocalyptic Jew, got his comeuppance. We cannot use the second-century recasting of Paul's story in the Acts of the Apostles to imagine what really happened to him. In fact, using Paul's own words (Galatians 1:13–

16) is difficult enough. Paul tells us that he had a breakthrough insight, a paradigm shift, not simply in understanding Jesus, but more so in recognizing God. The shamed, executed criminal Jesus, who should have no ties to the pure God of Israel, Paul now sees as accepted by this God. Such an action disclosed that Paul never guessed where God could be—right in the very mess of human disaster and abandonment! I have often wondered if Paul's words in 1 Corinthians 14:24–25 reflect his own experience. Did he enter a meeting of the people he was harassing and find "the secrets of his heart exposed"? And did he then conclude "God is really present"? I have no way of proving this. But it is suggestive. For Paul may have finally found that his deepest hopes came alive in places he never imagined.

In short, biblical scholarship, particularly since the aftermath of World War II, has provided us with a dismantling of the monotony of tradition. No longer, then, do the traditions unearthed cushion the blows of our lives. Instead, they give us strategies of transformation. They do not absorb, keep at bay or demystify the shockwave; rather, they encourage us to ride it into a deeper dimension of experience.

But will we continue on this tradition of discovery in the midst of terror and upheaval? Will we have the heart for it? I am reminded of a wonderful twist from an earlier shock to the world, that of the slave revolution in Haiti (See *Hegel, Haiti, and Universal History*, by Susan Buck-Morss (Pittsburgh University Press, 2009). The unthinkable happened there. For the savants of the Enlightenment what was culturally impossible came true. Among "wild, uneducated barbarians," who had "yet to undergo the process of education," the dream of freedom took hold. In fact, when French soldiers, sent by Napoleon to put down the rebellion, approached the army of self-liberated slaves, they heard a murmur coming from the black crowd. Could it be some sort of tribal chant? As they got closer they heard a song that had been banned by Napoleon, a rallying cry that once galvanized the French Revolution—they heard the Haitians in full throat singing the Marseillaise. The French soldiers stopped. They wondered out loud which side they were on, for they found those on the other side reminding them of the very reason for their existence.

As someone once advised, those who have ears to hear, listen . . .

Under a violent arc 2013

A remarkable interview happened last summer. Reza Aslan thought he would be discussing the merits of his new book on Jesus. But the Fox interviewer, showing no interest in history or Aslan's credentials, never stopped asking why a Muslim would have any interest in Jesus. The interview, quickly dubbed as the "dumbest interview ever,"* went viral on the Internet and helped turn a scholarly study into a best seller.

Reputation is not the final arbiter of scholarship. Fifteen-second sound-bites are no substitute for genuine thought. Honoring a scholar's work entails critically examining the claims, inspecting the evidence presented, and detecting any unspoken frames and assumptions.

Zealot, The Life and Times of Jesus of Nazareth strategically begins with the savage assassination of the high priest Jonathan only a few years before the Jewish revolt. From the outset of the book Aslan frames his case for Jesus under the overarching narrative of a revolutionary "era marked by the slow burn of a revolt against Rome." Despite acknowledging that Jesus was not a member of the Zealot party (which would not exist until thirty years after his death), Aslan contends that Jesus grew up in the aftermath of Rome's traumatic suppression of the revolt of Judas the Galilean in 4 BCE, took his initial lead from the radical voice of John the Baptizer, and zealously led a failed nationalistic revolutionary movement.

Aslan's contention that this perspective on the historical Jesus can be unearthed from subsequent attempts of the later Jesus traditions to cover up both the failure and the apocalyptic project of the man who would be Messiah is not new. Samuel Reimarus led the charge in the eighteenth century, while at the beginning of the twentieth century, Albert Schweitzer argued for Jesus' apocalyptic debacle. More recently, Bart Ehrman produced a Schweitzer-lite reprise. By situating the story of Jesus within the frame of the Jewish rebellion against Rome, Aslan graphically throws the reader into what he sees as Israel's bloody saga.

Aslan's Jesus is a predictable pastiche. He accepts the "cleansing of the Temple" as fact; then he moves quickly to Jesus' association with the Baptizer, then on to a brief messianic career. While he notes the existence of Q as well as the various other gospels, there is little indication of a consistent use of critical criteria to determine whether a saying or an act of Jesus might be historical. He picks and chooses evidence to fit his profile of Jesus. Aslan, for example, reads the story of "A man going down from Jerusalem" as an example story (thereby uncritically accepting Luke's redaction of the parable) of loving one's neighbor and a scolding of the Temple authorities. But the bite of the parable is lost; Aslan does not see the story's challenge to tribal thinking, in which one falls into the hands of the enemy and comes out the better for it.

The canny speech of Jesus falls on deaf ears. There is no sense that Jesus provoked his listeners, even toyed with how God's empire could be imagined. Instead, Aslan's Jesus "merely reiterates what the zealots have been preaching for years" (118), looking forward to a reality in which "God's wrath rains down" on the rich and powerful. Because Jesus was a Jew, his God was "the same God whom the Bible calls 'a man of war' (Exodus 15:3), the slaughtering god, the blood-splattered God (Psalm 68:21–23)." "That," Aslan contends, "is the only God that Jesus knew and the sole God he worshipped" (122).

An ancient proverb advises: *to a hammer everything is a nail.* Aslan has nailed the evidence for the historical Jesus by pinning difficult fragments to a tailored outline. But where is the shrewd peasant offering his listeners an unexpected vision of God's presence? What of the healings and table-fellowship that were inextricably tied up with that surprising vision? Was it really all about the would-be messiah? What about the people discovering the atmosphere of God in their lives?

Tellingly Aslan never mentions Jesus' saying about a God who delivers benefits unconditionally, not in the future, but in the present (Matthew 5:45). Such a God was embedded in the complexity, and wisdom of human life—not a hoped-for, purifying avenger. Perhaps that is because, for Aslan, the God of Jesus had never left Babylon. The God ascribed to Jesus is actually the well-known warlord, who eviscerated his mother Tiamat, insuring cosmic order and justice through controlled violence. The decision to frame the story of Jesus within the seething cauldron of the Jewish War takes on a deeper perspective. The God Aslan discloses still survives through the centuries: there is no other god but Marduk.

---

*www.youtube.com/watch?v=Jt1cOnNrY5s

Donut theology

Recently I was invited by a small religious community to talk on the non-canonical gospels. As we sipped coffee and munched on donuts around the kitchen table, their opening questions were less about the various gospels than over some more fundamental questions such as: How did it happen that some texts were selected and others consigned to oblivion? Who determined what was important? Why weren't we taught about all this?

Before I answered their questions, I held up one of the donuts on the table. I asked them to consider what was missing in this donut. After a few seconds of bemused silence, one woman said, "Do you mean the hole?"

Precisely. To answer their questions it was important to realize both what was before us and what was missing, what was said and what was unspoken. Simple pious clichés, such as "it's God's will" or "the church has always taught this" cannot satisfactorily answer those exacting questions.

So I returned to the donut. Much of who we are was shaped long ago. We have inherited not just the "flotsam and jetsam of history" but also the very ways in which we view that history. Our understanding of what is essential has been fashioned greatly by decisions we usually never imagine. I asked them to consider something that was hovering in the background of many of their questions. Take a look at how the Nicene Creed cast a particular light on Christian traditions. "The Nicene formula is very much like this donut," I offered. Puzzled stares. They had asked why some things have been overlooked or neglected by the church. What were those decisions that had long-range effects? And what does all this have to do with donuts?

The Nicene formula was not a simple statement of the faith of the church. A council, called by an unbaptized emperor, attempted to resolve the Arian controversy and, in so doing, unify an unwieldy empire. Having recognized Christianity as a legal religion, Constantine was now using its very episcopal structure to help solidify his reign.

But the Nicene formula was more than a loyalty oath. Its very language discloses not simply the Greek penchant for abstraction but, even more, a fascination with power. God is the "all powerful Father, the maker of all." Jesus is properly entitled as "Lord, Son of God," anointed with the finest pedigree: "the only-begotten begotten from the Father, God from God, light from light, true God from true God." Indeed all that the Father made was done "through him." It is only after such an exalted status report that we hear how Jesus entered the human scene: "he came down and became incarnate, became human, suffered and rose up on the third day, went up into the heavens." For one brief shining moment, there was Camelot. The Holy Spirit is then quickly noted before passing over to the formula's operational intent: to deliver an anathema to all who would deny this divine connection.

If this formula were the only scrap of information we had about early Christianity we could easily detect that the story sounds very much like the other divine visitation stories of the Greco-Roman world. The divine touches down, but only momentarily, the way the emperor passes through a city.

But we do know more. We know that the Nicene formula attempted to resolve how the ambiguous biblical tradition was to be read. Arius, reading the Gospel of Mark, argued that Jesus became God's son at his baptism, while his opponents preferred the pre-existent identity of the Logos in the Gospel of John. The resolution came about through adopting the larger conceptual frame that coincided nicely with the way power was wielded in the fourth century. The divinity of Jesus can be exponentially expanded from his public career to eternity by enfolding the Markan narrative within the larger Johannine frame. Indeed, this re-reading of the gospel of Mark reflected the growing experience of power by the fourth-century church. The church now read its tradition along the establishment's power lines. And so the Johannine image of Jesus appropriating the lesser Markan Jesus mimicked the imperial assimilation of power.

But there was something dramatically missing in this resolution: the words and deeds of the historical Jesus. The formula of "Father, Son, Spirit, and Anathema," circulating like an endless ring, provided a well-constructed litmus test. And, as long as we are content with slipping on this ring of power, we can refrain from those nagging aphorisms and social faux pas in the gospels. As long as we enjoy abstracting ourselves from the mess and muck of time and place, we can continue with the usual power plays.

But what if we notice what is *not* there? What if we detect the donut hole? What happens when we trip over the words and deeds of Jesus? How long can our imaginations remain content to maintain the political status quo when we cross his trip-wire of metaphor? What happens to our theologies when we discover that the historical Jesus was not obsessed with himself? How do we live on this planet when we discern that he risked all by imagining with others how to live in the atmosphere of God?

▌ Chew on this!   2014

▌ Ever since I was young, two scenes in the Gospel of Matthew have bewildered me. The first is that curious coda (Matthew 22:11-14) to the story of the king who gave a wedding feast. After having been rebuffed by the invited guests, the furious king dragoons all sorts of people in from the street. The king then notices that one of those pressed into the feast is not wearing proper attire. Before the poor fellow has a chance to nibble on an hors d'oeuvre, he is tied up and tossed out of the party! I could imagine that man dumped like trash in an alley asking himself, "What was that all about?"

The second scene is the judgment of the sheep and the goats (Matthew 25:31-46). Here the "Human One" accompanied by his messengers, sitting upon a throne, divides all the peoples assembled before him into two groups. One group inherits the "empire prepared from the foundation of the world." The other group is condemned to everlasting punishment. Now the judgment in itself is not terrifying. Even when I was young it made sense to talk in terms of rewards and punishments. But what was confounding was the fact that the rewards and punishments were doled out for actions that neither group was aware of having performed! This struck me as quite unfair, if not arbitrary.

By the time I was doing my graduate studies I realized that the parable of the great feast came to Matthew from one of his sources, the Q Gospel, but that Matthew himself had written the scene about the man lacking proper attire, and then tacked it on to the end of the parable. Matthew had designed this scene as a message to his own community. He was issuing an allegorical warning that they could not rest on their laurels, that simply being a member of that Jesus community was no guarantee. OK, I get that. But the Sheep and Goats scene still reeked of a gratuitous air.

The Gospel of Matthew is very much a Jewish creation. Written for a community that saw itself as the vanguard of Judaism in the aftermath of the Temple's destruction, this Gospel stood as a competitive alternative to the developing Rabbinic movement. Matthew's Jesus is not the new Moses but the embodiment of Wisdom (Matthew 23:34; compare to Luke 11:49), who remains in the heart of the community (Matthew 18:20 and 28:20). Furthermore, this Gospel is saturated with the Jewish sense of justice. And that is why the scene of reward and punishment in chapter 25 appears so unbelievable. A first-century Jew would assume that keeping the covenant would merit a reward, while failing to do so would end in punishment. But in order to keep the covenant one needed to be aware that one was doing so. Otherwise, where is the justice? So, along with the ancient Jew, I continued to be puzzled by what appears to be a capricious selection.

Perhaps this puzzlement is a clue. Such a scene in Matthew is what is known in Judaism as *midrash*. It is a fiction composed out of traditional verses or images. In fact, this scene is a collage of apocalyptic elements. The root of the word *midrash* means to "chew" or "think over." A *midrash* is then something to chew on.

But chewing on this scene still seemed rather unpalatable. Until I went over what the sheep did and the goats did not. Each action in itself was hardly worth mentioning. In fact, some of the actions would get you involved with people of uncertain character. In terms of the first century's notion of honor and shame, these were not the kind of deeds that would get the gods' attention. You were, in a word, *wasting* your time in doing them.

And yet Matthew constructs a future scene that revolves around these unlikely deeds. What was he thinking? Was this scene not a vision held up to his community to chew on? He used their Jewish sense of justice to provoke them to think about something right in front of them. He brought this future vision into their present and asked them to discover *that it was their wasted moments, where they gave themselves away to others, that counted in the long run*. The tension created by this long-range vision was designed to get the community to reflect on their life together. He was asking them to chew on what really mattered in their lives.

But the more I chew on this the more it becomes unsettling. What if I were to test this out? What I cannot do is to take the various actions mentioned and simply form a checklist of what I need to do. People have done this and have given us what the Catholic tradition calls the "Corporal Works of Mercy." But that actually deflates the tension of the scene. If I am operating by a protocol of mercy I am quite aware of what I'm doing. Ironically, I am no longer wasting my time.

If Matthew wanted his community to reflect on the depths of their life together, perhaps the way to go is likewise to consider those moments in my life that I would describe as "wasted." It might take a while, precisely because that which we little value, we hardly remember.

But if we remember, and if we are honest, we discover something priceless. We discover that it is those "throw-away" moments, when we carelessly gave ourselves to others, or when others wasted their time on us, that meant everything. In fact, our very lives often depend on those unsung moments. These are the moments that are not recorded in the annual update or that make the nightly news hour. Because of what is usually valued in our consumer world, we ourselves overlook those very moments that keep the world working. We forget that those moments in which our hearts opened echo forever in the lives we touched.

▌ Filling in the blanks ...   2015

As the Lenten season inevitably revolves Christian memory back to that death in Jerusalem, I am struck once again by the shadow side of that ancient tale. Despite the chapped-lip-service given to history by Bill O'Reilly's *Killing Jesus*, very few Bible readers want to know what really went on. "We know the story and we're sticking to it."

But if you took the time to read the various accounts (from Mark, Matthew, Luke, John, *and* Peter), you would find that the most certain facts are two: Jesus was crucified and that his death was at the hands of Rome. Everything else in the various narratives is up for interpretive grabs. For example, the dramatic scene (first found in Mark) where Jesus prays in the garden is very much a later construction by the Markan community. (Think about it: how did the sleeping disciples know what Jesus said while praying?) In fact, most New Testament scholars point out that Mark portrayed Jesus as a martyr and that the garden scene allows the later community to place their own prayers on Jesus' lips. As with the other gospels, Mark filled in the blanks surrounding the fate of Jesus.

Indeed, the entire structure of the passion narrative (found in each version) existed prior to the time of Jesus. The Tale of the Trial and Vindication of the Innocent One had been in existence since the Jews responded to the shock and awe of the Seleucid (Hellenistic Syrian) overlord, Antiochus Epiphanes IV around 165 BCE. While some Jews (such as the Maccabees and their followers) fought against the occupying Syrian forces, a number of scribes were shattered by the loss of so many innocent people who had remained faithful to the traditions of Israel and were summarily executed. Where was God? How could God not protect those who kept the covenant? The scribes answered with the Tale of the Innocent One who is ultimately vindicated by God despite ordeal, trial, and (sometimes) death. It is within this Jewish fiction format that the gospel writers set the death of Jesus.

But if that is so, then Bill O'Reilly and so many others got it wrong. Instead of treating the gospel versions as eyewitness documents, brimming with facts, one can detect a creative hand at work. Jews would call this *midrash*, a fictional weaving to make sense of things.

This gets us to the shadow side. To choose to tell the story of the death of Jesus along the structural lines of the Tale of the Innocent One meant that some unknown Jewish writer was responding to a disastrous situation and used the literary repertoire at his disposal. Crucifixion in the Roman Empire was in fact the worst fate of all. The true horror story of the ancient world, crucifixion represented the ultimate isolation and liquidation of a person. The naked victim was shamed publicly and any memory was to be erased. Even the remains were usually thrown into a mass grave and dissolved with lye. Upper-class Roman writers would only allude to crucifixion. Those who raised a sandal against the empire were condemned to such a "disappearance."

Christians usually gloss over these historical considerations. Familiarity with the amalgamated story allows one to glide quickly over the nasty parts. We let the momentum of the tale sweep us away from ground zero. What would happen if we stood still for a moment and asked why those early gospel writers (either Peter or Mark) chose such a narrative pattern? The Tale of the Innocent One was invoked by a real trauma, the crucifixion of Jesus of Nazareth. The selection of this Tale meant a radical Jewish response to what would have been seen as a total disaster. Rome had loudly and definitely spoken by torturing this Jew to death. His fate was to be annihilated, not just physically, but erased from human memory.

But his followers would not let him go. The essence of torture is to break a human being, to dominate so that a person is reduced to incoherence and despair. The torturer can taunt, "Cry out as loud as you can, no one can hear you!" Torture works on our deepest and oldest fear: that we are utterly abandoned. Some of the followers of Jesus refused to deny the depths of that trauma. They returned to the cavity of a lost life. They returned to that foul and filthy scene. They returned to fill in the blanks.

The followers' choice of the Tale of the Innocent picked up the echo of the torture chamber. But the story they told refused to reduce the victim to a single cry of despair. Even as they themselves felt the tremors of suffering and death, they remembered the trust out of which Jesus lived, and they continued in that contrary confidence. Their experience gave sorrow words.

The death story of Jesus, then, was not a simple assemblage of facts. Rather the original choice arose from a sense of creative solidarity. The early Jewish followers refused to forget the one who imagined an atmosphere in which the lost of the world could breathe and grow. They told of his death to upend the forces of domination and annihilation that continued to play out in their lives. They told and retold the story as they breathed life into that locus of death. They would not allow abandonment to be the final word.

9

Reports from the Trenches

These commentaries are truly dispatches from the educational front. I usually began with what I've learned from my interactions with students or with the various strategies I've employed in the classroom. While teaching undergraduate and graduate students at Xavier University, I also had the pleasure of teaching classes on the historical Jesus to seventh and eighth graders at Mercy Montessori. The occasion of university commencement has given me the opportunities to reflect on the "firefly moments" of the intellectual adventure. I've hoped again and again to lead students to see what is "not there," to experience the Zen of interpretation.

The subtle path of wisdom 1998

For the last few years I've been involved in an educational experiment, teaching theology, not religion, to seventh and eighth grade students at a private Montessori school.

The very first class began with a Greek fragment. Although the students knew no Greek, once they had the rudiments of the Greek alphabet, they made successive stabs leading them to detect that the fragment came from the first chapter of the Gospel of Matthew.

Over the years I've taken the insights of critical biblical thought into the junior high. We have looked at the question of the historical Jesus. Thirteen- and fourteen-year olds become quite adept at discerning the voiceprint of Jesus of Nazareth as well as nimble readers of the developing Gospel tradition.

We have even composed parables, proverbs, and aphorisms, learning from within the creative juices of Jewish Wisdom. Twice my junior high classes have made impressive presentations before my college students. This year they have embedded their wise sayings in several dramatic pieces. Bound together both in print and on film, their creations have become their own testament, to be handed down to future classes.

Recently the seventh graders met with me about next year. They want to explore the troubling relationship between the Bible and science, to confront the questions of death and life after death, and to face squarely the enigma "why things are so messed up."

At a time when we're obsessed with test scores, levies, and state controls, with documenting the failures of education, it would be well for us to notice those quite neglected by the public frenzy. Could it be that we, the adults, lack the imagination to see that the students can tutor us in the subtle path of Wisdom?

A theological experiment 1998

Over the last eighteen years of teaching scripture it has become clear to me that the real bible of our culture, the text consistently consulted for cues to behavior and insight into life, is film. Despite the protests of televangelists or the worries of mainline churches, people across the nation find their fundamental stories, which provide orientation and identity, in theaters and on VCRs.

Recently a student of mine wrote that her brother, educated in Hebrew school, never bothers with Torah when faced with a life question. Instead, he goes directly to the celluloid poets. In a world where long ago the biblical bubble burst, and the vacuum of space stares coldly on all sides, "Star Wars" speaks volumes to him.

Let's continue that theological lead with *The Truman Show*. Despite superlative reviews, audiences seem uncomfortable with the film. Teenagers are understandably upset that Jim Carry is not himself. Now those who stay with the film sense a deeper tension. Horror grows insistently as we see a human being so manipulated, so deceived. And yet we sit fascinated, hoping that somehow Truman will break through.

I don't want to give the story away to those who haven't seen it. Yet consider: Truman's entire life has been constructed to entertain others living vicariously through him. The director would attempt everything to keep Truman confined to the dome of his artificial world even to the point of risking his death.

Is there not lurking here a God who would sacrifice his son to keep a vast salvation enterprise in business? What are we to make of Truman's defiant cry to that ambivalent God: "Is that all you've got?" And why do we feel as we do when Truman takes his fateful step?

Could it be that this film touches what sacred scripture used to intimate: that terrible and tender surprise of being human?

▌The wrong box 2000

▌Boy, did they ever get the wrong guy. I was sent not one but two Private School Teacher Questionnaires from the U.S. Census. The second came within two weeks and a warning note of the first.

Eight years ago I volunteered to bring the insights and challenges of critical biblical scholarship to teenagers. Occasionally my Montessori students teach one of my classes at the University. My college classes are usually awed by such confident and creative junior high students.

But the forty-nine-page questionnaire was not interested in such wild educational gambits. What they wanted was an X in the appropriate box. Not until page thirty-four were students even mentioned. I first had to classify myself, despite the fact that none of the categories fit. Then came details on teaching certificates, class structures, students' use of computers, organizational policies, and working conditions.

Finally question 55 dealt with students. Has a student ever threatened you? Has a student ever attacked you? Question 60 listed eighteen different student problems, from tardiness to pregnancy, from robbery to apathy. As the questionnaire ended, I was asked to wonder aloud whether I would be a teacher if I could go back to college and start all over again.

Staggering through this slow death march of the mind, I realized that whoever concocted this instrument either had never taught or had had long ago a traumatic classroom experience. Ever see a student's eyes gently shocked by understanding? All Washington wanted was more numbers for an educational lotto.

Teaching is an art, where something mysterious and fragile conspires even in the worst of conditions. Perhaps I ask too much in taking teaching passionately but not seriously, for then the questionnaire would have been a poem.

Dunces among
the doldrums   2000

Now is the doldrums of the academic year. Exams and blue books pile up incessantly, pouting for attention. Even imaginative essays can become tedious when your eyes start to ache. You have to recognize those first tell-tale signs of sanctimonious overcorrecting, when red ink inundates the page. How could they have missed such an obvious point?

Twenty years ago I found a way through this slow death march of the mind. No one tells you about these things in graduate school. So I stumbled upon *A Confederacy of Dunces* by the ill-fated writer John Kennedy Toole.

By the end of the first page my cheeks were drenched from laughter. I was no longer in the examination's little ease. I roamed the topsy-turvy world of Ignatius J. Reilly, a collision between

Aquinas and Oliver Hardy, voluminously filling out a flannel shirt and tweed trousers, thirty years old, still at home in New Orleans, writing his manifestoes against the world on Big Chief Tablets. With a green hunting cap squeezed over the balloon of his head, and a burly black mustache, whose corners were filled with disapproval and potato chip crumbs, this Quixote of the sixties took on nothing less than the madness of the modern world.

Ignatius' weighty presence anywhere guaranteed disaster. Hawking wieners for the Paradise hotdog company somehow led Ignatius to Boethius' *Consolation of Philosophy* and his subsequent ramming the hotdog cart into a customer's crotch.

Enough for now. Time for me to return to the blue books. My students won't know that throughout this night of the living dead I'll keep sane by recalling those immortal words of Ignatius J. Reilly, "Is my paranoia getting completely out of hand?"

The fragile tremors of this planet
2000

Long ago in the lecture halls of medieval Paris, Thomas Aquinas confidently argued that theology was the summit of knowledge. This could be demonstrated by its effects. Indeed, all one had to do was to see how great an influence a doctor of theology had upon future teachers and pastors of Christendom.

Today the world has revolved well beyond that ancient synthesis. Business schools now buck to exert their quality control over the educated population. The same hubris that afflicted medieval theologians now undermines those who would write commentaries on the revelations of Greenspan.

But there is a deeper change in this global venture. I see it every time my students return from their international experience. They don't go on business junkets. Rather they live among the poor. They return from Central America, India, and Africa with an exacting honesty and a precious sense of life.

Today one of my students returns to El Salvador. During her years at Xavier Kristen had the opportunity to experience life outside the pale of her Cincinnati heritage. Now this young graduate, whose feminine nature Aquinas thought too soft to receive the clear imprint of ordination, flies to live generously again among the victims of that conveniently forgotten disaster of a war.

There is a legend that Aquinas had a vision which reduced all of his work to "straw." He never dictated again to his four secretaries. I've never had a vision but I have seen my students' eyes. They keep me honest and alive to the fragile tremors of this planet.

Do the math 2001

Sometimes it is good to go back to school. Now, I am not talking about summer school—a sweaty prospect in humid Cincinnati. Let's experiment a bit with what I've learned from the dramatist Simon McBurney.

Imagine your first day at school. Go back there. Do you recall what you were wearing? Look down at your shoes. Now look to your right and notice that your mother holds your hand. Turn to your left and see your father holding your other hand. Now here is where it gets weird. Look back behind your parents and see your grandparents. Then look farther back and notice your eight great grandparents.

But don't stop there. Go back to the beginning of the nineteenth century. There a line of 256 ancestors stares directly at you. Assuming no kinship ties, the beginning of the seventeenth century greets you with over sixty-five thousand relatives. At the start of the sixteenth century there are over 1,048,000. And a thousand years ago there would be 1,099,511,627,776 ancestors, which is probably more than all the people that have been born. You could push back to the dawn of human history but I think you get the picture. Such numbers are obviously not possible. And things become even more complicated when you realize that you're not the only one with connections.

In the last few months many Cincinnatians—including the mayor—have been dumbfounded by the fissures within our community. But you don't have to pass the ninth grade proficiency test to detect the lines of division in our town.

It's time to sit again in those awkward, elementary seats and do some simple multiplication. It's time to look at one another and do the math. We might finally learn that we are connected to everyone else.

Vita mutatur, non tollitur[*]   2004

This morning as I sit through Xavier University's commencement I shall be thinking of cicadas. Although one might be tempted to compare sitting through the seemingly endless list of names with the cicada nymphs' waiting for years underground, there is another facet of their life cycle that occupies me today.

In Cincinnati our cicadas take their time. After spending seventeen years underground, the mature nymphs crawl out of the ground and climb up tree trunks. They delicately remove themselves from their nymphal skin. If they emerge unsuccessfully — if their wings are deformed or shriveled — they will eventually fall to their deaths, get baked by the sun or eaten by scavengers. But if they succeed life is beautiful.

So here I sit thinking about cicadas — and the final exam of a student who cast off his fundamentalist Christian upbringing. He realized that his authoritarian past prevented him from tasting the truth of his experience.

Already a successful entrepreneur, he has found that the scientific world gave him room to grow. He observed that we humans are made of the same stuff as the rest of the universe, and that, since all matter is conserved, we really do not have the power to create or destroy. Instead, the material of the universe changes form.

Then he sagely delivered:

Everything and everyone that has come or that is to come is already here, waiting, in a moment of transition, to be born in a moment of revelation.

I think his wings have come out quite well.

A parable in ribbons   2004

Recently when I made a suggestion to an audience they were noticeably stunned. This had nothing to do with any wardrobe malfunction. No, it was about what many of us see every day as we drive about.

People nowadays don't wear their hearts on their sleeves. Instead they tattoo their convictions to the backsides of their cars. Magnetized yellow ribbons urge one and all to "Support

Our Troops," pink ribbons call for solidarity with victims of breast cancer. The tri-colors of our flag signal a patriotic ruffle.

So, when I tried out my experiment with one audience after another, showing them another red, white and blue ribbon with words embroidered in green, the reactions were telling.

I had wanted to speak to the Christian memory of a nation that had so recently espoused moral values. Would not the very words of Jesus be as warmly received as the other public appeals?

But many cautioned that the magnet wouldn't last long on my car. Others advised that such a ribbon would get my car keyed or vandalized.

Why were these thoughtful audiences gun shy? What could Jesus have said so long ago that still makes people dyspeptic? What cannot be printed on these cutouts of compassion?

Why is it so difficult to read on a red, white and blue background the words "Love your enemies"?

---

*"Life is changed, not taken away."

Those firefly moments   2005

The poet T. S. Eliot advises in his "Four Quartets":

> Do not let me hear
> Of the wisdom of old men, but rather of their folly,
> Their fear of fear and frenzy ...

I take these words to heart, not only because there is constant evidence of their truth all around us, but also because, as I get older, I sense quite keenly how courage can escape.

As professors pass from those initial electric classroom years, there comes the harder task of middle age. This is the time when contact can be lost. This is the time when you look into the searching eyes of twenty-one-year-olds and are challenged to your very core.

Students do not want the ready-made response. They easily sniff out inauthenticity. They want someone who lives in life's debris and can challenge them to dive even more deeply into the abyss.

Despite their ungainly self-absorption, their sometimes rude and thoughtless words, you can learn again from them what you thought was lost long ago. While you find yourself now in a different place, you honor those firefly moments when minds become incandescent, getting wondrously lost in arguments and ageless conversations.

And there you see how they gain courage—by relying on your trembling efforts never to lie to them.

Rattling the cage 2005

Three weeks ago fourteen graduate students joined me in an adventure that has gone far beyond *The Da Vinci Code*. We began reading all the ancient gospel texts—not just the ones embalmed in the New Testament but anything that remains from the first three centuries.

The effect of reading fragmentary evidence within the context of the ancient world has been staggering. Assumptions, some engrained since childhood, some buoyed up by ecclesial insouciance, have fallen away. We discovered that the early Jesus followers were not homogenized ditto-heads, but, quite the contrary, humans who used their imagination to carve out varied responses to the fate of that artisan of words.

They have caught that this is a politically charged murder story: a peasant liquidated by an Empire. Things should have stopped. But the vision of a God, indiscriminately offering benefits to bad and good, just and unjust, leaked out. Then they found that over a generation later a writer finally imagined the death of Jesus in solidarity with other innocent victims.

They have also seen how later authorities tried to channel and then freeze this abundant stream. When we chip through the ice we see the costly debris. The skeletons of the apostles Mary of Magdala and Junia still rattle the cage of the age-old patriarchal cover-up.

Sand castles 2007

This past week has brought wave upon wave of sorrow. The usual tranquil atmosphere of a campus was devastated beyond repair. Meanwhile, in Iraq the equivalent of three Blacksburg massacres occurred daily. Of, course, the weather only compounded this general sense of shock and awe.

Frankly the world is too much with me. I wince whenever the radio wakes me in the morning, expecting more or even worse. At night I lose myself if possible in some baseball game or mystery.

But last week there was another campus event that stopped me right in my tracks.

A group of Tibetan monks constructed a sand mandala in the Xavier university library. Mandala is the Sanskrit word for "world in harmony." In fact, as the mandala was painstakingly funneled out, it became an imaginary space for contemplation. It is the very essence of a transient performance art.

Beginning on Tuesday the monks chanted, played flutes and drum and blessed the area for their work of meditation. After the initial ceremony they immediately got down to drawing the exacting lines of the mandala design.

Then they began to pour out the sand—millions of grains of sand in wondrous colors—through vibrating metal funnels—grain by grain. For the next four and a half days they continued to create the imaginary palace of Compassion, where the lotus flower of the Buddha floated in the center. The monks explained the various elements and prescribed structures of the piece. The inner circle was squared. The square was encircled. The circle was squared as it moved outwards.

As soon as the last part of the outer rim was finished, the chanting began again. The flutes and drum played. The head monk circled the board.

Then he reached into the center of the mandala and picked up the sand lotus blossom, letting it run through his fingers. What had taken days of absorbed concentration was gone in an instant. Then he drew four lines through the mandala, then four more, cutting it like a birthday cake. Another monk brought a brush and began to sweep up the sand, pushing it to the center. Soon there was nothing but a pile of sand, whose colors formed a subtle heather tone.

The monks collected half of the sand to pour out into the Ohio River in order to continue the flow of compassion begun by this art work. Small bags of the remaining sand were distributed to those who witnessed the final ceremony.

How could this seemingly futile and transient activity help a fractured world?

By giving each of us the space to concentrate, to realize what attention can mean. As we watched the imperceptible happening before us, we fell silent, we slowed down. We sensed a deeper harmony running out.

Beyond the beauty, beyond the pain, in the very destruction of the mandala, I realized that nothing was lost. We all were involved in a deeper, rarer, finer life.

So now when I turn the radio on, or scan the headlines, I see the sands run through those fingers and detect for a moment the infinite trace and task of compassion.

▋ Blue book special 2008

Reading examination blue books is more than an acquired taste. Often the experience is like walking through a mine field. At any time one's confidence of being an effective guide, leading students through the debris of the past, can be blown to bits. You get used to miss-spelt youth's over-reliance upon spell-check and the inevitable transmutation of Pontius Pilate into an Hispanic boat captain Ponchos Pilot. But when a summary of the investigation of the facts of the death of Jesus concludes: "Tacitus and Josephus independently assisted in Jesus' crucifixion under Pontius Pilate," your mind descends into a vortex of amazement. How did these Roman and Jewish historians turn into anachronistic aiders and abettors of Jesus' execution? Is this simply a residue of poorly taken notes or has that student entered into some virtual reality?

Yet there are moments of lucidity. In commenting upon the cultural reality of the infancy stories of Jesus, a student wrote:

> In Jesus' time those who hold power are unworldly. Caesar Augustus was born of a God, Alexander the Great as well. The ones exhibiting uncanny abilities, abilities not associated with mere humans, are crowned with divinity. Jesus' fate was very similar. That from which Jesus seemed to be trying to separate himself, the tradition of Jesus draws him straight back into—the dominant culture and society of the ancient world. As communities formed around him after his death, a tradition of spectacular stories and events began to gather about him, and the tradition grew into otherworldliness.

Kevin Brophy had taken our discussions to heart. And he introduced a term that we had not used in class— "otherworldliness." Of course, this term has long been part of the traditional categories of Christianity, underscoring a dualism of this world and the heavenly realm. What Kevin had done was to link the experience of the uncanny with the power conduits of the ancient world.

The world in which Jesus lived can be characterized as a pyramid of power. The top 15 percent of the population (with the governing Roman elite at 5 percent) lived off the remaining 85 percent. Economic historians call it an "extractive economy." Yet, the underlying theology for this domination system relied upon the notion that the divine realm supplied the benefits (*charis*) to extraordinary individuals who maintained the cycle of benefits by giving thanks (*eucharis*) through sacrifice to these gracious gods. Thus, the elite were on top because of divine favor, while the 85 percent who serviced them had somehow incurred the displeasure of the gods. The world worked because people believed that this was how things came about.

When an unusual person appeared the only way to account for someone who exceeded social expectations was to invoke this benefit cycle. Arrian in his *Anabasis* (7.30.2) aptly put it: "It seems to me that a man who is different from all other humans could not have come into being apart from divinity."

Not only had Kevin captured Arrian well but he also delivered a very critical nuance. In using the terms "unworldly" and "otherworldliness" Kevin exposed what has enticed Christians through the centuries, allowing them to forget the vision of the historical Jesus.

The Jesus Seminar reached a consensus that the historical Jesus actually congratulated the poor, declaring that God's Empire was theirs. He also imagined a God who promiscuously gave benefits to good and bad, unjust and just. Such a vision violated the system. Even the poor would have a hard time adjusting to Jesus' cultural dyslexia. Who would dare imagine that the rarefied atmosphere breathed in only by the elite and the favored could be inhaled by sweaty peasants? If God was effectively present with the losers, who would hold up the world of the winners? God needs to be in heaven so that all will be right with the empire.

What Kevin detected was that the realm of the uncanny, the "unworldly," was really part of the way power was brokered in the ancient world. As long as the elite were the conduits and agents of benefits to those below, as long as this trickle down theology was in play, the majority were in abject dependence upon those who dominated them. Yet, for a while there were murmurings from below. Surprising words were exchanged over bread and wine. Some people began to pick up on what Jesus was gesturing at. They too played with his words and discovered worth in their expendable lives.

Later on, as the Jesus Movement grew, the charge of atheism was leveled at them. What is often lost by modern readers is that this accusation was not a rhetorical flourish. It came from a realization that these Jesus followers were not playing by the same rules. They were not harnessing their power from the sanctioned sources. They found it in their lives together in tenement houses, not in the magnificent temples.

But this peculiar stance did not last. Even by the end of the first century Jesus began to be couched in an unworldly glow. He had joined the heavenly hall of fame. By the fourth century Christianity had taken on the official trappings of the empire. Eyes looked once more into the heavens instead of across the table at one another.

Where do we go from here? If our historical investigations have any merit, we can detect some uncomfortable possibilities. Do we really want to play in a game that goes out of bounds? What will happen to our known universe? Dare we try again the shrewd wisdom of that uppity peasant?

When did the gospel stop being news? 2005

At least once a semester in my classes, or occasionally in lectures on the road, I ask whether those who still go to church regularly ever fear that they might be endangering themselves by going to services. Usually people quizzically stare back at me. Where is the danger in such familiar activity? Surely you don't mean a bumper mishap as people drive out of the parking lot?

Before some minds wander to the threat of paper cuts from bingo sheets or spilled coffee during fellowship, I stir the conversation back to the first century. What happened to those early followers of Jesus as they walked out of the tenement house or home of a hosting family after they had gathered for a meal in memory of the Anointed Jesus? Were the cobblestones they walked on the same as when they entered? Or, did the world seem different because of their evening together?

I do not start this line of questioning to romanticize the early followers of Jesus. Yet, in order to come to grips with the fragments of the first century, it is necessary to engage in some thought experiment. We need to put some skin and muscle on those bare bones. We need to be aware of the acoustics, the surroundings, in and against which the sounds, now mute on the New Testament pages, echoed and played. Indeed, when we do this we begin to understand what attracted those unknown followers in various towns and cities around the Mediterranean.

What happened, for example, when the person (perhaps Phoebe—see Romans 16:1) who carried Paul's letter to the Romans got up after the meal and delivered his words to the gathering? How did those opening words strike the eardrums of people well accustomed to imperial trumpets and proclamations? How did they react to Paul's introducing himself as an "envoy appointed to announce God's gospel (*euaggelion*)"?

Due to our familiarity with the word "gospel (*euaggelion*)" we usually move right along with Paul's opening words. But would the original audience have done so? Or would they have grown uneasy with such a word? Would they have been roused or stunned on hearing the "news" about a "son of God," who had been enthroned by God's action? Such language was not unknown in the heart of the Empire. *Euaggelion* bore the imperial brand. This was the word Rome used to announce the state of things, how the world held together. The gospel of Rome was carved in bronze and stone throughout the world. It reinforced and echoed the cadence of the armies. It proclaimed peace and prosperity under a world order maintained through controlled violence. It summed up a victorious narrative beginning with the figure of Rome's founder, faithful Aeneas, punctuated by the emperor Octavian's miraculous victory at Actium, exalted through the deifications of emperors, and preserved through the imperial lineage. From the countless sacrifices in temples to coins jingling in purses throughout the world the message was clear and indelible: the eagle of Rome flew triumphant.

The words of Paul, then, did not emerge from some religious ghetto; rather, they played off the public imperial saga, as sparks from an anvil. In fact, the upcoming Scholars Version of Paul's correspondence attempts to convey this by translating *euagge-lion* as "God's world changing news." Paul was announcing a counter-movement, declaring a seismic upheaval, namely that things were no longer the same, that a new world order was underway. Indeed, he included his audience among those in solidarity with the shamed state criminal whom Israel's God did not abandon. Now the nobodies of the world had an access and means of appeal to the heart of Reality. But such a ragtag regime contradicted the imposing story of Rome. Uttering such words risked the charge of treason and the inevitable consequences. In fact, Paul himself disappeared shortly after writing his letters with their treasonous overtones, as so many have done through the centuries under similar circumstances.

This is why I sometimes ask whether anyone has felt like they have come out of a nuclear reactor when they have left their Sunday service. Certainly I do not expect radiation poisoning; but do we ever experience a message that touches not only our lives but the way in which we construct our world? Do we ever sense that we are risking ourselves as we gather together? Do we ever become unnerved at the thought that we might be involved in a breathtaking possibility?

It would seem that I am not alone in wondering aloud about such things. The recent downturn in newspaper sales has led a number of writers to ask what is the function of "the news." News is more than the 24/7 hallucination that has overtaken our media. It is not the endless feeding of the electronic beast to keep a nation groggily content. The function of news is the constant critical search for and communication of the events that touch and affect our lives. In short, real news declares what is signifi-cant for people. News, then, cannot be a shilling for the estab-lishment or an advertisement for the status quo. Rather, in the best tradition of the Enlightenment, it provides that perspective, that moment of critical lucidity, which enables and empowers a people.

And so I ask again; do your knees grow weak when you en-ter your gathering of worship? Does your community promote the quest and detection of meaning? And if not, then has any-thing really changed?

Back to the future   2010

Recently a colleague walked into my office to discuss some departmental matter. After we solved the issue, I mentioned that I missed seeing his wife in the department. Elizabeth was on leave to write a book on theology and the environment and, as her husband noted, was getting more and more anxious over finishing the volume as the publisher's deadline approached. She regretted taking time away from being with their only child. But what was truly weighing on her (greatly due to the subject matter of her project) was the state of the earth itself. Her analysis and research had brought her almost to paralysis. Her meticulous social and scientific analysis had touched a nerve: Was there any future for her son, for all our daughters and sons?

I have been there. Back in the '80s when the Reagan administration was going great guns with nuclear weapons, I looked at my sleeping son and wondered for his future. I, too, had some released time for research and writing, but I was spiraling down in slow despair. There seemed to be nothing to stop this mindless momentum. Then two things occurred. First, I slowly realized that if I gave into this downward flight then I would have let the mushroom cloud go off in my heart. The forces of destruction would have won without firing a shot. Second, I heard of a crazy physician from Australia (Helen Caldicott) who was mounting a campaign against this nuclear plague. Then more news came—from an unexpected region. Soviet scientists began to speak out. (Little did I know that Gorbachev was tunneling his way from within the very Soviet system; nor could I imagine that Reagan could shake free of his script.) From within and from the other side of the planet I gained the courage to imagine and write. I began giving lectures and workshops on the "Bible and the Bomb." I felt I was no longer alone in facing the nuclear reaper.

I mention these two incidents because I have been wondering aloud with friends and colleagues over the value of religion in the twenty-first century. Certainly critics of religion have no lack of evidence for the mindless violence of those who would speak and act in the name of particular religions. But often their critique demonstrates the critics' superficial understanding of religion. In fact, while I can often agree with their atheistic denunciations of a controlling, unjust god, I am left quite frequently with an impression that these same critics display little appreciation for the human dimensions of the religious experience.

In fact, every time I imaginatively enter the ancient world, trying to sense the texture of their texts or stones, I recognize even from the fragmentary evidence that religion for the ancients was ripe with human complexity and depth. For them religion was not an academic game. It was certainly about power. It was about recognizing that human beings often got into situations beyond their control. It was about those moments when people would invoke gods. They had a language at the ready to give them a sense that, in the midst of chaos and conflict, meaning could be woven. They felt they participated in something far greater than themselves. They did not deny the powers that shaped their lives, for the gods had names and life was negotiable.

Of course, we are no longer in that world. Photos from the Hubble telescope do not reveal a three tiered universe. The planets and moons, as Galileo spied, are not intelligent spirits but rock and matter. We now feel disconnected and adrift in an ever-expanding universe. And the words we once confidently used to connect come out of our mouths like cartoon balloons and simply pop in our faces. Even Nietzsche's daring declaration (God is dead!) has been subject to mass distribution by *Time Magazine*.

So I return once more to where I have been and where my colleague stands. With the planet spinning away on its galactic arc, as we humans continue to construct havoc and catastrophe for life as we know it, I am brought back to the question: Is there a future for us? What will our great grandchildren inherit?

From an ancient perspective these are religious questions. And we are in a situation that is beyond our control. We cannot dodge the issue by separating science from religion. Nor can we ignore matters by opting for some heavenly deus ex machina. We need to help one another to find new words and illuminating metaphors in the midst of social disruption and environmental collapse. Indeed, we need to learn from each other once again that we are not alone on this planet. The temptation is to think that it is all about us. But our older brother Paul reminds us in Romans (chapters 8–11) that it is not about us; it is about how everything—how the universe—will be redeemed. Our task rather is to discover how we can participate in this unfinished work. The question of planetary survival thus stands as the religious quest for our time. I am heartened that I am not alone in this effort. Howard Zinn, who knew what it meant to take on apparently impossible causes, offers a veteran's encouragement:

> Revolutionary change does not come as one cataclysmic moment (beware of such moments!) but as an endless succession of surprises, moving zigzag toward a more decent society. We don't have to engage in grand, heroic actions to participate in the process of change. Small acts, when multiplied by millions of people, can quietly become a power no government can suppress, a power than can transform the world. ... If we see only the worst, it destroys our capacity to do something. If we remember those times and places— and there are so many—where people have behaved magnificently, it energizes us to act, and raises at least the possibility of sending this spinning top of a world in a different direction.*

* *A Power Governments Cannot Suppress* (San Francisco: City Lights Books, 2007), 100.

Moments of parting and torment 2011

Reading undergraduate essays and examinations is less an acquired taste than an occupational hazard. Occasionally a sentence leaps out, shouts or hits you right between the eyes. Is this line profound, an awkward expression, or an invitation to a brain aneurism: "There is much more to reading the Bible than just reading it"? What of this insouciant attempt to describe the various Gospel sources: "Signs, Mark, and L seem to compose the Miracle *Catena*, which was written by St. Thomas Aquinas"? On the other hand I was considerably heartened by this biting observation: "If by some miracle the writers and audiences of the gospels were able to observe the state of Christianity today, they would most likely associate it with the very institution that was persecuting them in the late first century."

But as I recently gave my course on the Death of Jesus I was struck especially by two voices that seemed to speak for a significant number of my students. One young woman wrote: "I believed God protected Jesus during his crucifixion and raised his spirit to the heavens without any suffering. I viewed his death as a symbolic death, not as an actual occurrence." She later added, "The death of Jesus was itself a miracle; Jesus could not have suffered because he was not human." A second essayist included this: "I never considered that Jesus was a human who would be under immense pain." Then in her essay towards the end of the semester the second writer maturely reflected on what she had encountered in the course by noting: "Reading the Gospel narratives from a fictional but historical perspective would also have some positive consequences on the Christian faith. Instead of hiding behind Scripture for explanations, Christians would actually be forced to investigate their hopes and fears in life."

With the exception of one or two students not identifying themselves with a Christian background, the rest of my two sections came out of what they would have loosely termed "traditional forms of Christianity." It became apparent that almost all suffered from a severe lack of historical imagination. Jesus, at best, was a first century Clark Kent, not really human, from another world, and invulnerable. Twenty-first-century Docetism, right here in Ohio, the heart of it all.

Things started to get complicated when a student's research presentation on the torture of crucifixion in the Roman Empire riveted his classmates' attention. I noticed that a number of students, both male and female, were visibly affected as we drew out the gruesome details of this method of legal suffocation. Embed this image within the honor/shame Mediterranean world and one can begin to appreciate the lasting horror and understandable repulsion to the entire execution. No noble Roman would waste time writing about this. It was beneath them.

Indeed, the earliest Gospel source (Q) seems not to be overly distressed by the death of Jesus. In the Sayings Gospel Jesus' death is alluded to as a death of a prophet. Rather the paramount interest seems to be on Jesus' words and wisdom. Thomas shows no concern about Jesus' death. For that matter, the Didache also has little to say. *It is only in the pre-Pauline material* that we can begin to see that some followers of Jesus (probably Syrian Jews) began to take on the trauma of his death. They transformed a shame-filled public execution into a heroic end. Jesus died like other Jewish martyrs. They became convinced that this man's trust in God was vindicated. Paul would take this understanding and, in his own dramatic way, focus sharply upon the trustworthiness of God in the midst of this disaster. It is only later in the century with either an early version of the Gospel of Peter or Mark that the full-blown narrative of the death of Jesus emerges on the historical scene. Either the writer of Peter or Mark reached back to the well-known story of the Suffering and Vindication of the Innocent. This fiction conceived in the second century BCE attempts to redress the question of suffering of the innocent and the justice of God. In fact, Mark uses this story format not to isolate the fate of Jesus but to point to his solidarity with all those other sufferers, especially in the wake of the devastating Jewish Revolt (70 CE).

In short the tradition of the death of Jesus did not begin full-blown. Instead, some Jesus followers courageously and creatively came to grips with the harsh and disconcerting reality of his end. Those nameless Syrian Jews refused to let the Empire of Rome have the final, liquidating word. The attempt to "disappear" Jesus was frustrated by Jews who created "gaps" in the official record. Borrowing a stylus from an older Jewish hand, they composed a story about a peasant, who called on his listeners to live out of trust and was convinced in his vision to the very end. The later full-length narrative of the Innocent Sufferer continued this subversive trend. The story that Christians today carry forward is not a record of facts but a refusal at the historical outset to give up on the meaningful depths that humans discovered in their engagement with Jesus of Nazareth. It took time and a multitude of experiences to revisit his death. But isn't that always the case with us? A contemporary Russian novelist captures much of such an attempt:

> Death seems terrible, but it sows the most kind and useful harvest in the souls of the living, and from the seed of mystery and decay develops the seed of life and understanding. Look, think, and have ceremonies and rites! Man is not alone. There are many countrymen in his skin, like men in a boat rowing from shore to shore, and the true person appears per-

haps only in the moments of parting and torment—here he is, remember him.

—Valentin Rasputin, *Farewell to Matyora*

▌ Only a game 2012

▌ Recently I was invited to a "Lifeboat Debate" by some undergraduate students. Evidently this debate program has been making the rounds of college campuses. The format comes right out of Reality TV: Imagine that civilization, as we have known it, has come to an end. There is a lifeboat with one remaining place. And there bobbing in the water are various professors. Who will win a place on board? Each professor is asked to defend his or her discipline. In addition, there is a devil's advocate who will have the last word. The students in the audience (with pizza and soft drinks available during the voting period) select the winner.

The auditorium was packed. What made that unusual was that the professors engaged did not stipulate that their students should attend; no extra points were given. Yet the students came. A chemist, a philosopher, a mathematician, a literary pro, and I filled the field. The economist tellingly never appeared.

My colleagues defended their disciplines with both wit and humor. The devil's advocate provided a delightful caricature of each discipline, although his resume of the presentations paid less attention to the actual arguments than to his prefabricated autopsy of the disciplines.

I must confess that I did not play the game.

You may well ask why then I accepted the invitation. I did so for two reasons. First, upon thinking of the format with its imagined situation, I saw that this was an old and tired game. It was the premise of the TV show *Survivor*. It also has haunted the field of economics for some time. This was the threat of scarcity along with the attendant ideology of the survival of the fittest. I saw the opportunity to present an alternative voice. And that opened up my second quixotic reason: this could become a teachable moment.

So I began my defense by making none. Although I could have spoken at length on behalf of the "Queen of the Sciences" (that note alone brought considerable hooting), I made it clear that I denied both the premise and the imagined situation.

I noted that this format was akin to the show *Survivor* which has always struck me as a most irrational show. No one wanting to survive would simply play the game of "last man standing." That is not survival; it is a suicidal course. Such a show enacts the gladiatorial combats of old without the messiness of blood dripping on the sand. It plays well in the race for ratings, keeps sponsors happy and couch potatoes entertained, but does little to teach any of us about how we are to live together on this planet.

So instead I told stories. I told of the Inuit from Greenland who refused a European's thanks when he shared his walrus meat after the latter had been unsuccessful in his hunting. "Up in our country," he said, "we are human! And since we are human we help each other. We don't like to hear anybody say thanks for that. What I get today you may get tomorrow."

I went on to the well-known story of the monk being chased by a tiger. The monk, backed to the edge of cliff, fell and, by chance, caught a vine a few feet down. As he looked above at the snarling cat, he noticed a mouse that had crawled onto the vine and had begun to gnaw away at it. What would the monk do? He looked beyond the vine and below the tiger and saw something growing and said, "Ah, strawberries!"

Finally, I told of a story from a friend who survived the Holocaust. There was a sadistic Nazi officer who determined who would live. He saw an old man pleading for his grandson's life. The officer went to him and offered to let the grandson live (and the old man would take his place) if the old man could tell which eye of his was real. The officer was proud of his life-like glass eye. The old man accepted and studied the face of the German. Then he said, "It is the right one." The officer said, "Yes, it is. How could you tell?" The old man said, "Because the other eye looks human."

I then added that I was taking the advice of a peasant artisan from long ago, someone who risked everything on words and refused to let go of people. He challenged his listeners: "Do not respond on the same level to someone who intends you harm." The usual translation "Do not resist evil" of Matt 5:39 fails to notice the shrewd peasant advice and, instead, turns it into an impossible order. Actually it is a jujitsu move of the imagination. It does not advocate passivity; rather, it suggests that we have more than two ways to deal with life. Can you think of a third or fourth alternative? Can you imagine the other as more than a demonic threat? Can we think of a conversation format that does not play into the capitalistic spasm of unremitting competition? Can we see that there is more to our being here on this planet than meets the eye?

So I ended this rosary of quotes with the sly epigram of Edwin Markham:

> They drew a circle and shut me out,
> A heretic, a rebel, a thing to flout,
> But Love and I had the wit to win—
> We drew a circle and took them in.

By the way, the vote was quite clear: the devil's advocate's trashing of the disciplines won the night. The students played the game to the end. No one made it aboard.

▌The Zen of interpretation   2012

For the last two years I have opened my course on the early Christian writings by showing the opening battle of the film *Gladiator*. Despite the liberties that the director Ridley Scott takes with history (like turning the Roman battle lines into a Western cavalry charge), the scene's shock-and-awe, coupled with some salient remarks ("Strength and honor," "A people should know when they are conquered"), help me set the atmosphere for the course. Students are too often introduced to the New Testament not only without sufficient historical context but also without any sense of the rhythm and beat of that ancient world. When the word *euaggelion* ("gospel" or, better, "world transforming message") was heard across the Mediterranean there was no original association with Matthew, Mark, Luke, and John. Instead, from the time of Augustus the word was out that (as Russell Crowe, who plays the film's gladiator, exclaims) "*Roma victa*": Rome had won the world. From inscriptions to temple entablatures, from the propaganda of Virgil to the imperial coins, from the bread basket of Egypt to a marketplace off the Tiber, the word was out: *Roma victa*. And, when this message of divine favor could be backed up with legions strategically poised to respond quickly and with overwhelming force, then the message of Rome determined and reinforced the assumptions, aspirations, and dreams of daily life.

I begin with such a weighty counterpoise because I have long been convinced that the act of interpretation is not simply a matter of discerning what is in front of me—a text, an inscription, an archeological site—no, it is fundamentally a matter of detecting what is not there, what is unspoken. In a Zen garden there are rocks and sand. But there is more—there is the space, the emptiness in which the rocks and sand take on their intimate inflection. If you catch this you are stunned into insight.

My task then is to call students to what they do not see, have not imagined. Through a variety of presentations I ask them to rearrange their mental furniture, or better, to rebuild from the foundations. I want them to walk "again, for the first time," into the ancient marketplace, to hear the competing calls that cried out for survival, to catch the incense masking the bloodied butchery on the nearby altar, to smell the garlic from the shaded tavern.

But this is not a tourist excursion. There is danger in this enterprise. If you become acquainted with what was taken to be real, then you also can become trapped in that prevailing atmosphere. You may miss what was actually unspoken and unnoticed in that ancient world. After we have watched and commented on the opening of *Gladiator*, and after some discussion on "Gospel of Rome," I then return to those *Germani* ("barbarians" to the Romans) who refused to "know when they are conquered." There was little in the film about them save their raw and fearful rush to oblivion. But they also had a world of meaning, something for which they went to their deaths. What was their "gospel"?

In fact, the *euaggelion* proclaimed by Paul and the early writers should be seen in just such a light. Their *euaggelion* was definitely a minority report, a cheeky affront to the eternal message of Rome. Because such a message went against the prevailing status report, the early Jesus followers were considered atheists (*atheoi*). This offbeat message by unheard-of followers was not part of the unrelenting humdrum of the world. Yet, when, under Constantine, Christianity became the religion of the Empire, the gospel was transposed, piped to a military air. Nevertheless, that surprising arrhythmia was not wholly lost. It fled into the desert. Mystics and peasants, heretics and reformers in subsequent centuries occasionally caught and danced to that unheard beat.

But the Zen of interpretation does not end with these historical observations. There is even further danger in falling under this dark art of interpretation. If you start to detect what has not been spoken, what has not been noticed in the ancient world, you could begin to re-imagine what is happening in your own. No longer enthralled by the sight of dinosaurs, you catch sight of those tiny mammals that survived those ancient beasts. You begin to hear cries of those who should never be heard from again—whether from the sands of the pyramids or from under the tanks rolling over nameless protestors. Indeed, the world you inhabit is no longer empty, drained by some financial ledger or existential dread, but enriched by laughter coming from unexpected banquets. The various verities that head-line our days lose their electric attraction. Instead, you are shocked by the fate of those who have been passed over in silence. And when you return once more to the Bible, you realize that this text has become quite vexing with complexity and import for you. It is haunted with human hunger and hope, with hands you never realized were there, but nevertheless are there and, as Dante learned, help you crack the ice of hell.

▌ A report from the trenches   2012

This past spring I have been fully engaged in teaching three courses at my university as well as delivering three Jesus Seminars on the Road. Usually I am greatly energized by teaching and lecturing. But a close re-reading of my students' final essays left me somewhat stunned. Now, the final results actually were quite good; the students had genuinely made some progress in their critical trek through scripture. But there was a singularly disturbing note in those essays. In one class of thirty students, 90 percent declared that they had had significant religious education through high school (most of which was from Catholic institutions) and yet not one had any glimmer of the complexity and context of the New Testament. In the honors class sixty-eight percent registered the same point. With one or two exceptions, however, no one had heard in their classrooms or from the pulpit anything that dealt with the historical meaning of the New Testament. Instead, many were brought up with the impression "that God and Jesus were these ever-loving, all knowing beings that wanted all people to do service and to never let your angry side show." Jesus was "a miracle man." "Thirteen years of Catholic education left one with the impression that scripture was the *strict* word of God." A few had finally begun to question their tradition, especially a gay student who declared that "the shenanigans of the church" left him greatly "conflicted and alienated." Some others indicated their growing distance from their church. But none of them had any way or means for reconsidering their tradition.

Some might find these observations unsurprising. But for someone who has been teaching scripture for over thirty years it signaled more than a cautionary light. What had happened to all the educational reforms stemming from Vatican II? And why, if these students, according to our recruiters, were entering college with ever-increasing test scores, did they have so little ability to read a simple text with a sense of complexity and surprise? While some of this is undoubtedly due to the influence of the digital age, there is something else involved. For most of the students their tradition not only had been uncritically accepted but had been consistently presented to keep them in a pediatric condition. I remember a time when a majority of my students would begin their reading of a scriptural text with a modest amount of skepticism. Now that is the exception. Indeed, a number of the university's alumni and major donors have become increasingly vociferous in demanding that the theology department confine itself to catechetical instruction. In short, what once seemed to be an enormous but rewarding project of goading young minds to reconfigure their tradition, has become a daunting prospect that beggars the imagination. At the risk of sounding like a theological geezer, could it be that the barbarians are no longer at the gates but already inside?

But that is only from one front. Interspersed through the semester I have journeyed to Tacoma, Tucson, and Long Island with Westar Fellows and have found interested and questing people. Of course, the groups are self-selected. Only those who are provoked by the subject matter show up for the weekend lectures. Nevertheless, again and again there is the confirmation that an intelligent reappraisal of the Christian traditions is taking place throughout North America but very much under the radar of the news media. And then there is the fact that the majority of the participants come in various shades of gray. Some might dismiss all this as a final gasp of a dying tradition, but

I do not share that opinion. What I have learned from those I have met and thought along with is that these are the courageous ones who soldier on, who have taken their experience seriously, and who keep finding that their questions continue to open them up to a deeper sense of life together on this planet. This country, sadly, has quite forgotten that civilizations live not from trends but out of wisdom. And I have detected much wisdom in the eyes I have met. Indeed, I shall never forget the sure eyes of an eighty-year-old woman, who some years ago drove to Atlanta from Florida to catch the accent of the historical Jesus. She knew she had only months left to live, but this discussion to her was worth her tiring but gallant effort.

And so I continue on. The task of biblical literacy is still a major concern. I am encouraged by the *elders* throughout this continent. They refuse to go away. They will continue to seek and find meaning. They have discovered that their quest is hardly over.

And for my college students? I end with a story. Before the semester began a student-to-be was warned by her ultra-orthodox Catholic peers that she should avoid "that Dewey" at all costs, but, if she did take my class, she should not listen to what I said. Simply do the readings, write the essays, and get the grade. It did not prove to be that simple. She became intrigued by what she called "an annoying trait" of mine. She could not understand how someone so demonic, a destroyer of faith and tradition, could be so interested in all the details of the New Testament. Why would someone so perverse spend so much time worrying about Jesus? If that provocateur were so intent on undermining faith, why make the effort to detect the historical context from the fragmentary evidence? Her own curiosity got the better of her. Despite her own health issues (she was operated on a few days after graduation), she wrote two sets of essays that indicated that she realized that she was as complicated and as adventuresome as those captivating Jesus followers.

Light and shadows 2013

I usually begin my spring semester courses by reminding my students of an ancient anniversary. Three hundred and three years ago Galileo discovered three of Jupiter's four largest moons: Io, Europa, and Callisto. He discovered Ganymede four nights later. He noted that the moons would appear and disappear periodically, an observation he attributed to their movement behind Jupiter, and concluded that they were orbiting the planet. Galileo was the first to report lunar mountains and craters, whose existence he deduced from the patterns of light and shadow on the Moon's surface. He even estimated the mountains' heights from these observations. This led him to the conclusion that the Moon was "rough and uneven, and just like the surface of the Earth itself," rather than a perfect sphere as Aristotle had claimed.

Due to these observations all heaven broke loose. Usually the Catholic Church's complaint against Galileo focuses upon the question of whether the Earth revolves around the sun. But it was not a simple matter of location. It was actually the question of *matter*. From his observations Galileo had detected that the heavenly bodies were not spirit, but "rough and uneven" like the Earth. Matter now was scattered through the universe.

Until then the heavens were assumed to be the realm of the Spirit. Plato declared that noble souls became stars. Julius Caesar was so extraordinary that he was transformed into a comet, as Roman coins attest. Roman emperors rode eagles to the heavenly hall of fame. Jesus ascended in competition with the greats of the ancient world. There were reports of his mother launching after her son. Dante embodied the medieval cosmology as he journeyed from hell to heaven.

All this was undermined from Galileo's deductions from light and shadows. The empyrean no longer hosted angels as the stargazing projects of centuries began to tumble to earth like aging satellites. Does this not mean that we are now alone in an infinite universe? It all seems like cold comfort. John Donne summed it up nicely:

The new philosophy calls all in doubt,
the element of fire is quite put out.

Yet, despite the fact that my students appear to live in a modern cosmology, many of them still continue to read the New Testament as if the three-tiered universe of the first century was more than a virtual reality. They somehow compartmentalize their worlds, separating their religious experience from their actual business of living. Of course there are a few who are not at all troubled by such contradictions, since these issues are actually of no concern to them. And there are those science majors who simply dismiss the ancient world views as antiquated fossils. But the majority, once the problem is pointed out, begins for the first time to consider the consequences of living with both the New Testament remnants and the conclusions of Galileo. How can a redeemer come "down" if there is no "up"? Where did the ascending Jesus go? In short, what remains of the early Christian stories when the very cosmos in which they were spun has changed utterly? For many coming to grips with this cosmological collision dramatically recapitulates Rudolf Bultmann's challenge to demythologize our interpretation of Christian tradition. Can any meaning survive the crossing of the cosmological no-man's land?

Even as our minds are spinning from such dizzying questions, there is further cosmological news. Just around the anniversary of Galileo's observations, astronomers announced at the 221st meeting of the American Astronomical Society that there are a total of seventeen billion (that's 17,000,000,000!) Earth-sized planets within our galaxy. Nasa's Kepler space observatory has been staring at a fixed part of the sky and (taking a cue from Galileo) has been detecting the minute dip in light coming from a star if a planet passes in front of it (a "transit"). Astronomers have made corrections for any possible transits caused by something other than a planet. The results suggest that 17 percent of stars host a planet up to 1.25 times the size of the Earth, in close orbits lasting just eighty-five days or fewer—much like the planet Mercury. That means our Milky Way galaxy hosts at least seventeen billion Earth-sized planets.

Moreover, Christopher Burke of the SETI (Search for Extraterrestrial Intelligence) Institute filled in the picture more by announcing 461 new candidate planets, a substantial fraction of which were Earth-sized or not much larger—planets that have until now been particularly difficult to detect. He even noted that there are four new planets—less than twice the size of Earth—that are potentially in the habitable zone, the location around a star where a planet could potentially have liquid water to sustain life. In fact, one planet (KOI 172.02) was very much in the Goldilocks' zone (just at the right distance from its sun). Scientists are becoming more adept at detecting the frontiers of potentially life-bearing planets. Indeed, the most important aspect of the Kepler mission is to find not another Earth but many Earths.

Such possibilities will begin to hover over the surface of this planet. The forlorn perspective of a lonely planet, shorn of its spirit cocoon, may once again be transformed. What would happen if we began to take seriously the possibility that we are not alone in the universe? But this time it is not gods that we anticipate, but something like us. What does that do to the stories we tell ourselves? How do we begin to understand our origins, unless we address these seemingly unimaginable possibilities? We are stepping into, no, we are in a universe that continues to beggar our speech. Will we recognize that these data provide the occasion for genuine religious reflection? That the religious imaginations of the entire planet are already put in jeopardy by these findings? Will we finally begin to recognize that we are indeed "stardust, we are golden, we are billion year old carbon" (Joni Mitchell, Woodstock)? Are we not just at the beginning of recognizing that the universe may well be a genuine chorus of light years dimensions?

A devil's exercise   2014

About eighteen months ago a colleague invited me on an adventure. Would I being willing to re-imagine the *Spiritual Exercises of Ignatius* in a team of two women and two men? Although I had intimate knowledge of the *Exercises* constructed by the sixteenth century Basque courtier, soldier and mystic, my experience of the thirty-day Ignatian retreat and the ideological assumptions structuring the *Exercises* gave me pause.

Iñigo de Loyola had been a man on the make, using court life and soldiering as a way to get ahead in the Spain of the Conquistadors. Only a severe battle injury prevented his career plans. His prolonged convalescence gave him a chance to profoundly reassess his life. He decided that, even with a limp, he could do "great things" for his newly chosen sovereign Jesus. He would soon thereafter put together notes of his ascetical and mystical experiences in a small volume that would lead a person to discover, in conversation with a retreat guide, what was one's true desire and whether an encounter with a narrative of the life of Jesus would go anywhere. This intensive and guided meditation conducted over a few weeks produced remarkable results. The earliest companions of Iñigo all went through these *Exercises*. They founded a company focused on Jesus, earning the name "Jesuits." In fact, it was the *Exercises* that provided the motivational basis for the various counter-reformation attempts by the Jesuits throughout Europe.

I agreed to join only under certain conditions. I would bring my long-standing research on the historical Jesus as well as an appreciation of historical limitations and an abiding critical skepticism to the conversation. My colleagues actually hoped that that would be my angle of approach. So we began.

From the outset I was acutely aware of Iñigo's latent machismo of the world of the Conquistadors. His use of the New Testament was not unexpectedly naïve and literal. But perhaps the most perplexing aspect of the *Exercises* is that, while they concentrate on the life of Jesus, not one of the sayings of Jesus appears. Of course, various retreat directors over time have introduced various sayings and those making the retreat are encouraged to imagine what Jesus might be saying in a scene. But it is quite telling that the *Exercises* actually make no mention. It was action not words that seemed to count.

And so the devil entered into me as we discussed the *Exercises*. I suggested that we take seriously some of the wisdom sayings of the historical Jesus. We began examining what happens to us when we test "What you treasure is your heart's true measure." I pointed out that as an itinerant sage Jesus would have challenged his listeners to determine whether what he was saying had any merit. They had to figure it out. They had to "get it." If they saw wisdom in his words they would remember them, live out of them and pass them on to challenge subsequent audiences. This was how the conspiracy of the atmosphere of God grew.

The aphorisms and parables of Jesus provided a number of incandescent moments. When my colleagues began to read the saying of "God sending sun and rain upon the good and bad, just and unjust" (Matthew 5:45) from the point of view of a first-century peasant, their imaginations began to catch fire. Here was a vision of a God unreservedly showering benefits on those who "don't deserve it" according to the norms of the first century. The story of "A man going down from Jerusalem" (Luke 10:30–35) no longer served as an example story but as a shocking revelation that your enemy could be human, indeed human enough to entrust your life to him. Such words transgressed boundaries, just as the God envisioned by Jesus could mercifully encompass just and unjust. Even the "eye of the needle" aphorism (Mark 10:25) was detected no longer as a simple critique of wealth but as a comic undermining of a cultural assumption shared by poor and rich alike—that wealth was an indicator of God's favor. Life, rather, could be lived out of a fundamental trust, as simply as the wild lilies in the field (Luke 12:27).

Working with the words of Jesus is not everyone's cup of tea. The results are not predictable; the engagement is not simple. Some of my students who have joined me in the *Exercises* resisted the task of working with the words. They would rather have me tell them what the words mean. Others did not like that some sayings run sharply against their presumed image of Jesus. They did not want words that can bite. Moreover, they resisted the burden of putting these words in historical context and having to ask whether the words still have any meaning for the present. Why not simply imitate "buddy Jesus" and leave the thinking out of the picture?

On the other hand, my experience with my colleagues and many students who have dared to struggle with the words and put them into play has convinced me that something quite real is afoot. We do not simply repeat the words of Jesus when we remember them. Instead, we chew on them, taste them, discover in them possibilities that fly against and beyond the fearful constrictions of our world. In knocking our heads together over those fragmentary utterances from a hauntingly creative voice, we pick something up. We discover how to reframe the very conditions of our life together.

Seven sonnets encircling wisdom
A running commentary*   2014

> Wisdom has built her house
> She has hewn her seven pillars
> She has slaughtered her animals
> She has mixed her wine
> She has also set her table
> She has sent out her servant girls,
> She calls from the highest places in the town

You simpletons, turn in here!
To those without sense she says
Come, eat of my bread
And drink of the wine I have mixed
Lay aside immaturity and live
And walk in the way of insight
— Proverbs 9:1–6

I. *In Medias Res*
None of us today deserves to be here.
No calculus exists for what we've done.
Some think that the narrative is quite clear –
an arc stretching from senior to freshman.
But nothing could be farther from the facts.
We who dared know otherwise; that haunting
chill still climbs steadily upon our backs
when for the first time we risked everything,
fell down an unexpected rabbit hole,
saw Neverland sprout in a petri dish,
walked through a minefield in a beggar's bowl,
discovered worlds are built upon a wish.
So many times our breath was lost from fear;
but we adjusted to that atmosphere.

2. The X Factor
Wisdom never comes in preprogramed ways.
No algorithm finds her in advance.
We catch her off the corners of our eyes,
in the odd moment, through a backward glance,
nothing left but a trace upon the heart,
beating out something wild and wonderful.
While the ancients figured each step a part
of something much larger, some cosmic role,
we're left with metaphysical debris.
We no longer dance with constellations.
Shock and awe from the outset seem to be
why white noise hisses from the farthest points.
Are static echoes from those depths of space
enough to conjure meaning for our race?

3. Back to Earth
Before we get quite tangled in the stars,
let's keep our feet upon this shrinking sphere.
Did Proverbs' sage mislead with metaphors –
seven columned splendor, bricks and mortar
or is that the take of corporate dons
with vision shrink-wrapped to the bottom line?
Scarcity bleeds their boardrooms and their brains,
risk averse, yet unable to decline
the latest trends, or what they guess the world
craves to stay ahead of every fear.
Imagination falls to a brand unfurled
as flowcharts paint a future very clear.
Mow the lawns, advertise the golden rule:
a saintly bronze beside the business school.

4. Wisdom's Favela
Wisdom still plies her trade, seducing us
to settle for nothing less than the real.
She sees through our academic circus,
the clowns in gowns, the snob and mob appeal.
She yawns through all that highfalutin praise.
She entertains in no luxury box,
has no need for pomp, nor delicacies.
Well-upholstered suits are not what she seeks.
"Run away," she purrs, "come on home with me,
Break that alarm that circumscribes your life.
Enter this, my shantytown, and you will see
that there is more than constant fear and strife.
Find out why the poor and unimportant say:
'Wisdom comes when you give yourself away.'"

5. Wisdom's Partisans
Sometimes there is nothing left for us but words,
bread crumbs dropped, despite destiny and death,
insouciantly along the boulevards.
Who but the mad pick them up, test their worth?
The likes of Tolstoy, Gandhi, M.L.K.

experiment with human dynamite,
to see if our dreams do more than decay,
to learn if hope is still within our sight.
The aphorisms of an artisan
have leaked out on a planetary scale,
speak to lives of constant desperation,
unsettling experts with a twice-told tale.
What happens to this maddened world if we
unmask our fears and love the enemy?

6. A Blaze of Solidarity
Some say Wisdom flares like a burning nun,
enigmatic to the corporate gaze,
sitting, an incandescent Buddhist sun
that calls in question all our nights and days.
She topples over, ever silently;
soldiers rush in to occupy the spot
replacing any ash of memory
with mindless discipline that serves to blot
the inconvenience of her smoking bones.
Again they're too late to put the fire out.
Those searing images heat up the phones.
From a nameless street comes a primal shout:
empires try to pick you off one by one,
by snuffing out the hope we're not alone.

7. The Play of Wisdom
We all are caught in a midsummer's dream.
Our cosmic nightmare takes a comic twist:
Is there no bottom to the primal scream?
Do we keep falling for the story's gist?
Or can we see beyond the bottom line,
by taking seriously our child's play?
Is this where Wisdom wants us all to dine
with all our fears and foibles on display?
There is no certainty in all of this,
no guarantee we ever get it right;
nor is there any everlasting bliss

as we disintegrate from day to night.
Still Wisdom teases, daring us to dance,
to come alive, at least to take the chance.

---

*Occasionally in these columns I had made "reports from the front," detailing my experience with students. At the closing of the current academic year at Xavier University, I was invited to give the Honors Convocation Address. Instead of congratulating the students, faculty, and parents, I wondered with them whether Wisdom is still possible. Here is my foray into that no man's land.

On a Personal Note

In these commentaries I have shared some of the dearest moments of my life. My experience has shown that whatever insights I come by are soon used to help others. One never knows when, but it does happen. Our lives are curiously tied together. Those singular moments, where our hearts open, usually from pain and hurt, somehow reveal what we can say to others. Often these episodes trigger memories that lead in directions I have only begun to discern. A second cup of tea, a reluctant dryer, a broken-legged robin, even a mother-in-law's eulogy, have shaken my world. I conclude with a letter addressed to my great, great, great grand-children. My words for them, like these commentaries, are like light from stars long gone. I only ask that future readers will look up and keep whatever is beautiful before their eyes to create even more precious visions for our planet.

Ghosts in the machine   1996

Recently my older son needed clean jeans. Because of time constraints, this meant a midnight laundry. I told him to put his clothes in, go to bed, and I would take care of it. Halfway through the dryer's cycle, everything stopped.

Panic ensued. Images of repair bills or new dryers loomed large. But right now the insistent problem was: how to dry those jeans? Oddly I recalled what my mother used to do: iron out the damp clothes. So at 1:30 in the morning I found myself frantically ironing jeans.

The rhythm of the iron brought back memories of my mother's labor and of her stories of her father, which she would recite over the hiss of the iron.

She often told of how my grandfather left home. In the 1890s many working class women of Boston hung their laundry up on the roofs. His mother, pregnant with her second child, tripped tragically on the hem of her dress coming down stairs one Monday morning. Within two years of her death, his father remarried—to the "Belle of the Cove," as she was called. But his father continued to grieve and play songs on the violin his new wife knew were not meant for her ears. Within months of this marriage, his father was killed saving two men by holding up a collapsing iron gate long enough to free them. A few days after his father's funeral, my twelve-year-old grandfather fled the house of the beautiful ice queen.

These haunting images halted as I realized that the jeans were not responding to my desperate measures. Hoping against hope I tried the dryer again. Eerily it creaked and began working. Why it had stopped and then began again still startles me. Perhaps it was time to listen to those ghosts in the machine; those generations tumbling over and over in memory.

An anniversary   1997

The baby boy had been brought home to die. Conceived in the booming aftermath of World War II, his premature birth on April 1 seemed too cruel a joke to play upon a woman who had been told she would never have a child. After enduring two months in an incubator, but with little chance of survival, he was brought home. It would be better that way.

Immediately he was carried to the parish church for baptism. Aware of the inevitable, the priest could only suggest a final desperate attempt: trust more deeply than you ever have before, act without any visible means of support.

So the sleepless days and nights began. She could hold her son in one hand. So tiny, yet she could detect her husband's features. Since breastfeeding was discouraged in those days, she prepared formula around the clock, feeding him two or three drops every fifteen minutes.

Today is the anniversary of my faraway baptism. I was startled into remembering that time when my life was totally in another's hands by the stirring words of a young Rabbi. Recently I had brought seventh and eighth grade students to visit a synagogue. Before we finished our visit we paused at the Holocaust memorial. In it we saw the aching memory of death contend with the cry of life. Rabbi Daniel spoke directly to his young audience: "If anyone ever tells you that you are worthless, that you are nothing, know that God doesn't create garbage, know that God is creating you."

I cannot think of any finer commentary for this anniversary.

▌ Those trembling lights

1997

For someone who has always lived in Ohio, summer arrives with fireflies. They just show up one night, surprising you out of spring. Hovering so invisibly near to you, they blink out the inevitable, phosphorescent pulse of summer.

Nothing you can do to them seems to have a lasting effect on their insistent mating. My sons have gone through all the hunter-gatherer stages. For a number of summers they became adept at snatching fireflies out of midair. At first the fireflies were bottled and we all watched the glass glow, until the light weakened and we released the survivors to the air. And there were times when a jar was liberated in the house. My sons would go to sleep mesmerized by a solitary rhythm of light.

But my sons are spoiled. Having lived in Ohio all of their lives, they do not understand a summer without fireflies. But I do. I grew up with the annoying hum of mosquitoes drowning out the tranquility of sitting in the dark. A firefly was rare. To see stars or fireflies you had to drive out to the country, sometimes twenty or thirty miles away from Metropolitan Boston.

But in Ohio, yes in Cincinnati, they are in your backyard. Recently, as I walked in from the garage after returning from an evening class, they caught me off guard again. They brought back a wondrous night, sixteen years ago. My wife and I had driven to a birthing class and parked near a field teeming with fireflies. I do not remember the particulars of the class but, walking back to the car through that sparkling field, I was convinced that we were caught up in something as subtle and as fragile as those trembling lights.

A second cup of tea   1998

Recently, one morning after dropping off my wife at work, I returned home for a second cup of tea. On the way to the pantry to get some tea, I found two remote control vehicles blocking my path. A sleek, metallic blue-gray Evader S7, a futuristic Delorean, was backed up by a flaming red, big-wheeled 4x4 Hot Machine. They stopped me in my tracks.

Ordinarily I would step over the debris, making a mental note to ask their owners to put them away. But, for some reason, those remote control cars triggered more than annoyance.

I heard myself saying, "The boys are home." With these words issued a sense of quiet excitement. Immediately my mind raced to memories—to my mother's obvious joy whenever her children visit. I now understood why she stands still for a moment, intently holding her hands, in the midst of a noisy reunion.

More deeply than ever before I realized how that heartfelt moment can slip in, when the mindless rush of the everyday slows down before the gentle reality of love.

This moment of intersection, of memory and meaning, would soon be dissipated by the humidity of a Cincinnati August day. The boys would eventually get up and stare hungrily into the refrigerator. The older would drive his brother crazy again with his teasing.

But, for the moment, in a world brimming with pettiness and chaos, I can gratefully whisper, "The boys are home."

Drinking all this in with my second cup of tea ...

Out of the teenage mouth 1999

"It will happen again. It will happen again, if they don't listen." The words of my seventeen-year-old son kept me awake. He first heard of the Colorado shooting while working out at the Y. Throughout the evening he kept close watch on CNN.

Meanwhile my wife called her sister in Denver. My brother-in-law Butch answered. We were worried about him, a retired principal, who keeps going back to school for one reason or another. Besides, his daughters, Paula and Lynn, might be teaching in that school district. Fortunately none of them were at Columbine. But Butch knew the principle, who had done his student teaching under him. Two seasoned teachers fell silent imagining what that man must be going through.

It was almost midnight when I got off the phone. This is the time when teenagers begin to talk. Geoff had been upset by the cable talking heads, who rushed in to fill the horrible gap. He sat on the floor in my study and shook his head, "It's going to happen again." His words did not come out of fear but from conviction:

> I know what it means to feel alone. I've been beaten up because of my color. A couple of months ago a transfer student was mouthing off at everyone in the caf. Nobody wanted to talk to him, just rag on him. He blew me off once. When he did it again, I sat down and told him I wouldn't leave until he said something. Now we're friends. That's what you need to do, listen, reach out.

Instead of calling for yet another commission, why not do the unimaginable? Find wisdom in the mouth of a teenager.

The wounded and the wild 1999

My younger son pointed to a thrashing in our ginkgo tree. A robin hung upside down twisting desperately. One leg was caught in a string meant for a nest, now coiled around a branch, a slipknot for extinction.

How long the bird could survive we didn't know. Nor did we have any idea how to get it down. The branch was too high for our modest ladder. Enter Tim, our neighbor, who gets the MacGyver award. With garden clippers duct-taped to bamboo poles he stretched as far as he could on the top of a ladder commandeered from another neighbor. After a few sweaty moments he cut the bird free.

The left leg was horribly broken. Again we had no idea what to do. A call to the SPCA brought hope: "There's a group called Second Chance Wildlife." Not long afterward I was in the home of Lana in St. Bernard. Holding the frightened creature, she knew the leg was lost. If the bird survived the night, there was a chance. Then Lana told me of a quiet underground of care. Over fifty people around Cincinnati are mindful of the broken ones.

In fact, Pat, on the west side, has a greenhouse where she nurses amputee birds back to health. When they're strong enough, they're released to the trees around her house. And the magic lingers on, for, when healthy birds nest in her trees, the broken ones uncharacteristically fill in for the overburdened parents. Birds of different feathers actually do flock together.

Who would have thought such desperate thrashing about would have brought me into this peaceable kingdom of the wounded and the wild?

By the way, the robin survived the night.

▌ Emporium of serendipity   1999

The Basement is bankrupt. Filene's Bargain Basement, that emporium of serendipity, where anything could turn up, and, if you waited for four weeks, you could have it for a song, is on the financial ropes.

But I've known it's been in trouble for some time. Though living in Cincinnati, I've had an inside informer—my mother. For the last few years she has noted that Filene's doesn't have the sales it once did. Macy's, the former Jordan Marsh, has "much better buys." So, I've known Filene's was in trouble.

In its heyday Filene's was Boston's real Combat Zone. No punches were pulled, no holds barred, in getting to items. The year I was born over seventeen thousand women broke down the doors to salvage the merchandise on sale from a Neiman Marcus fire.

As you descended from the street on the escalator you discovered a scene as wild as Waterloo: skirmishes everywhere—

among the hats, the stockings, the shoes, the shirts, the suits, the ties.

Years before Victoria's Secret, children dragged along could witness the unimaginable as matrons pulled bras and girdles off tables and strenuously fitted themselves in the aisles still in their clothes.

My brother and I retreated to the luggage. We would play with the locks, imagining being anywhere else. I fancied London. Nearby stood the only oasis of calm. There we were often bribed with a paper cup of vanilla ice cream sprinkled with chocolate "jimmies."

A few months before my wedding my mother came home with her biggest coup. Patiently stalking the automatic mark-down, she made her move. Reaching for a dress she unerringly knew would fit, out of the grasp of another veteran huntress, she found the ultimate buy: a thousand dollar wedding dress marked down to ten dollars.

▌ Out of the cave   2000

In less than two weeks I'll be teaching on the edge. Gandhi would call it an "experiment in truth." No, it's not going to be some sort of public spectacle. It's more subversive than that. Seventh and eighth graders and I will be reading a selection from Plato—the allegory of the cave—and then compare it to the visually stunning film, *The Matrix*.

A few days ago I got an intimation of what may happen. My thirteen-year-old son couldn't sleep. The Christmas vacation had taken its toll on his nightly routine. A story didn't work. Neither did a 1:00 a.m. snack. So, I took advantage of his weakened condition. I suggested reading the "allegory of the cave." After he read it through and we cleared up some of the archaic translations, I asked him what was going on. He grasped the scene: people chained from birth in a cave and forced to think that the only reality was the shadows and sounds coming from the facing wall. Then freed and wrenched from the shadowbox of the cave, the liberated one discovered the ordinary wonders of the earth and sun.

And if he were to return to the cave? Here Nick thought awhile and remembered *The Matrix*. "They wouldn't believe him. He threatens what they think is real." Then I asked him to go back to the beginning of Plato. What was the story of the cave really about? "Education," he read, then smiled, recognizing he had made the connection.

I wonder what will happen when he gets back to school.

▌ Where our wealth is found 2000

▌ The boys are sleeping in. After dropping off my wife at work, I return home this early June morning. It's been humid for the last few days. The sun is subtly winking on the morning dew. Time for a second cup of tea before I start my research.

The applause of their graduations has died down. I see Geoffrey again, on leaving the stage with his high school diploma, raise his fist and bring it down—yes! The faculty enjoyed what was the only visible disturbance of the evening's protocol. Nicholas, our giant teddy bear, sporting a yellow tie against a black jacket, basked in his eighth grade ceremony with a calm and steady gaze.

For Geoff the last eighteen months have been a survival course. He now knows that nothing he will face in college will be as daunting as the hell he went through. A Dante of the third millennium, he walked out of the adolescent inferno.

In formal terms ("Dear Mother and Father") Nick wrote us a note of thanks for being there for him. As he went on, I was struck by his assessment of the constant sibling feud. His honest longhand intimates how he will meet the future.

Last night, as we sorted out our bills, trying once again to keep the ship of professorial poverty afloat, we never wondered aloud where the money went. We've known for years where our wealth is found.

And this morning it's sleeping in.

▌ My own worst nightmare 2000

▌ Did you ever fall asleep with the radio on? Or have it turn on when you were dreaming?

Last week it happened to me. Somehow I was involved in a panel discussion about Buddhism. Every time I would offer a word, I was cut off by what seemed to be a non-sequitur. When I finally got my say, I found myself in a totally different situation with people all around me wondering why this babbling about mortality.

My father used to fall asleep listening to the ball game. Was this his field of dreams? But, considering it was the Boston Red Sox, it was probably "Nightmare on Yawkey Way" with Bucky Dent ever hitting the ball over the Green Monster or the baseball scurrying ad infinitum through Bill Buckner's hobbled legs.

While serving on jury duty a couple of years ago I met a woman, who, on recognizing me, said that she liked waking up with me. Another chimed in, saying unabashedly, if not infelicitously, that she enjoyed me in her shower.

I used to think that a professor's worst nightmare was to be condemned to read the lecture notes of his students. But things could be worse! I might be in your dream right now—a poor man's Picasso! A voice shrink wrapped by your *id*. In fact, talk about invading your dream might induce a dream within a dream.

And, if I were to be sleeping when this commentary airs, I could become my own worst nightmare!

Perhaps the best thing is to issue a disclaimer: Neither I nor this station nor any of its underwriters take responsibility for what might be presently occurring in your dreams.

But, let's be honest, are not all commentaries woven from such shuffling frustrations and waking dreams?

At the thought of human contact 2002

He stood in front of the campus chapel with a Bible in his raised right hand. For whatever reason, he had come to bring the University back from the edge of perdition. This thirty-something preacher in a business suit set his face like flint against the inevitable remarks of passing sophomores. He stood his ground for God and the literal truth against the liberal laxity of this so-called Christian institution.

Some passing co-eds felt uncomfortable under his intense inspection. Other students meekly accepted his leaflets, only to toss them away when they got to class. A few simply gawked, marveling at how this guy was "so into God." And there were some who felt inexplicably that he might be onto something.

Even the campus police were at a loss. How should they handle this? What choice did they have in their repertoire of control? They feared that whatever steps they took would only bring him back again.

All the while Geoff studied this scene. A fledgling psychology major, he brought a perspective that knew what it was like to live in hell. Even in his last year in high school he grasped that Dante had gotten it right so long ago.

So what did that preacher want? What was it that others were too busy, too afraid, too preoccupied, to see?

Geoff approached the man and asked for a hug. He told the stunned evangelist that he would listen to what he had to say after giving him a hug.

"No, I'm no homosexual," the preacher yelled. He fled in fear; surprised that someone actually would come close. The Word of God screeches to a halt at the thought of human contact, doesn't it?

▌ Fathers and sons 2002

▌ Yesterday we celebrated the birthday of my older son. Twenty-one years ago I walked out of Good Samaritan Hospital into the afternoon sun and discovered that I saw children in a profoundly different light. To put it awkwardly, I began to see children from the inside out. No longer was a child a "cute kid." Each carried the human mystery in every unsteady movement.

Because of what I learned from my son I began to take the nuclear buildup in the '80s personally. And I rejoiced to see how many people around the world shared this refusal to give up on human life together.

My son still leads me on. In this time when fear is our national mascot, when critical thought is replaced by ideological rant, and when discussion of the common good is lost in profit-taking moves, I wonder what will soon be happening to our children.

The neon signs of war have been blinking for some time. If you listened to the Sunday morning talk shows you would think only the unpatriotic or the criminally insane could imagine a scenario where the US would not go to war with Iraq.

At least in the Gulf War of 1991 there was lip service paid to fighting a "just war." Today we don't need such moral niceties. Even when Scott Ritter, the former UN inspector in Iraq and a card-carrying Republican, publicly declares that there is no basis for the Administration's warmongering, when European allies and Arab states vehemently disagree with America's military proposals, nothing seems to sink in.

Donald Rumsfeld, unable to justify his military flight of fancy, stubbornly replies with a Clintonesque dodge: "Absence of evidence is not evidence of absence."

Actually there is evidence but not what the Administration wants known. The Third Marine Expeditionary Force in California is preparing to have twenty thousand Marines deployed in Iraq for ground combat operations by mid-October. We could also mention, for example, Boeing's accelerated production of GPS satellite kits for the targeting of bombs for late September.

Others can rehearse these tactical designs. I want to stay with fathers and sons. How many will be lost in the desert sands because one son simply wants to finish what his father started?

▌ Tea leaves 2004

As I washed out my Brown Betty teapot, I became absorbed in the splash of tea leaves on the bottom of the sink. For a moment I peered down trying to do what my mother instinctively does. For years she has squinted at tea leaves at the bottom of a cup and has made uncanny observations.

Last summer as I got out of a cab I looked down the street to see her walking with my brother back to her apartment. She stopped and stared. For she had seen the scene already—in the bottom of a tea cup. The late afternoon sun silhouetted me and my bags on the sidewalk beside the standing cab. Once more those wet, black specks inside a china cup had grown to human size.

What my mother does is not so unusual. What is extraordinary is her success rate. Taking her time, with pursed lips, she angles the cup to catch the lamplight. From the most meager shreds she detects meaning that hits home.

As I said, what she does is not so unusual. As the presidential campaigns begin to heat up, we'll see an overabundance of political soothsayers, witlessly rushing to ride the tidal wave of cable TV.

But a deeper and more reaching scrutiny is already underway. Yet how many of us will catch what the Hubble telescope reveals? What do we make of all those spiraling galaxies? What future do we read in those specks of the past, stardust in the teacup of the universe?

Is this heaven? No, it's Iowa! 2004

Just a few weeks ago as the Boston Red Sox began to reverse their curse by stunning the Yankees with four straight wins and as the Sox pitchers continued their magic upon the vaunted Cardinals' lineup, I journeyed with my wife back to southwestern Iowa for her mother's funeral.

Verna Davis had lived long and prospered for ninety-five years. She had survived two husbands, raised four children, and taught grammar school for over thirty years. Verna was my mother-in-law and a Republican whom I respected and with whom I often agreed.

She loved sports, wore Nebraska red, and watched baseball the day before she died.

Verna could well have been the model for Iowa's new state quarter, featuring a country schoolhouse and a teacher with her pupil.

So there I was in the Holiday Inn the night before her funeral, watching the Sox win it all under the blood red eclipse of the moon. The dashed and ever-recurring dreams of generations welled up in me as Foulke threw to first for the final out. While my wife read and dozed, I celebrated what my father never lived to see with an A&W root beer from the soda machine.

Then I sat down to write Verna's eulogy. For a second I wondered, "Is this Heaven?" "No, it's Iowa."

A gift outright 2005

A true story as our country descends into the darkness of the bottom line

It was Mother's Day 1986. Kevin had simply told his parents he would be there for dinner. His folks had finally decided to retire and would be facing an uncertain future. His father had worked twenty-seven years for a milk company that went under after illegally devouring the workers' pensions. For the next fourteen years he had worked tending cars and elderly priests at Boston College. Rita, having worked her way from waitress to director of an executive dining room, had the good sense to know that she had worked long enough.

They had rented all their married life. Their money flowed out with the needs of their children. Their present apartment was getting more and more expensive to heat.

Now, ten years before, Kevin, the impractical artist and dancer—not telling a soul—spent all his savings, making a down payment on a tiny condo in Boston's North End. Leasing the condo out, he rented a hole-in-the-wall for himself and waited for the right time. A month before Mother's Day he sold the condo and with the profit paid off the mortgage and purchased outright another, somewhat larger, condo.

On that Sunday after dinner, he handed the deed of 8 Wiget Street to his mother.

▌The kaleidoscope of care 2005

Even if I had all the talent in the world, I could not paint a portrait of my mother. My brother and sister, both artists, have attempted that labor of love numerous times. But I never got beyond a clumsy calamity of paint and paper.

Moreover, what are portraits really all about? Historically they were social indicators of the elite. They tipped off viewers that the subject on canvas had a dominating position.

Since the mid-nineteenth century the photograph has led a democratic revolution. Now anyone can hold a likeness of loved ones.

But the photograph came as part of a new world where the multiplicity of angles and perspectives confirm what physicists suggest.

The story of a face is no longer a simple line. Each human point is an intersection of an infinite number of lines; each human life is an event that extends simultaneously throughout the universe.

Consider a young mother with a child so small that she can hold him in one hand. Revise the scene every fifteen minutes for feeding a few drops. And wonder how far her words sink into that premature babe, when she whispers, "Everything's all right."

The painting shifts again and again in the kaleidoscope of care. And, as it shifts, what do we detect about the heartbeat of the universe?

▍ So light I cried   2005

Every time I return home to Boston I tremble. Intellectually I know that the years take a toll on all of us; that as we age our bodies diminish; that women particularly suffer from telling calcium loss.

But, when I go home, it is hardly a head-trip. Delicately leaning forward in her hallway, my mother greets me as I climb the stairs.

Then it happens. As we hug I feel her curving back, detecting less and less fat about her bones. I have held dazed robins in my hands, felt the insistent throbbing of their life. My mother is becoming a little bird.

As my visit continues I feel as if I have entered a Zen garden, where emptiness holds sway, where a pebble speaks wonders in a sea of sand.

And so I sit, listen, and see.

I hear her singing in the kitchen. The same giddy tunes whenever her children come home. She insists on making the tea and sets the table on the porch.

As she raises her teacup to mine, I ache in understanding well the words of Ishikawa Takuboku, a nineteenth-century Japanese poet:

> For fun I carried my mother on my back
> She was so light I cried
> And couldn't take three steps.

▍ Nashville blues   2005

It seemed like a win-win situation. My younger son had received tickets to the Raiders-Titans game in Nashville. The weekend weather looked promising. He and his girl friend would go to the game, my wife would visit the Frist Center for the Visual Arts and I would return to the Parthenon.

Originally built in plaster and wood for Tennessee's 1897 Centennial Exposition, this life-size replica of the Parthenon in Athens was saved from its temporary fate by the citizens of Nashville. By 1931, after ten years of reconstruction, it stood proudly as the centerpiece of Centennial Park.

But there is more than just a magnificent building. If you go inside you come upon the daunting forty-two-foot statue of Athena, in her helmet, with the goddess Nike in her right hand and her enormous shield at her left side. Her skin is painted in ivory; gold leaf details her dress, helmet, and shield. You stand there looking up, stunned, in awe.

That was the plan. But, after walking around Centennial Lake, I found the entrance locked. The Parthenon is closed on Sundays after summer ends.

Well, then off to the Frist. Before I entered the galleries, I noticed some museum catalogues. In one I spied Albert Bierstadt's misty landscape of Mount Tamalpais near San Francisco. Having been there often, I wanted to see what the painting offered.

I appeared to be in luck. Master works from painters of the Hudson River School were on display. Bierstadt was one of those nineteenth-century discoverers of what nature could reveal.

But *Mt. Tamalpais* was not there. The haunting works of Cole, Wadsworth, Church, Durand, and Bierstadt were there. Sunsets that set achingly behind mountains, pastoral interludes on distant shores, panoramas that caught great and small, spectacular vistas and crystalline lakes, all these and more were there.

But where was *Mt. Tamalpais*? I went back to the catalog. The painting had been shown recently at the Frist, but it was now back where it was housed permanently—in The Parthenon!

Fatherhood—from the inside out
2006

It's just not the same with us, with men, that is. We don't get a nine months head start in parenting as mothers do. There is no umbilical cord to tie us to our children. In fact, from my own experience, we are a bit obtuse. It takes us time to realize what's going on.

I know when it hit me. After leaving the delivery room and making the obligatory calls to family and friends, I walked out into the Saturday afternoon sunshine. I noticed some children playing across the street from the hospital. Unlike W. C. Fields, I've always enjoyed children. But on that afternoon a light went on within.

A sense of gratitude had been welling up ever since my son had taken his first breath. Where this thankfulness came from I could not tell. But something in me was set in motion and bathed the children across the street in a new light. I saw that life truly was lived from the inside out. It was no longer a matter of some easy notions and ideas about kids; no, I knew that from now on I was in the compelling world of care.

That moment launched me into the future. I began to see that what was to come was not simply scripted for me. So, I began to work against the prospect of a nuclear winter. For I could not shake off the worry that my generation would leave our children and their untold children to come with a miserable existence.

This inside-out epiphany also led me to reread the ancient account of Abraham and Isaac.

Wilfred Owen, writing shortly before his death in World War I, rewrote that tale. From his vantage point in the muck and mire of the trenches, with the heavens declaring only death from above, he saw old man Abraham, refusing the angel's stay of execution, and instead "slew his son, And half the seed of Europe, one by one."

I must admit that it seems the various offspring of Abraham today are following in their father's bloody footsteps.

But then I looked again—from the inside. The story of the sacrifice of Isaac is a very primitive piece. In fact, many scholars have pointed out that this story represents the passage away from human sacrifice.

Yet this is a story of a father and a son, not just an anthropological flyover. And from it I began to discover my own way into it. Notwithstanding the ways later generations would draw Abraham and his loyalty to God, this story goes deeper than making nice with the "Powers That Be." Nor is it merely a "transitional phase in human development."

No, this is a story about fatherhood. It finally dawned on Abraham that he had a son, not an installment on a promise. We can notice that the angel's interruption was how the ancient mind projected what we today would find within. Indeed, there was enormous turmoil within. A father broke through the lies and lures of a sacrificial culture in which he was embedded. For a split second he saw "the way things were" as sharply edged as a dagger, because his son's life was on the chopping block. He finally got it and realized what fatherhood meant in flesh and blood.

It sometimes takes men a lifetime to come to this. I recall my brother saying that in the days before he died, my father, when asked what he was thinking, simply said he was remembering his children. As he slipped away from us, he finally was at peace, being a father.

▌An ancient fear 2006

In what seems like a lifetime ago I feared I would become a dinosaur. No, I was not dreaming of Jurassic Park. Rather, I was considering my future. Would plunging into New Testament studies keep me "forever amber," a professorial fossil, an academic museum piece, occasionally exhibited to remind people of what had become culturally irrelevant?

At times, especially at national professional meetings, I can feel the hot breath of that lingering fear. I recall one time walking from my distant hotel to the convention site in New Orleans. After my first encounter with grits, I spied the *Picayune Times* headline. A California Congressman was missing in Guyana. Then, in the succeeding days, the news of the mass suicide of James Jones's followers became my morning ticker tape. As far as I could see there was little notice of this among the thousands seeking the elusive Assistant Professor position or the panels rehearsing the recherché.

I knew that could happen. Certainly it is a commonplace to observe that humans thrive on distractions and miss not only the obvious but also—tragically often—the crucial.

Yet I did not start my studies naively. I had already read the letters of Paul in Greek and had discovered from that utopian thinker that the human act of trust was the basic tissue of our life together. Again and again I would experiment with that insight. Often surprising things would happen. I also realized that I would be spending my time with radioactive material. This stuff merited caution. It had somehow detonated an Empire. I also noted how often apologists in the tradition would suffer from mental meltdowns.

And then there was that figure of Jesus. After spending some weeks with Joachim Jeremias' *Parables of Jesus*, I caught a breath of fresh air. The poetry of that peasant artisan intrigued me so much that, as Holmes would put it, "the game was afoot."

But I knew from the outset that these studies were not just about me. To enter into biblical studies meant dealing with the reality and resistance of cultural memory. I knew that I would be forever caught in the flotsam and jetsam of two worlds. Antiquity and modernity would pull me every which way. My work was a Janus task: to hold onto both ends of the dangling conversation.

But I would not be alone. The Jesus Seminar rescued me from any slide into fossilization. Bob Funk saw to that by realizing that our national fortune was inextricably linked to the Judeo-Christian mythos. By keeping critical religious discourse out of the public domain, we, as a nation, were "dumbing" ourselves down. It was thus our responsibility as scholars of religion to speak to this withering silence. Each of us began to see that what seemed to be remote work had an enormous payoff for anyone interested in the future of our cultural conversation.

People took notice. With the attention of the national news media, this critical group of scholars was no longer flying under the radar. It became even fashionable to think seriously about Christian origins. And this was years before *The Da Vinci Code*!

But what has been more significant is the growing number of Associates and advocates of the Seminar's work. Their continued interest and hard questioning challenge the Fellows to grow and become as honest as possible. From the Associates came the Jesus Seminars on the Road. What the media overlook are the many people hungering for a critical and open discussion of religion. Again and again people at the JSORs have found that they do not have to sacrifice their brains to maintain their hearts. A critical re-appraisal of the first century does not consign our traditions to the dumpster. Instead, people have begun to pick up strategies of survival from noticing those early communities.

Now we are at the outset of a new Seminar. Begun in Miami last spring, the Seminar on Christian Origins may prove in the long run to be the most explosive.

One thing I had forgotten when I began to fear becoming a dinosaur. While the dinosaurs went extinct, the unnoticed and underfoot, the mammals, survived.

Reflection between painkillers

2008

For some time Bishop John Spong has reminded Christians that they are facing what he would call an incredible creed. In a variety of books he has made a cogent case. Indeed, he has gone beyond complaint to construction, to an articulation of what Jesus and God mean to him in his present experience. Utilizing the theological efforts of Paul Tillich, Spong has translated the outdated credo into the poetry of critical realism.

I wonder if that is as far as one can go.

This question came home forcefully to me as I was in the hospital for gall bladder surgery. In the midst of procedures, x-rays, endoscopies, and surgery, some of the nurses found out what I did for a living. Even though they were not supposed to bring up religious matters, I found myself being asked questions on the Bible and what I believed in. You become rather honest on the days before surgery.

At the same time the students of my Senior Seminar were left to their own devices. In fact, I took the occasion to encourage academic revolution, namely, that they take over the class and experience co-operative learning in my absence. I had them read two books over the summer. One was a book on the new cosmology; the other, entitled *The Human Web*, caught up the flow of human history in one volume, emphasizing the intersections of human civilization through time around the globe.

My Senior Seminar began with some introductory remarks from a professor who was obviously jaundiced. Later that afternoon I was having blood drawn. The next day brought the emergency ward. I was able to send orders for the students to try to compose a creed from their initial theses on the new cosmology. Reports from one of my "spies" in the class indicated what I thought would happen. They debated, argued and collided. They could come up with little more than "Here we are." They had undermined their own positions, while at the same time they had overlooked a major assumption—the notion of the creed itself.

Meanwhile after three days of draining, surgery revealed more gall stones than anticipated and thus more complicated surgery and a larger scar. Four days later I was home. Time on my hands. Time to recuperate, to sleep, to wake, to sleep, to get up and take some pain medicine, time to sleep, to wake, to invent mischief.

I asked my students to continue the creedal madness. I asked them to go back through the chapters of *The Human Web* and to compose creeds for each of the civilizations that emerged through time and space. I also gave them a working definition of creed: *the symbolic expression of how we think the cosmos works.* I then asked them to compose two more creeds: a creed for the gas-guzzling world and a one for an alternative green world. This is where they are right now—in the midst of coming to grips with three imaginative constructions. I wanted them to see that a creed has never been a personal expression but an articulation of a communal vision. A creed is not a simple religious artifact that theologians can poke and prod to get some information. It is more a synapse binding many facets of life on the planet at a certain time and place. It is an expression of how we imagine the world works.

When I was asked in the hospital what I believed, I was thrust back on what I had worked through all these years. I found that the Catholic chaplain with his plastic covered prayer book was a sympathetic but comically distant figure; that the Rabbi spoke my language of being caught in the very midst of things; that Matt, the "personal care assistant" on the overnight shift, who loved jazz, had an autistic younger brother and a baby out of wedlock, carried compassion in his bones. I told the nurses who wondered about the Bible that things were more complicated and that the vision of Jesus was not some proposition but an abiding trust. Through the numerous conversations I struck up with personal care assistants, housekeepers, nurses, and doctors, through the interminable waiting, painful nights, endless blood work, I saw that I was involved in a very fine tissue of care, certainly never perfect, but constantly trying to do the right thing. I got a glimpse on how the world painfully works.

So, with a laptop on my legs, underneath the stitches, along with my students and all those hospital workers, I attempt to sketch out how I imagine the cosmos works. We are not in just one world anymore. Nor have we fully digested the view from the Hubble Telescope. Indeed, we are caught in worlds that presage a future—the world of the dinosaur to which we are addicted and an ill-defined alternative that senses the radical connection of everything. In fact, these very words I type attempt to articulate that radical tissue of trust I experienced so forcefully this week.

Perhaps this is where the "creedal question" is going. As each of us begins to perceive the seismic shifts on our lives, we try to communicate to one another the painstaking experience of being human to one another.

Lost (and found) in translation 2010

A few days ago a graduate student I was tutoring interrupted our conversation over the possible sources in the story of Jacob's dream in Genesis 28 by asking: how did I decide to become a biblical scholar? The question was not some sort of delaying tactic; he was truly curious. I knew he has been wondering about his own future and we had already rehearsed the harsh realities of job prospects for Bible scholars in the present economic climate. I also realized that he was catching glimpses of unexpected horizons as we made our way through various texts. It seemed quite appropriate, then, to bring my own past out of the shadows. Just as Jacob's story did not start at Bethel but extended backwards into a hectic past and stretched into an uncertain future, so each human story wends its precarious way through time and space.

My story began with being flummoxed. Actually it began about a year before that when I was twelve. I had finally done something right in school and ended up eating rubber chicken at a Kiwanis Club luncheon. My mother wanted to encourage this edging into the academic by declaring that I could have anything I wanted. Since we had little money, certain items were out of the question. I did, however, consider a forbidden thing. And, as I contemplated it, my desire for it grew. Now this was in pre-Vatican II days. What could I ask for that would not cost an arm and a leg but would give my mother pause? Of course! A Bible! Catholics often featured gilt edged Bibles on their coffee tables. But they never opened them except to mark an occasional baptism or wedding. (We didn't even have that kind.) Only Protestants read the Bible and everyone knew where they're going. My request did stop my mother in her tracks. Yet, she swallowed hard and surprised me a few days later with my first Bible.

Without having read the Bible I was already a biblical literalist. I believed that the Truth would make me free. All I had to do was to read the Bible and things would be perfectly clear. So I began eagerly with Genesis and moved on into Exodus with increasing enthusiasm. By the time I got to Leviticus I was talking to myself. I had no idea what was going on. Then the histories of the land of Canaan spilled more than milk and honey in my lap. Repetition, unexplained customs and cruelties, a nagging suspicion that I might be missing some joke (there must be some humor there, right?), and those names, some running more wildly than the rivers, all this and more kept my mind off the ever-tragic Red Sox (but not for long). The prophets' kaleidoscopic visions were tantalizing but out of my league. Nor did the Wisdom writings sound that wise to an almost-teen. I thought I found relief when I reached the New Testament. Surely here things would get straightened out. But no. Jesus didn't sound at all like what I had imagined him. In fact, he seemed to be speaking out of both sides of his mouth (which he actually seemed to do in Revelation!). I honestly don't even remember what I thought of Paul. He just seemed to go on and on. When I finally finished with the Apocalypse I had wild and crazy images rumbling through my brain. It had taken me about a year of determined slogging. I would finish that book just as I finished so many limping novels and uninspiring biographies (such as Zebulon Pike).

Some would say that this was hardly a promising start for a biblical career. But it was the best thing for a stubborn twelve year old to fling his wit and will so wildly on that mute text. Nothing was resolved. And many questions kept nagging me, although never in some overwhelming way. But they were there, like unseen critters in the woods.

All of those efforts got lost through my college years. Or so I thought. I entered an MDiv program with the intention of doing a joint doctoral program in religion and literature. But then I had lunch with George MacRae. George had taught me in his course on Hebrews. Over the mousaka and Ouzo in a Cambridge Greek restaurant, he asked what I wanted to do with my life. No one had ever asked me this. I told him of my plans. He dismissed them saying that I would never find a position with such a hybrid degree. I then asked him somewhat defensively what I should study. He answered directly: New Testament. George hit a nerve deep within. I never thought a lay person could consider such a career. I countered with various objections, including all the languages I would have to know. But he beat back everyone, ending with, "You like languages; it's just a matter of sitting down and learning." That summer I read the letters of Paul in Greek with George. I slowly began not only to understand what Paul meant by *pistis* (trust) but also to realize how life itself is woven out of a delicate tissue of trust.

All of this seems so long ago. But now, after years of work with Roy Hoover, Lane McGaughy, and Daryl Schmidt to produce *The Authentic Letters of Paul*, I realize that I would have never been part of that exhilarating wrestling with the text without a mother who entrusted a Bible to a naughty twelve-year old and a teacher who confided his student with the truth.

Awkward openings 2013

It can happen anywhere. Often it is awkward. Your mouth has been forced open with an array of dental devices, Novocain slowly creeps into your gums and lips, and the dentist says, "You're a Bible scholar; what do you think of what they're saying about Jesus?" Or, it might be shortly after a gall bladder operation, and, while you're trying to get what little rest you can steal between blood pressure checks and pill dispensing, a nurse inquires sheepishly, "I know we shouldn't ask these questions, but what do you think about God?" Perhaps the most uncomfortable situation occurs in the fetid "little ease" of an intercontinental flight, when the person beside you opens with, "I see that you are reading a book about Revelation,..." and then proceeds to lay out a detailed flowchart of the final days. Unless this disquisition is interrupted by the food cart or warnings of turbulence, the inevitable question comes, "So, what do you think about *that*?"

Now, one could simply observe that all this is just part of the job of being a scholar of religion. It is the price scholars pay for getting involved in such matters. But curiously no one asking these questions ever worries about a consulting fee! Some years ago when Proctor and Gamble was bothered by the uproar over their "Moon and Stars" logo, a vice president called me, asking if I could explain the symbolism of the logo and its possible religious connotations. I told him I could, and remembering that my business school colleagues received a consulting fee from P&G, I cheekily added that I would expect a fee upon submission of my report. He demurred and never called back. *Religious questions are apparently worth asking, but are they really worth anything?* Actually I am not distressed over such awkward openings about things that matter. In fact, I am often reminded of the rabbinic challenge: that one should be able to encapsulate the entire meaning of Torah while standing on one leg! Such unexpected raids of the inarticulate compel me to gain some clarity about what in the world I am doing.

Indeed, let me repeat the question: *What in the world am I doing?* Such a question often ricochets about the brain when you are stunned by events, when you are thrown for a loss of words. It also intimates that whatever I am doing involves a "world." Somehow a larger picture is entailed. And even the words I use are part of an ongoing conversation I am having with others. Despite the scholarly temptation to remain a comfortable recluse, I succumb to being bothered by the questions others offer me. Perhaps this weakness is congenital; it certainly is habitual. For I have gotten into the habit of being stunned. I have found that my experiences with others have continued to stretch me so much that I often have described *theology* untraditionally as *the reflection upon the depths of our experience.* I have tried to face honestly whatever emerges from the encounters of my life. I have recognized that I am not alone on this planet and that the resources to make sense of things are not limited to either the present time or place. I can thus attempt to listen sensitively to the variety of voices, past and present, which sometimes form a modulating chorus, sometimes reverberate with a callous cacophony. So, when unexpected questions detonate around me, I hunker down in the crater left by their impact, and feel my way along the inevitable aftershocks.

As you can tell, I've lapsed into metaphors. But this is no frosting on the rhetorical cake. Metaphors move us onto the no man's land of speech, where we use sounds we know for what beggars our speech. We return from the depths of our experience with words that gesture beyond themselves. What we sighted—was it a grail?—comes back with us only on our lips. And when we listen to the speech of religious traditions we begin to see with new ears. Our very synapses begin to mirror the treks others have made. Somehow the clasped hands on an ancient funeral stele reach into our brains. Stone touches our flesh.

But that is not all that happens. These connecting jolts expose and often shatter our world. Every journey we make into the interior of our religious traditions disentangles us from the assumptions that determine our world. We can go home again, back to our world; but our perspective has changed. Perhaps for the first time we see the fishbowl we have ever been swimming in. Plato talked about returning back to the cave and taking the measure of the shadow show. *The Matrix*, the 1999 science fiction film, reprises that platonic spelunking. Another way of saying this is that our journey has taken a critical turn. We have become amphibians, conscious that our world is not the end of it all; nor is the world that intrigues us the final word.

But, because of those fragmentary contacts, nothing is ever the same. We can no longer read our world just along familiar lines. What we have seen, what visions and dreams we have glimpsed in our border crossings, haunt us. Worlds collide in us. We begin to notice that others, both in the present and in the past, also perpetrated such "breaking and entering." Jesus of Nazareth, for example, very much embodies this in his parabolic dyslexia. In fact, if we continue to make frequent and disquieting crossings, we shall find ourselves in a most interesting predicament. We shall become "maladjusted," as Martin Luther King, Jr. in an early speech on non-violence challenged his listeners to become:

> as maladjusted as Amos who in the midst of the injustices of his day cried out in words that echo across the generation.... As maladjusted as Abraham Lincoln who had the vision to see that this nation could not exist half slave and half free.... As maladjusted as Jesus of Nazareth who dreamed a dream of the fatherhood of God and the brotherhood of man.*

---

* Martin Luther King, Jr., "The Power of Non-violence," June 4, 1957.

▌A vacation reverie   2013

My dear great, great, great grandchildren,

I trust that somehow, by some incredible luck, my words have reached you. I write to you with some modicum of hope, perhaps because I am far from the usual din and incessant madness of city life. I have found a few days of quiet in a little town on the side of a mountain in La Verna, Italy. Among these rocks an almost blind Francesco of Assisi, distraught over what his friars had done to his original vision and so physically worn out that he would die two years later at forty-four, hunkered down in the crevices and moss to detect the mystery of his life.

I have not had to sleep in caves but I have become as quiet as these woods. Moments of silence and centering have brought me to the edge of my fears and hopes. Maybe I'm crazy but I have dared to put a human face on the oncoming future. So, this is my feeble attempt to write to you, so many years away, to tell you that many of us really have been concerned and almost paralyzed about what the future holds for you, our descendants, our offspring.

Our leaders have been in denial, negligent and even obstructive in providing living solutions to the changes in climate. Unable to think in the long term, they do not want to disturb their economic universe, nor the profit-making concerns of their financial backers. Neither do they genuinely encourage concerned citizens to work collaboratively for a genuine response to these dire threats.

The ordinary person feels either trapped or unable to do anything that may significantly help matters. Many simply have become numb, avoiding any thinking about it. And many others run from the prospect, looking instead to the short term, gathering their pitiful profits in the hope that the disasters will come after they are gone, or, if they are still around, that they will be sheltered in their gated communities or private islands far from the calamity to come.

But, of course, the lives of most of us on the planet are and will continue to be in desperate straits. There will be increasing conflicts over the precious water on this planet. Communities of the "haves" already are defending their "rights and property" while abandoning all those who were unfortunate enough not to gamble wisely in the crumbling financial markets. As the waters rise, massive migrations and panic will inevitably occur. Already countless millions are starving. I can only shudder at what will be the cost in human lives.

My only hope is that something will come from where the movers and shakers of the world least expect. Perhaps the frayed burlap remains of Francesco have had an effect on me. Could the poor and all those with little to lose be the ones who will see that there is a possibility for concerted, collaborative action, not for mindless revenge? Will people rise up like the Argentine *madres* whose children were "disappeared"?

How this will work out I haven't a clue. I fear, indeed, that the oligarchs around the planet will use their power and government forces as well as their private police to put down any threat.

But I am crazy enough to hope that a certain creative shrewdness will emerge from the "little ones" of the world. It happened once with an exodus of slaves from Egypt; then, years later that wordsmith and artisan, Jesus, aroused the poor with the dream that God's Empire was theirs and carried forward the revolution. For a while things were turned upside down by peasants and nobodies who took such wild speech to heart. People began to live out of the conviction that the deepest power resides among the nameless, the powerless, despite the propaganda of the dominating elite. Some of us can still remember how Gandhi renewed the impact of those courageous words. Martin Luther King, Jr. continued the experiment. Nelson Mandela, cut off from contact for almost three decades by the government, still kept abreast of things by listening to what the authorities never imagined to be important: the tribal drums! Will some of us in the twenty-first century carry on this rag tag zigzag of imagination and hope?

I strain to hear that there are others around the globe, unknown to me, who will become comrades in hope from all and any background and mount drives that will take inspiration from Gandhi and King, Caldecott and Sakharov, Tutu and Mandela. If this happens on a worldwide scale there just may be hope for you.

We do not need for everyone on the planet to stand together. A courageous minority, on a number of global fronts, could begin to turn the tide. Many major battles have been won when a little band refused to break and held their ground. Who will be there to refuse to give in to the incessant pressure to do so? Refuse we must, holding the ground against ignorance, greed, and shortsightedness.

Maybe we can finally learn from history and recognize that real change does not come in some grand gesture or cataclysmic event, but in those small acts of courage which, when multiplied in endless surprises across the planet, can overwhelm the powers that be.

If you are reading this (again, I am thinking crazy!) somehow, somewhere humans refused to give in and found ways to act that surprised even themselves. You have fortunately survived the crisis—at least to some degree.

Forgive us our debts, for we have burdened you with so much. I hope that whatever positive efforts we have made will have lightened your burden. I suspect that, if there has been some success in warding off the harshness of the climate changes, you will still have much work to do and that there will be people who will still prefer to look out for themselves. Do not fall prey to their mindless behavior, for it is precisely their attempts to control and hold on that brought humanity to its knees again and again.

Continue to look forward and trust that things will work out. Be on watch for the little things that are essential for any lasting solution. I always marveled at how the mammals, unnoticed and underfoot, survived the age of the dinosaurs. If we humans survive it will not be because of the "great ones" but because of the unsung wisdom and creativity of countless, nameless people.

Honor us insofar as what we did gave you a chance to carry on. Forgive us for everything we saddled you with. Remember that you also carry in your genes the "blind spots" that need mutual care and correction. Look up at night and recall that some of the light that reaches you comes from stars long gone. Keep whatever is beautiful from us before your eyes and create even more precious work for your grandchildren.

Remember us who refused to forget you.
Hope and love from
An old and foolish great, great, great grandfather.

Index

About the Author

Arthur J. Dewey (Th.D., Harvard University) is Professor of Theology at Xavier University in Cincinnati. A distinguished teacher, writer, translator and commentator, he is the author of *Remembering the Death of Jesus* (forthcoming Fall 2016) and co-author of *The Complete Gospel Parallels* (with Robert J. Miller, 2011) and *The Authentic Letters of Paul* (with Roy W. Hoover, Lane C. McGaughy, and Daryl D. Schmidt, 2010). Dewey's poetry has appeared in *Christian Century* and his poetic perspective aired on the Saturday Morning Edition on Public Radio Station WVXU (91.7) in Cincinnati for more than a dozen years.